THE SPANISH MAIN

The House of the Inquisition, Cartagena.

THE SPANISH MAIN
FOCUS OF ENVY
1492–1700

BY

PHILIP AINSWORTH MEANS

OFICIAL DE LA ORDEN
DE
EL SOL DEL PERÚ

NEW YORK
GORDIAN PRESS, INC.
1965

Originally Published 1931
Reprinted 1965

Published by Gordian Press, Inc., by
Arrangement with Mrs. Philip Ainsworth Means
Library of Congress Catalog Card No. 65-24994

Printed in U.S.A. by
EDWARDS BROTHERS, INC.
Ann Arbor, Michigan

A LUISITA
CARA ESPOSA MÍA

PREFACE

"THE SPANISH MAIN" is a term to which various meanings have been given from time to time, with the result that it is anything but precise. Perhaps the most narrow definition of it would be as follows: The Spanish Main comprises the northern coast of South America from Panama on the west to Trinidad on the east and also the waters along that coast. Originally, no doubt, "The Spanish Main" was intended to indicate "The Spanish Mainland," which the Spaniards themselves called "Tierra Firme." But, in English, the word "main" applies as well to a broad sweep of sea as to a broad sweep of land. Bearing this in mind, I have ventured, in this book, to use the term, "The Spanish Main," in a wider sense than is customary. Therefore, it is hereinafter employed to designate the entire Caribbean Sea and the southern half of the Gulf of Mexico, together with the islands in those waters and the mainland adjacent thereto, in a word, the whole vast area where Spanish power in America had its inception and where its vital arteries of commerce and of administration lay throughout the colonial period. Used in this sense, "The Spanish Main" indicates, therefore, not only the central and crucial part of the Spanish empire in America but also the area in' which Spain's enemies concentrated the majority of their efforts to destroy that empire. It is the history of The Spanish Main—Focus of Envy—which we shall study in the following pages.

As in the case of my two earlier books, *Ancient Civilizations of the Andes* (1931) and *Fall of the Inca Empire* (1932), I have drawn upon materials studied and knowledge gained during many years of research in many countries. The fundamental purpose of the present volume is to show forth some of the chief aspects of Spanish colonial rule in America and to display the nature of Spain's long conflict with her principal rivals. I hope, in later volumes, to be able to set forth other and less known parts of the colonial labors of Spain, of Portugal, and of other European nations in the colossal task of opening up the New World to European influences, following this with a study of Spain and her rivals in America during the eighteenth century, and ending up with a work on *The Origins of the Hispanic American Nations.*

In the present book, as in its predecessors, I have been much aided in many ways by many people. I am particularly indebted to Mr. Francis Russell Hart and to Mr. Robert Niles, Jr., for their generosity in placing illustrations at my disposal. Mrs. Robert Niles, Jr. (Blair Niles), has also stimulated me greatly by her interest in my former work and her wish to see the present book finished. To Mr. Lawrence Wroth, Librarian of The John Carter Brown Library, and to the assistants in that great treasure-house of materials for historical research, I am more deeply grateful than I can say for all their unremitting aid and encouragement. In like manner I am under great obligations to Mr. Clarence Brigham, of the American Antiquarian Society, and to the staff there, who, both before and since my receiving the honor of election to that distinguished Society, have often shown me greatest kindness. Mr. H. M. Lydenberg, Director of the New York Public Library, and particularly the staff of Room 300 in that great institution, have taken much trouble in helping me to find materials that I needed. At Harvard, Yale, and the Library of Congress, also, I have been much aided and encouraged, so that my gratitude to all those centers of learning is profound. In a very special sense I am indebted, and deeply indebted, to Professor Wilbur Cortez Abbott and to Mr. R. V. Coleman for their aid in steering me through troubled waters. Some of my research has been much aided by Mr. Stetson Conn, of Washington, D. C., and by Dr. Richard Pattee, of the University of Puerto Rico. Of foreign correspondents I may gratefully mention Mr. William Charles Cooke, of Bishopstown, Cork, Ireland, and Professors F. A. Kirkpatrick and Edgar Prestage, of London. Miss Irene A. Wright, of Seville, has also greatly helped me on sundry occasions. Finally, to my wife I am eternally grateful for her unceasing encouragement.

PHILIP AINSWORTH MEANS.

POMFRET, CONNECTICUT.
August 14th, 1935.

CONTENTS

ILLUSTRATIONS

MAPS

THE SPANISH MAIN

CHAPTER I

SPAIN ARRIVES

1. America, on October 10th, 1492

VAST, diverse, and rather sparsely peopled, the continental land-masses which we call North America, Central America, and South America extended their bulk almost from pole to pole, a world having its own peoples but nearly free, for countless centuries, from alien visitors. The isolation of the American hemisphere and of its native inhabitants from contact with other regions of the earth is a fact that cannot be too much emphasized. It explains not only the highly individual character of the native American cultures but also the shock that they received when, two days after the date written above, they began to receive a great and steadily increasing inflow of strange folk and of strange civilization the like of which was quite without precedent in their experience.

Geographically considered the almost landlocked seas which we call the Caribbean and the Gulf of Mexico were the focus of the native population of America. In that mid-continental area, or near it, were represented all the chief grades and kinds of native culture, and the corresponding grades and kinds of environment were represented there likewise. On the islands and along the coasts of those bodies of water there were tropical conditions which offer the sharpest contrast to the temperate conditions prevailing wherever mountains and table-lands of sufficient elevation occur. In tropical regions native culture could not progress beyond the stage which modern science calls "intermediate" or "archaic"; that is, a stage in which are found the incipient forms of such elements as agriculture, permanent architecture, ceramics, textiles, perchance a knowledge of how to work gold, and also rudimentary forms of government, law, and religion. In temperate regions,

3

on the other hand, there was a notable development in all these matters, so that civilizations of the sorts peculiar to America were developed by its native race.

The chief cause of the contrast mentioned is the factor of environment. Culture progresses from a moderate development to a high because men have the vigor and intelligence to enable them to make a full and increasing use of the raw materials in the country around them. If, because of adverse conditions such as too-warm air, too-great dampness, too-vigorous vegetation, and too-limited a horizon, the energies of the people are lowered, a stunted growth of ideas results, and no progress is possible. Their ideas may grow laterally, as it were, and may achieve considerable elaboration. They do not grow upwards towards a certain measure of dominance over the environment and towards a resultant perfecting of the work begun on the intermediate or archaic plane of culture.

This accounts for one of the major facts of America as it was on October 10th, 1492: A huge percentage of her people, most of them living either in forests or else in open country poor in the raw-materials wherewith to build culture, had never risen far from earth, had never sought in their philosophies Sun, Moon, and Stars, still less had ever imagined Something even beyond those bodies. Such gods as they had were creatures of the soil, of little height, and, too often, lurkers among shadows. Nowhere in native America's forested areas, whether in what is now the eastern part of our country or in the verdant islands of the Caribbean, or in the tangled jungles of Amazonia and of other regions, did a highly developed polity take its rise. It could not; the enviroment imperiously forbade ideas to reach a sufficient height.

In America, as in other continents, the higher civilizations came into being only in open regions where sunlight falls freely upon mankind, where the air circulates generously, where a clear blue vault of sky invites the gaze upwards from the level of earth. Such regions may be in either highlands or lowlands, so be it there is an abundance of flowing water—or of water which man can cause to flow in accordance with his will. In America the regions which have produced the highest native civilizations fulfill these requirements.

The highlands of Mexico, for example, were the seat of advanced civilization for at least twelve hundred years before the coming of Columbus. There, in abundance, were found fine clays for pottery, good stone for building, many wild plants which could be nurtured and tended by a steadily improving agricultural technique and many other raw materials which could be used for the improvement of the arts of living. Furthermore, the climatic and other natural conditions were such that the energies and the mentalities of the people could be maintained at a high level permitting them to make the fullest use of the opportunities offered to them by their surroundings. Again, the eastern seaboard of Mexico, between 21° north and 22° north was a region where a certain amount of progress was made possible by relative dryness of the air. In that region the great Maya stock began its rise towards civilization, and part of that stock has lived there ever since. Another part, however, went southwards into the tropical country on the coast near the southernmost part of the Gulf of Mexico. It was there that the Tuxtlá Statuette, with an engraved date equivalent to 98 B.C., was found. The Mayas did not remain there, however, but in the next century or so continued their march, or perhaps rather their drift, southeastwardly, into the highlands of Guatemala where, during the first seven centuries of our era, they rose to a level of civilization in art, science, and government never surpassed in native America. This achievement was due to the beneficial effect of the environment in their ultimate home. When, afterwards, they spread northwards into the upper and tropical part of Yucatan they were culturally strong enough to resist the adverse conditions inherent in that lower and hotter country, and to continue on the high plane of civilization which they had reached on the Guatemalan highlands.

In South America, no less than in Mexico and in Central America, the highest culture was produced either in mountain country or in specially propitious shore country. On the plateau of Bogotá, in modern Colombia, for example, the widely distributed Chibcha stock attained to a growth more modest than that reached by the Mayas, but conspicuously higher than that of the Chibcha stock in less favorable regions. Finally, in the Andean area, from what is now northern Ecuador down through modern Peru and highland Bolivia and so into northern Chile and northwestern Argentina, there was a vast extent of territory destined to bear advanced civilizations. Both in the cool, bright mountain-lands and in the warm, dry, sunny, river-streaked coastal desert along the Pacific, peoples originally on the intermediate plane of culture were pushed irresistibly onwards and upwards by a felicitous interaction between natural advantages and human ideas which resulted in an astounding series of civilizations during the first fifteen centuries after Christ.

With the exceptions here noted all the peoples of America remained on the archaic or intermediate plane of culture. This was equally true of the low, damp, hot, enervating islands scattered about the Caribbean Sea, of the closely similar mainland shores of that sea, and of the great river-valleys lying within the mass of South America. Throughout the lower regions of the Orinoco, Amazon, and Paraná-La Plata drainages dwelt forest-folk whose culture, though intricate, was never advanced. Nor is it so today. On the Caribbean islands, which here particularly concern us, life on the intermediate plane, with simple agriculture, simple pottery, simple weaving, rudimentary architecture in wood, and a very simple tribal sort of government was so easy as to become a fixture, all the more so that there was nothing in the climate which could give the native peoples a vigor or an imagination capable of imagining that progress which, in other climes, was made. In short, the Caribbean, at the time of the Spaniards' coming, was one of the many areas where the native folk of America dwelt contentedly on the archaic plane of existence. But, to the west, to the southwest, and further to the south were areas of high culture which, eventually, would draw

Spaniards to them, and draw also the envious thoughts of other Europeans. Those delectable regions could only be reached, however, by first passing through the Caribbean or the great interior river-regions of South America. As it fell out, the Spaniards got there first, but this only stimulated their rivals to make prolonged efforts to follow in their footsteps. Thus the Caribbean became the focus of Envy, and of a great and long-lasting struggle.[1]

Such were our continent and its peoples on October 10th, 1492. Two days later began, for the native folk of this hemisphere, the greatest wave of alien influences they were ever to know. Had a throng of angels, of a civilization higher (in some respects) than the highest of theirs, come suddenly among them, the contact and the contrast might have generated naught but good to all concerned. But the invaders were men, varying greatly from devilry to angelhood (or something within measurable distance thereof). Consequently a situation immediately arose and began a long existence which we shall, in this book, examine, along with many other matters.

2. The Discoverer Comes. October 12th, 1492

Whether he was born in Italy, or in northern Spain, or in some other place, the man whom we call Christopher Columbus made, accidentally, the most portentous geographic discovery of all time. He was impelled theretowards by a series of motives most of which do him infinite credit: A wish to save the souls of the benighted heathen; a wish to enlarge and to foster trade; and, underlying the rest, a matchlessly dynamic curiosity which drove him past all obstacles until he stumbled on our continent while groping westward towards the Far East.[2]

At all events, the fate of America and its peoples was sealed in 1486 when Christopher Columbus, after years of pleading in the incredulous courts of Europe, first succeeded, at Córdoba, in stirring the interest of Queen Isabella of Castile in his plan for maritime exploration westwards. At that moment, however, naught came of the royal curiosity because the Catholic Sovereigns were engaged with all their might and resources in finishing a task of seven centuries, that is, the expelling of Moorish power from Spain. Only Granada, of all the Moslem kingdoms on Spanish soil, was still unhumbled, and to the pious purpose of destroying it all the Catholic monarchs' efforts were then, and for some years afterwards, fervently put forth.

Nevertheless, amid all the martial preoccupations arising from the final phase of the Reconquest, the Spanish monarchs—and more especially Queen Isabella of Castile—bore Columbus and his novel ideas in mind. Further interviews were granted to him, and the Queen hearkened to his long expositions with a steadily increasing attention. On Sunday, January 2nd, 1492, Moorish Granada at length opened its gates to the Catholic Sovereigns, Columbus being present at the time, and once more the Iberian peninsula was wholly Christian and Catholic, and Spain was finally triumphant in the long, heroic, and unifying crusade against the Infidel upon her soil. The supreme obstacle to the royal interest on behalf of the stirring plans of the great adventurer was now cleared away.[3]

The course of things was not destined to be unruffled between Columbus and Queen Isabella. The Queen, a woman of amazing intellectual strength, of great heart, and of penetrating mind, was now definitely in the grip of Columbus's ideas. But she, with her husband and with all the subjects of both rulers, had just finished a protracted and costly crusade, so that it was natural enough that she should be cautious concerning the engagements into which she entered. To the Queen the demands of Columbus concerning his future rights in whatever non-Christian lands he might come upon seemed, not unreasonably, exorbitant. Negotiations came to a dead stop, and Columbus had actually departed in a huff from the royal camp of Santa Fé, outside Granada, with the firm intention of selling his ideas and his services either to the King of France or to the King of England. Sharp wits and eloquent tongues were at work for him, however, in the Queen's presence, particularly those of two high officials, Luís de Santangel and Alfonso de Quintanilla. They brought the Queen around by skilful appeal to her best side. Hardly had Columbus gone two leagues from Santa Fé when a galloping messenger caught up with him to tell him that the Queen had reconsidered, and that all would now be well.[4]

Supported now by the increasingly enthusiastic Isabella of Castile, but receiving slight encouragement from Ferdinand of Aragón, Columbus, with less than 100 followers divided among three small ships, of which only one, the *Santa María*, was decked, left Palos on August 3rd, 1492. His first destination was Gomera, in the Canary archipelago. There the little fleet lingered for repairs and other business until September 8th. On this date the great voyage westwards began, and on October 12th, 1492, Columbus and his followers trod the strand of the isle of Guanahani, which he renamed San Salvador and which is now called Watling's Island. It is a tiny bit of land at 24° north, on the eastern side of the Bahama archipelago. Neither America nor the rest of the world ever knew an arrival more epochal.[5]

3. America and the World Enter a New Age

Then began a time of shocks and wonders, with a grand clashing of contrasted cultures, a period crowded with new knowledge and with essays in adjustment, an age filled with stresses and strains taxing equally the bodies and the spirits of both races concerned.

Between October 12th, 1492, and, let us say, 1550, the servitors of the Crown of Castile conquered for their sovereign the best parts of the New World. It is an oft-sung saga which cannot be repeated too often. Let us remember, therefore, that, on October 10th, 1492, no Spaniard walked beneath the American sky, and that, by the end of 1550, the King of Castile, through the persons of thousands of his subjects, owned *de facto* and in his own belief *de jure* as well, all parts of the Western Hemisphere which did not belong, in like sense, to the King of Portugal.

A point generally overlooked is the utter novelty of the situation in which the Spaniards found themselves in America during the first sixty years or so after the discovery. Prior to 1492 no Europeans, except the Portuguese explorers in Africa, had been brought face to face with low-cultured tropical peoples of a race unknown in the Old World. Exoticism had not been lacking, of course, in the previous experience of Spaniards; for centuries they had had commercial and cultural relations with North Africa and with the Levant, and, still more pointedly, their own land had been partly held during 700 years by a foreign people of an alien civilization and of a religion profoundly at variance with Christianity. Indeed, the long struggle to remove from Christian Spain this intrusive creed had engaged the energies of Spanish Christendom until the very eve of Columbus's little deal in futures with the Catholic Sovereigns.

In addition to their conflict with and conquest of the Moors the Spaniards had had a certain amount of preliminary training in forming colonies across the sea. Between about 1350 and 1479 the Spaniards established their rule over the Canary Islands. The native folk there, known as Guanches, though of modest, or rather backward, culture, were clearly of the white race and had social and political institutions which the Spaniards early learned to adapt to their needs as colonial administrators. From the first it was the policy of the Spanish crown to make the conquered islanders good Christians. Moreover, as there was no racial contrast between the Canarians and their invaders, the latter made a policy of regarding the former as their equals, maintaining their "kings" in a superior social class, and granting them various flattering favors. In a word, Spain's conquest of the Canary Islands shaped the colonial administrative philosophy which was to be hers in all her possessions across the ocean.[6]

It was, therefore, only with their arrival in the Antilles that

Spaniards came into touch with a race conspicuously different from their own and with people whose whole mode of living seemed to most of the invaders so artless as to be both contemptible and ridiculous, as well as downright wicked, in many respects. Steel-clad knights and fire-spouting arquebusiers of Spain with the memories of glorious Spanish cities fresh in their minds simply could not feel for the naked, club-wielding, arrow-shooting, hut-housed Antillian natives anything but scorn and dislike wholly unleavened by that respect and comprehension (however grudgingly conceded) that they had had for the Moors and even for the Canarians.

The environment in which the Spaniards found the unheard-of race of the New World was no less strange to them than were the people encountered. Never before had Spaniards seen tropical islands such as those in the Caribbean. The new scenes thus entered, together with the racial contrast and the foreignness of the people found there, must have been a sharp psychological jolt for the invaders who, expecting to enter the realm of the Grand Cham or of some other half-fabulous Oriental potentate whom they could have admired, found themselves instead among untutored children of an exuberant tropic world unlike anything previously known to them. True, that world contained many phenomena and many living things which by their novelty filled the newcomers with amazement, sometimes even shocking them as did the Cuban birds which nested and sat on the eggs at Christmas-tide;[7] but on the whole the commonalty of the Spaniards found nothing, or very little, imposing, lordly, grand which could compel them to respect the native folk and their culture. Added to this was the unfortunate fact that the plentiful golden ornaments, richly wrought and burnished by the aid of a bitumen process, upon the Antillians' persons awakened a burning cupidity in Spanish minds. Indeed, one aspect of the contrast between natives and strangers may be exemplified by their respective attitudes towards gold, the former esteeming it for its sightliness, the latter for its money-worth. So little did the Indians prize their gold that they gladly gave quantities of it and of yams and other foodstuffs in exchange for the most trifling novelties, such as beads, pins, and oddments of European crockery.[8]

Thus far we have been speaking of the impressions received by the less perceptive and less kindly element among the Spaniards. How was it with the more enlightened among them? How with the Catholic Sovereigns themselves? How, finally, did it all seem to the American natives?

Columbus himself early displayed an intense, but not always just and wise, preoccupation with the Indians. On the very first American island visited by him he forcibly took some native men as prisoners, afterwards carrying a number of them to Spain as exhibits, of whom only seven ever again saw a stately palm waving in a wild tropical wind. In spite of this high-handed action (which had as its purpose the training of interpreters), relations between Columbus and the Indians were often pleasant enough. He, in his turn, was impressed by some of the accomplishments of the Indian craftsmen, particularly by their large, swift, slender-waisted dug-out canoes.[9]

Nevertheless, it was early found that the Indians could be dangerous. This was particularly true of the Caribs who were an indomitable and warlike people of South American origin and who had made themselves dominant in many parts of the West Indies at the expense of the milder Arawak folk, likewise of South American origin. On his first voyage Columbus founded a little settlement called La Navidad on the north coast of Hispaniola, almost due east from the eastern tip of Cuba.* Rough cabins and a little fort were built at La Navidad, and a small garrison was left there by Columbus when he

---

*Today Hispaniola is divided between the republics of Haiti and Santo Domingo. Together with Cuba to the west, Jamaica, also to the west and so south of eastern Cuba, and Puerto Rico to the east of Hispaniola, it forms the group often called the Greater Antilles. The Lesser Antilles form a sickle-shaped archipelago of almost innumerable small islands running from east of Puerto Rico down to the northern coast of South America, and thence along that coast in a westwardly direction to the mouth of the Gulf of Maracaibo. The Greater and the Lesser Antilles are often called today the West Indies, but in Spanish colonial times that term was not seldom applied to all America. See Map I.

departed for the first time from America to Spain. Notwithstanding these precautions, when he came back on his second voyage, he found that La Navidad had been destroyed. This calamity seems to have been the product of a hostile attitude on the part of the natives as a principle, but it may have been provoked by outrages by the settlers. It is impossible to know which is true.[10]

In his Memorial to his Sovereigns, from Isabella (Hispaniola) during the second voyage, and sent home by the hand of Antonio de Torres, captain of one of the ships, Columbus speaks again of the great prestige given to the Spaniards by their well-managed ships, unlike anything the Indians had ever seen before, and he goes on to say that the Indians, if ruled with justice and kindly firmness, do willingly all things pleasing to the Spaniards. In their rejoinder to this the Catholic Sovereigns emphasize the desirability of bringing the natives to the Faith as quickly as possible, and in so doing the monarchs not only continue that policy which had been in force in the Canaries, but also lay down a principle destined to guide the theory, if not the practice, of their subjects in America in their own day and for the whole period of Spanish rule in the Western Hemisphere.[11]

On their side, the Indians seem to have believed that their visitors were strange beings from the sky. The beards, raiment, arms, ceremonies, chattels, customs, and technology of the strangers combined to fill them with awe equal to the astonishment caused in the voyagers by all the extraordinary things which they were beholding. Those Indians who were taken to Spain and later came home soon added to the reputation of the newcomers among the natives by telling in glowing terms the marvels and grandeurs which they had seen beyond the eastern waters. They discovered that the Admiral, howsoever great a being he might be, was but a servant to sovereigns of unparalleled splendor who lived in majestic palaces adorned with artistic embellishments beyond the previous experience of simple creatures like themselves; they walked through paved city streets crowded with colorfully arrayed people, and saw brightly apparelled horsemen on unknown beasts; they witnessed bull-fights, replete with pageantry; they saw cultivated fields producing crops of mysterious plant-life, cattle whose shapes were no less puzzling than were the purposes which they served; and they entered mighty and mountainous buildings, wrought in cunningly sculptured stone, which, they were told, were the mansions of the white men's God. In short, the far-wandering Indians were shown all the pomp and richness of Spanish life, and their natural intelligence was equal to the formidable task of comprehending in great measure this world so vastly more complex than their own; they even understood that the sovereigns were the apex of a system and that the throng of resplendent personages attendant upon the monarchs was made up of proud lords who, none the less, looked upwards to the King and Queen as these did to that Unseen Being who dwelt in the massive, towering stone temples.[12]

In short, two far asunder kinds of human life were brought into closest contact by the coming of the Spaniards among the American islanders. Friction and fusion, almost equal portions of each, and each taking sundry forms, were immediately set up. Unhappily even the fusion was too often fraught with woe for the invaded because, like some insidious poison, the gold in which the modestly developed Indian tribes were so rich corrupted the hearts of many Spaniards, causing them to regard the bedizened "savages" merely as creatures of bestial habits who were to be first despoiled of what they had and afterwards were to be forced to toil incessantly in search of more. At no time, be it remembered, was it in accordance with the will and intention, either of the Crown or of the Church, that this should be so; yet the glitter of the yellow stuff engendered in many men from Spain a gold-lust so overwhelming that it overbore their normal loyalty to the Crown and even their duty to God.

The consequence of the indicated situation was monstrous tragedy. In Hispaniola, to mention but one of many islands, the native population was reduced from at least 100,000 before

1492 to a bare 30,000 by 1514, and other islands saw analogous
carnage made all the worse by the growth of systematic hunting and kidnaping among the Indians in order to enslave
them.[13] In this we see the effect of a baneful combination of
factors: The complete novelty of being in contact with a
wholly distinct and hitherto unknown race; the comparative
weakness of that race in war against Europeans; and the visible presence of much gold in the hands of that race, with
many hints at the hidden presence of much more in the soil
of their islands. The Antillians and some of the folk on the
mainland first explored were foredoomed to misfortune; not
even the dauntless and never humbled Caribs (who constituted but a part of the whole) were able to resist permanently
the fate of being thrust aside into the less desirable islands,
and the Arawaks and other stocks, meeker and less resistant
than the Caribs, were killed off in job-lots, notwithstanding
the strenuous efforts of the Spanish government, of the
Church, and of compassionate individuals to save them.

How different was the case when the Spaniards arrived first
in Mexico and afterwards in Peru! *There* they found themselves in native states strongly organized for war and of
civilization in which they could find much to admire and to
seize upon for the purpose of constructing a bi-racial colonial
polity precisely as they had done in the Canary Islands and in
the Iberian peninsula during the Reconquest. The recurrence
in the pages of early chroniclers of Mexico and of Peru of
such words as "mosque," "great lord," "king," "castle,"
"citadel," "temple," and so on emphasizes the fact that the
Castilians viewed native Mexico and native Peru with much
the same perhaps unwilling respect that they had looked upon
the Moorish kingdoms in Spain. In Mexico and Peru, no less
than in the case of the Moslem states, reduction to obedience
to the King of Castile came as the result of subduing or capturing native rulers and of following that with a systematic
expropriation of their administrative machinery. In the first
fine flush of inexperience and cupidity the Spaniards slew in
order to take; later, more subtle methods were made necessary

by the superiority of the civilizations encountered, and they
were re-shaped, but not destroyed, to meet the Spaniards'
requirements.

4. Spain and Portugal Share the New World

The discovery of America produced a political problem of
unprecedented sort. Spain, through Columbus, had discovered
it. At first glance it might appear that, if the New World
was to belong to any European nation, it ought to belong to
Spain. Portugal, however, also had a claim to the New World,
arising out of her long series of discoveries in Africa and India.
In 1493 it was by no means certain that the countries seen by
Columbus were not a part of Africa or of India. The matter
of jurisdiction had, therefore, to be settled and apportioned by
the highest earthly authority, namely, His Holiness the Pope.
His paramountcy was then recognized and acknowledged by
all Christians in Europe.

At that time the Pope was Alexander VI, of the Spanish
house of Borgia (in Spanish, Borja). Not unnaturally, he
tended to favor Spain as much as possible, and this, coupled
with the inevitable weaknesses in his geographical knowledge,
brought about a good deal of experimenting during 1493, in
the course of which no less than four Papal Bulls were issued
in the attempt to adjust the claims of the two Iberian nations
with respect to the non-Christian parts of the entire world.
At last, on June 7th, 1494, the diplomats of Spain and Portugal, by the Treaty of Tordesillas, settled the matter by drawing a north-south line 370 leagues west of the Cape Verde
Islands, or, in modern terms, about 50° west from Greenwich.
All non-Christian lands discovered or to be discovered east of
this line were to belong to Portugal, and all those to the west
of it to Spain. As the line runs through the mouth of the
Amazon the country which we call Brazil was the only part
of the New World falling to Portugal. All the rest, by the
Pope's award and by the Treaty of Tordesillas, was to be
Spanish.[14]

Quite naturally, the Pope's award and that of Tordesillas, which grew out of it, failed to please every one. France, no less Catholic than Spain and Portugal, never accepted it and, after the rise of Protestantism, England and other northern peoples of Europe wholly denied the validity of the award. Furthermore, various native rulers of parts of America pointed out that the Pope had no sort of right to dispose of their realms. Inasmuch as many learned and devout Catholics, including ecclesiastics, held more or less the same opinion, we cannot but take it seriously.[15] The gist of Friar Francisco de Victoria's argument concerning the Pope's right or lack of right to dispose of the New World and of its people is found in a syllogism running thus:

The Pope has no temporal power over the Indian aborigines or over other unbelievers. . . . For he has no temporal power save such as subserves spiritual matters. But he has no spiritual power over them. . . . Therefore he has no temporal power either.[16]

Audacious and unshakable logic! Courageous words from a friar concerning the limitation of the Pope's authority! In a word, Friar Francisco de Victoria, founder of the basic part of our international law, belonged to the great school of Catholic thinkers who, in the face of the King and even of the Pope, fought for what they held to be justice towards the Indians. Friar Francisco, born in the little village of Victoria in the Basque provinces of northern Spain about 1483, was educated in celebrated Dominican colleges at Burgos and at Paris. He was in the French capital in 1506 and remained there some eighteen years, studying at the Sorbonne as well as in his own Order's college and later as a teacher of theology. After his return to Spain, about 1524, he made a distinguished professorial career at Valladolid and, especially, at the University of Salamanca, then the greatest centre of education in Spain. Until he died at Salamanca in 1546, Friar Francisco de Victoria was highly regarded not only by the students whom he served with utmost devotion but also by his king and by leaders in political life. True, his convictions more

than once led him to anger the king, but Charles I of Castile
(the Emperor Charles V) was big enough later to acknowledge
the intellectual stature and the moral rectitude of Friar
Francisco. Today he is all but forgotten by most of us, but
in his own time and for more than a century afterwards he
was honored most greatly both in Spain and elsewhere in
Europe because of his wisdom tempered by compassion in
many fields of thought. Victoria did by logical reasoning
and by quiet analytical exposition all that could be done to
save the Indians of America from injustice and oppression,
and to him must go a large share of the credit for the fact
that a desire for mercifulness became the central feature of
Spanish colonial theory. It is one of history's sardonic jests
that a much less intelligent and much less noble man, Friar
Bartolomé de la Casas, the over-advertised "Apostle of the
Indies," should have captured a great part of the credit that
Victoria ought to have received. To him we shall have to
refer on later pages.[17]

The practical and realistic title of Spain to huge areas in
America arose, therefore, neither from the act of a Pope dis-
posing of the whole nor from the Treaty of Tordesillas which
did likewise, but rather from the fact that subjects of the
Crown of Castile won, settled in, and organized those parts
of the New World which suited them.[18]

In short, Spain's emissaries—explorers, settlers, and administrators, as well as churchmen, won for her a sound title to
large parts of America. The claim to the whole non-
Portuguese part of the Western Hemisphere soon became,
however, only academic. This did not come to pass until
Spain had caused careful studies to be made of the northern
part of America's eastern coast-country as a result of which
she deliberately abandoned them except in theory. In 1523
King Charles I of Spain made an agreement with Lucás
Vásquez de Aillón whereby the latter, using two ships of his
own, made an exploring (and incidentally a slave-hunting)
voyage from Hispaniola northwards to 35° or 37°, thus
examining our coast as far as the mouth of the Chesapeake.

Not content with this, King Charles I employed a Portuguese navigator, Estéban Gómez, in 1524-1525, to make further investigations on behalf of Spain along what is now our entire Atlantic seaboard and onwards to what we call Nova Scotia. The motive, in part, of the Gómez voyage was the hope of discovering a strait which would cut through the still but little understood land-mass into the Pacific; but equally important was the wish of Charles to know what lay on and behind the Atlantic coast of what is now our country.

Nor was Charles the only European monarch to interest himself in that portion of the New World. As early as 1497 King Henry VII of England had sent John Cabot exploring in the same direction, and in 1500-1501 he had sent Gaspar Cortereal on a like errand. In 1523–1524 King Francis I of France was employing an expert Florentine navigator, Giovanni da Verrazano, to make voyages along the eastern side of North America, partly to find a short route to Cathay and partly to gain general knowledge. On the first of his two voyages Verrazano did not reach America at all; but he captured between the Azores and Spain a goodly part of the spoils of Montezuma, ruler of Mexico, which the conqueror Fernando Cortés had despatched to his master in June, 1522. On his second voyage Verrazano explored for Francis I the whole Atlantic coast from Cape Fear up to Nova Scotia, making his report from Dieppe under date of July 8th, 1524.

So far as Charles I of Spain was concerned North America turned out to be uninteresting, indeed repellant. There was no strait leading to Cathay; there were no gold-mines, no native civilizations awaiting his rule, no disciplined peoples fit for money-producing labor; there were only wildernesses, forests, and savages. As he already held the glittering realm of Mexico, and as he already may have heard the first whispers of Peru, it is natural enough that Charles should have turned his attention in those directions.[19]

In this survey of North America by Spain and in the subsequent lack of interest in the country then examined we see an unconscious response to a deep-seated natural truth:

Spaniards and Portuguese, being accustomed to the environment of southern Europe, felt themselves uneasy and lost in the colder climes of the New World. There was something in the very landscape of the northerly regions which repelled them. Here was no rich realm in which new kingdoms based on ancient polities and modified by institutions brought from Spain could be set up. There was, in fact, a line to the north of which it was not natural for Spaniards or Portuguese to make lasting settlements and to establish intensive occupation. That line, speaking in approximate terms, ran through the middle of the present United States from the Pacific to the Mississippi, and thence southeastwardly to what is now southern Georgia and so onwards out into the Atlantic. South of that line lay their natural and proper colonial sphere, and south of it they founded and maintained the vast fabric of their American empire. In the south, also, there was such a natural border-line, albeit less emphatically drawn by reason of the fact that no other European nation ever seriously attempted colonization in the austral regions of our continent. Still, south of 40° S., Spanish rule was at most a theory. Between the two lines defined, and only between them, lay the natural zone of Spanish and Portuguese expansion. The whole history of the career of those nationalities in America reveal, if unconsciously, the truth of this interpretation. The failure of the Spaniards firmly to hold Bermuda, and the later lack of real interest in Georgia, the Carolinas, and Virginia, prove the point.

Within their natural zone of colonial expansion, however, the Spaniards and the Portuguese justified their claim to ownership by solidifying their occupation and organization of regions discovered. In that process the Spaniards fulfilled the requirements defined by Friar Francisco de Victoria as constituting valid title. He held that mere discovery in America by Europeans conferred no more right than would have been conferred had American natives discovered Europe; he averred that "possession should follow discovery to ensure title," and that intrinsically the native states of America had the same degree of justness that the kingdoms of Europe had. He goes on to blast forever the opinion held in many interested quarters that the Indians were "natural" slaves. Unshakably he maintains the thesis that they were rational beings with immortal souls which must be saved and that they were "true owners (of their lands, etc.) both from the public and the private standpoint."[20]

It is not too much to say that, almost from the first hour of their presence in the New World the attention of the Spaniards was fixed chiefly upon the natives and upon the question of what to do about them. True to an old and honorable tradition the Catholic Sovereigns wished, from the beginning, to rule the Indians benignly and to bring them to the Faith. At first, however, they did not understand just how to go about it, the problem in the Indies being so very different, by reason of racial and cultural factors, from any encountered before. To meet the situation a variety of experiments was tried, chiefly in the Caribbean islands and mostly within the first thirty years.[21]

In the meanwhile, the unrobust Arawak Indians of the Islands were practically exterminated by gold-maddened Spaniards who betrayed the Crown's and the Church's intention. A great part of the tragedy was due to grossest abuse of institutions which were designed to regulate the work of the Indians and, fully as much, to ensure their conversion to Christianity. These were the *repartimiento* and the *encomienda,* terms whose meanings largely overlap. In the early years, and among the Antillians, chiefly among the Arawaks, as the more formidable Caribs either fled away or else fought successfully against invasion, the *encomienda* was a grace conferred upon some favored Spaniard, for his life and that of one heir, to receive the tribute of and to profit from the labor of a given number of Indians, with the obligation of providing them with religious instruction and likewise with the obligation of serving the king in war. Subsequently, when the Spanish government had got the situation more firmly in hand and had learned how to manage matters with greater skill, the *encomienda,* although its theoretical definition and functions remained as before, assumed in practice more the nature of a feudal grant (still for a limited number of lives) with a pronounced territorial aspect. This alteration of the factual character of the *encomienda* took place in the countries where there was strong native civilization itself having institutions roughly parallel to feudalism—as in Mexico and, still more, in Peru, also in Colombia.[22]

History, for the most part, is the record of the selfish naughtiness of men and of the efforts of some of them to contend against it. Spain in the New World worked through a host of her subjects who varied tremendously in point of moral character. Saints of purest ray dipped their food from the same stew-pot with sinners of darkest hue. Most conquerors stood between the extremes, blending a martial habit of mind with contempt for physical pain received or given in the service of Both Majesties, God and the King. To nearly all Spaniards the moral obligation to save the souls of the Indians —even amid the howls of homicidal dogs and the rattle of firearms and the rushing thumpety-thump of charging cavalry —was a vital reality. After all, what is the flesh? Dust, doomed to the worms. It is the impalpable soul which lives forever. Meanwhile, though they die, minions must work for the king and for his vassals, all to the glory of God. Thus they argued.

5. *Conclusion*

Whatever else the Spaniards were they were soldiers and men of unsurpassed virility who built an empire in a crusading spirit compounded equally of piety and intolerance. Judged by the standards of that time—which are the only standards that may be fairly used—both the piety and the intolerance of the Spaniards were laudable, and the title which they conferred upon the original conquerors of America was valid and remained so as long as the descendants of those conquerors could maintain it by force of war. European rivals were destined to come and to build lesser realms of their own in territories claimed by Spain, but wrested from her. The efforts of the rival nations to break up the Spanish empire in America were informed by a crusading spirit no less real and vigorous than that of Spain, and compounded of precisely the same ingredients, piety and intolerance. Moreover, Spain and her foes were alike also in the fact that they sought for wealth in America greater than that which any of them had known previously. Altogether, we may say that on all sides the religious motive, the motive to crush departure from an accepted pattern of righteousness, and a hunger for riches gave to all the contenders a deep-rooted determination to hold the chief place in the colonial game.

In short, Spain the first-comer soon became and long remained the target for furious attacks. Nevertheless, in spite of all her enemies, and in the face of tremendous calamities to her cause, Spain was to hold against all comers most of what she originally took through the vigor of her subjects, and she did so for over three hundred years. In other words, of the nearly 450 years that Europeans have known about America, 325 were years during which Spain was the dominant power in the most enviable parts of the Western Hemisphere. It is the amazing record of her defensive struggle that we shall study in succeeding chapters of this book.

Notes to Chapter I

[1] To select, from a veritable host of valuable works, two or three for specific citation in this connection may seem invidious. Nevertheless, because they have been supremely important for my studies of the broad, underlying facts about native American culture, I must cite four superlatively significant works: Dixon, 1928; Wissler, 1922 and 1926; and Toynbee, 1935. This last and very recent book, destined to be as important in the field of anthropological history as is Sir James Frazer's *Golden Bough* in that of folklore, Mr. Toynbee combs the entire earth and its peoples, and explains them with a vigorous yet serene criticism rarely equalled and never surpassed. There is not a page of his three volumes which does not illumine the subjects here touched upon, and his specific references to native American cultures are so numerous that to cite them individually would be vain.

2 The historians, great and small, who uphold the Genoese, or at least Ligurian, origin of Columbus are legion. Any college freshman can name the *decuriones* if not the *milites*. More recondite, and at the same time more consonant with my own secret convictions on the subject are certain writers whose works are all but unknown in this country. Among them are: Beltrán y Rózpide, 1918 (Columbus was Cristóbal Colón, not Cristóforo Colombo, a Genoese); Bogotte, 1904–1905 (Columbus was Spanish); Calzada, 1920 (Columbus a Spaniard of Galicia); Casanova, 1880 (Columbus a Corsican); Delgado Capeáns, 1924 (Columbus a Galician); García de la Riega, *circa* 1920 (Columbus came from northern Spain); Santelli, 1919 (Columbus a Corsican); Tavera Acosta, 1922 (Columbus a Spaniard). Jane, 1930–1933, lists all the more obvious works on Columbus.

3 Herrera, Dec. I, Ch. ix. López de Gómara, Chs. xiv and xv. Martyr d'Anghera, Bk. I., 1912, I, pp. 57–59. Casas, 1875–1876, Bk. I, Ch. xxix. Helps, Bk. II, Ch. i. Gaffarel, 1892, II. pp. 74–83. Jane, 1930–1933, I, Introduction, pp. liv–lix, lxiii, cii–ciii.

4 Herrera, Dec. I, Ch. viii. López de Gómara, Ch. xv. Helps, Bk. II, Ch. i. Gaffarel, 1892, II, pp. 84–85. Vignaud, 1911, II, pp. 47–134. Jane, 1930–1933, I, pp. lx–lxiii, II, pp. 106–108, where Columbus explains his motives for wishing to hold the government of the realms which he might find; they are good motives. Bourne, 1906. See also, Introduction of Jane, II, pp. xiii–lxxv for data on the preliminaries to the first voyage.

5 Helps, Bk. II, Ch. i. Gaffarel, 1892, II, pp. 84–107. Vignaud, 1911, II, pp. 135–210. Jane, 1930–1933, I, pp. cxii–cxvi and 2–3. Cronau, 1923, pp. 1–31. For a brilliant and magnificently documented study of the personnel of Columbus's crew, see: Gould y Quincy, 1925–1928, a great work too seldom cited. A valuable discussion of the character of the Spanish conquerors is Blanco Fombona, 1922. See also, Richman, 1919.

6 Abercromby, 1917. Espinosa, 1907. Torres Campos, 1901, especially pp. 37–45. Newton, 1933, pp. 1–5. Prestage, 1933, Ch. iii. Chapman, 1933, pp. 1–3 and 12.

7 Jane, 1930–1933, I, p. 42, citing the letter written by Dr. Diego Álvarez Chanca, physician of the second expedition, to the city of Seville. On this letter see: Jane, I, pp. cxliii–cxlv.

8 Jane, 1930–1933, I, pp. 46–58 and 64–65 (Álvarez Chanca), and 94, where Columbus, in his Memorial to Ferdinand and Isabella, dated from Isabella (Hispaniola) January 30th, 1495, stresses the allurement of gold, at the same time mentioning the ships of his fleet as a source of prestige among the natives and as a protection against them. Also see: I, pp. 71–73, where Dr. Álvarez Chanca, at the end of his account of the second voyage, promises the Catholic Sovereigns limitless golden wealth.

9 Jane, I, p. 11, where he quotes from Columbus's letter to the Catholic Sovereigns, written off the Canaries on February 15th, 1493, with a postscript written at Lisbon, March 4th. Martyr, Dec. I, Bk. III, 1912, I, p. 95, states that Columbus treated the captured Indians with kindness.

10 Jane, 1930–1933, I, p. 38, where Dr. Álvarez Chanca speaks of the Caribs as being different from the rest of the Indians, and I, pp. 46–56, where the same authority relates the affair of La Navidad.

11 Jane, II, p. 91, quoting Columbus's Memorial from Isabella, January 30th, 1495, and from the marginal comments of the King and Queen.

12 Jane, 1930–1933, I, p. 156, quoting from Andrés Bernáldez's *Historia de los Reyes Católicos Don Fernando y Doña Isabel.* This great work, written in the years down to 1513, was first published by Don Miguel Lafuente y Alcántara at Granada, 1856, in two volumes, and afterwards by the Sociedad de Bibliófilos Andaluces, Seville, 1870–1875, 2 vols. Jane gives the original Spanish and an English translation of chapters 123–131, relating to the second voyage of Columbus.

13 It is, of course, impossible to know what the original number of people was in the island of Hispaniola. The figure offered in the text is a conservative guess based on: Simpson, 1929, p. 48; A. L. Kroeber, "Native American Populations," in *American Anthropologist,* XXXVI, pp. 1–25, and one or two other studies of the kind. Particularly important is Angel Rosenblat, *El desarollo de la publicación indígena de América,* being published in the new Spanish periodical, *Tierra Firme,* Madrid, 1935.

14 Prestage, 1933, pp. 238–244. Newton, 1933, pp. 7–10. Chapman, 1933, pp. 14–15. Kirkpatrick, 1934, pp. 23–24. Andrews, 1934, pp. 13–15. In 1506 Pope Julius II, a Pontiff worthy indeed of his unique office, confirmed the arrangement made at Tordesillas.

15 Friar Francisco de Victoria (or Vitoria), in the edition of James Brown Scott (hereinafter cited as Scott-Victoria, 1934). Both Dr. Scott's editorship of this volume and the translation of Victoria's work by John Pawley Bate are nothing short of faultless in their scholarship and in the sympathy which they display for the great man whom they interpret to this modern world which, although it has forgotten him, owes him an enormous debt. Friar Francisco de Victoria had one of the greatest intellects—and one of the most compassionate hearts—that ever sought to serve humankind.

10 Friar Francisco de Victoria, in *De Indis Noviter Inventis,* quoted from translated version in Scott-Victoria, 1934, Appendix A, p. xxiii. Also see pp. 119–125, especially 125. A whole library could be formed of the tomes in which this subject and allied subjects have been argued back and forth, up and down. Native chieftains of America sometimes called in question the validity of the Pope's and of the King's jurisdiction over them, as in the case of that Indian lord who declared that "The Pope must have been drunk and the King of Spain was an idiot." This tart comment is preserved in Fernández de Enciso, 1519.

17 Scott-Victoria, 1934, Ch. iii. Nys, 1889. MacNutt, 1909. Simpson, 1929. Means, 1932, pp. 229–232, 253, 269, 291.

18 Estimates of the numbers of Spaniards in the New World vary as greatly as do the estimates of the Indian population. An ultra-cautious figure is that of Luís Rubio y Moreno, who holds that, between 1492 and 1592, only 7,846 Spaniards went to the New World. (Chapman, 1933, p. 92, citing Rubio). But other estimates assert that, by or after 1574, there were over 150,000 Spaniards and more than 200 Spanish towns in the Americas, which seems altogether more probable. (Chapman, 1933, p. 127. Bourne, 1904, pp. 250–251). If, as one gathers, Señor Rubio was basing his calculations on the *registered* passengers going from Spain to the Indies, the discrepancy is in part

explained by the probability that many people crossed over without going through all the proper legal formalities of registration. Spain in the fifteenth to eighteenth centuries was certainly not overpopulated, consequently there was no such irresistible pressure leading to emigration of huge masses of people as certain modern nations have known. Therefore, only the more dynamic and ambitious types of men went to seek their fortunes in the Indies, they being in some respects the best, rather than the worst, of the Spaniards. Conditions in America, however, too often brought out in them unlovely qualities which had not been in evidence at home in Spain.

[19] For the Spanish reaction to the reports brought back by Gómez and Vásquez de Aillón see: Martyr, Dec. VIII, Bk. X, 1912, p. 419. The voyages are well described, with rich documentation, in Medina, 1908b, pp. 63–111. See also: Brebner, 1933, p. 32; Wilgus, 1931, p. 84. Verrazano's voyages are well described in Brevoort, 1874, and in Winship, 1905, pp. 1–23, to mention but two of almost innumerable sources. Andrews, 1934, pp. 144–145, tells us how, as late as 1610, the Spanish government still believed that Virginia was unfit for settlement even by Englishmen. See also, Bourne, 1906.

[20] Scott-Victoria, 1934, pp. 106–115, 125–126.

[21] Hanke, 1935, entire, and 1935a, Chs. i–vi. It is not generally known that the Catholic Sovereigns once contemplated the establishment in the West Indies of a colony for criminals from Spain. In a decree of June 22nd, 1497, they legalized this scheme, as set forth in Ramírez, 1503. Luckily nothing came of it.

[22] The character of the *encomienda*, in fact as contrasted with theory, will be found discussed in Means, 1932, where the territorial aspect which it came to have in Peru is duly emphasized on pp. 150–160 and elsewhere. Very important for this subject are: Markham's remarks at p. 72 of Simón, 1861; Wright, 1916, pp. 5–10; and Simpson, 1929, pp. 78, 92–93; and 139.

CHAPTER II

SPANISH CONQUESTS AND SETTLEMENTS

1. Spain's Conquest of the Northern Part of the Caribbean

DURING the first sixty years or so after the advent of Columbus the Spanish advance into the New World was a slow and somewhat jerky progress in a generally westward direction. Beginning, as far as intensive and permanent occupation was concerned, in the Greater Antilles, in Cuba, Hispaniola, Puerto Rico, and less carefully in Jamaica, Spanish power first took the land, then attempted to clamp down upon the natives new forms of rule and of economy, and finally introduced a new and intricate and morally exalted Faith, as well as a general approximation to Spanish civilization.

It was the second and third of these steps, especially, which resulted in the near-extermination of the island natives. This sad fact arose from the inexperience of Spaniards in dealing with modestly cultured folk in a tropical environment rather than from any innate wickedness and cruelty on the part of the Spaniards. It is as foolish and as superficial to charge the Spaniards with more than usual cruelty because some of them like bull-fighting as it would be to bring the same charge against Englishmen because some of them are fond of fox-hunting.* Again the gory deeds of the Inquisition—much exaggerated in the modern imagination of things past—do no more to demonstrate a collective fierceness on the part of Spaniards than do parallel manifestations of fanaticism on the part of Englishmen. As already stated, the previous dealings

*Bull-baiting, cock-fighting and other cruel sports involving animals, not to mention boxing without gloves, were as frequently, if not as ornamentally, carried out in England as they were in Spain until the middle of the eighteenth century; yet none of them has been used as a "proof" of English cruelty, nor should it be.

27

of Spaniards with alien folk had been either with the Moors
in Spain itself, who were the equals if not the superiors of
Christian Spaniards in point of civilization, or else with the
white natives of the Canary Islands whose culture, though
backward, permitted a relatively easy establishment of Spanish institutions and rule among them and whose country
was not widely different from that to which the Spaniards
were accustomed at home.

On arriving in the Greater Antilles, however, the Spaniards
stepped into a complex of conditions wholly novel to them.
Used to a temperate, open, semi-arid country where the energies of men are readily and normally maintained at a high
point permitting arduous labor and a free play of thought,
the Spaniards suddenly found themselves in a hot, damp, enervating climate which lowered their vigor conspicuously,
making it impossible for them to live and to toil as they had
done in Spain. Moreover, they rapidly became subject to
maladies of sorts unknown at home. Many Spaniards succumbed to yellow-fever, dysentery, and other ills to which,
comparatively speaking, the natives were immune. In time,
of course, the Spaniards also attained to a relative immunity
if they and their descendants remained long enough in the
Caribbean area; but, throughout the colonial period, Spaniards
and other Europeans arriving in those parts had to go through
a process of physiological adjustment to the prevailing conditions and, as usual, only the fittest survived.

Added to the environmental factor was the human element
encountered. The modestly cultured natives who previously
had led indolent and happy lives in the manner natural to
them suddenly had to face unwonted conditions brought in
by the newcomers. The latter, finding it impossible themselves
to labor in the fields or in the gold-mines, inevitably sought
to put the natives to hard work for their enrichment. The
Indians, however, died away under the burdens laid upon
their unwilling shoulders. At the same time they showed
themselves to be psychologically unable to absorb either the
religion or the general culture of their new masters, in spite

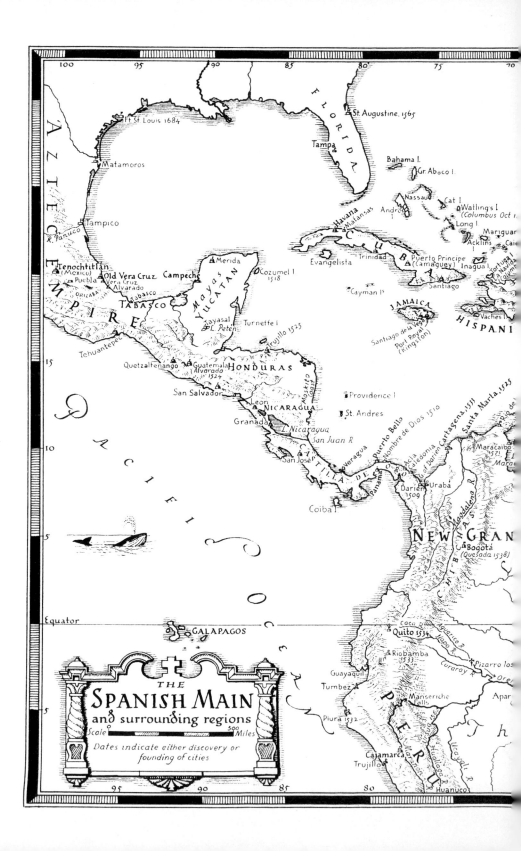

THE
SPANISH MAIN
and surrounding regions

Scale 0   500 Miles

Dates indicate either discovery or
founding of cities

THE ISTHMUS

Scale 0 ___ 50 Miles

Inset map labels (THE ISTHMUS)

Ft San Lorenzo
Colón (modern)
Puerto Bello
Nombre de Dios 1510
Slaughter I.
G. of San Blas
Port Phaesant?
Acla
Caledonia
Chagres R.
Venta Cruces
Gold Road
Old Panama
Perlas Is.
Gulf de S. Miguel
(Balboa 1513)

Main map labels

ATLANTIC OCEAN

San Germán 1508
San Juan 1511
St Thomas
Tortola
Anguilla
St Martin
Barbuda
Vieques
Saba
St Eustatius
Antiqua
St Cristobal
(1628 Br.) Nevis
Montserrat
Guadalupe
Marie Galante
Dominica
Martinique
Sta Lucia
Barbados
St Vincent
Grenada
PUERTO RICO (BORIQUEN)

Aire
Curata
Guayra 1566
Tortuga
Margarita I.
Cubagua
Caracas 1566
Cumana 1520
Tobago
TRINIDAD (Columbus 1498)

Line of Jordesillas 1494

COUNTRY
BARQUICANA
St Thome 1595
GUIANA COUNTRY
Coroni R.
Essequibo R.
MANOA
ELDORADO of
Martin 1593

Orellana Aug 24 1542
Aguirre 1561

Rio Negro
Orellana 1542
Aguirre 1561
Amazon R.
Ursua killed 1561
OMAGUA'S DOMAIN
RO'S
LIN
Purus R.
R. Madeira
reat Forest
BRAZIL

Raisz

of the incessant and conscientious efforts of the Spanish government to confer these benefits upon them. This inability suddenly to make the leap from an intermediate stage of culture to high civilization produced, among some Spanish conquerors, doubts as to whether the Indians were truly human. Others, to be sure, had no such doubts. Nevertheless, the inability remained, except perhaps in a few individual cases, and its working was disastrous to the population of the islands.[1]

Consequent to the decimation of the native folk of the Greater Antilles, there grew up the practice of slave-hunting. It began on the larger islands themselves and proceeded in ever-widening circles to the Bahamas and the Lesser Antilles, and eventually to the mainland shores north, west and south of the Caribbean. Concurrently, beginning as early as 1501, Negro slaves were brought over in rapidly increasing numbers to take the place of the vanishing Indians.[2]

These gloomy, deplorable, but inescapable processes retained the westward march of Spanish intensive occupation in the Greater Antilles down to about 1517. Gold, in moderate quantities, was to be found in those islands, and it must be collected at all costs. Besides, it was necessary to establish centres whence Spanish rule could be extended and where nascent Spanish commerce could find havens from storms or from possible attack. Thus it came about that the city of Santo Domingo was founded on the south coast of Hispaniola in 1504, becoming the first capital of Spanish America. This was but the first step in the process of permanent and intensive settlement. Under the rule of Governor Don Nicolás de Ovando the city of Santo Domingo became not only the seat of political authority but also of ecclesiastical. Moreover, in the island of Hispaniola generally farming was introduced and encouraged so that European crops as well as native plants were cultivated on a large scale. Great attention was paid also to cattle-breeding and to horse-breeding, the animals grown there being long considered to be the best in Spanish America. In like manner, the island which we call Puerto

Rico, and which its native Carib folk called Boriquén, or Land of the Valiant Lord, saw the foundation of San Germán, in 1508, by act of Juan Ponce de León. Afterwards, in 1511, San Juan de Puerto Rico was founded near the northeast corner of that almost rectangular island.[3]

On the large island of Cuba the active and vigorous Governor Diego Velásquez founded Havana on the north coast in 1511 and Santiago on the south coast near its eastern end in 1514. There were beside various other settlements made at this period or soon after in Cuba. Each of the foundations named partook of the same general character, which will be described more fully a little further on.[4]

Early in 1517 there began a westward shift of the centre of Spanish interest. Governor Diego Velásquez of Cuba had a marked curiosity regarding the wonders that might be awaiting discovery in the west. Under his auspices and in swift succession three expeditions visited, studied, and gained knowledge of the mainland coast of Yucatan, Tabasco, and Mexico. Francisco Fernández de Córdoba in 1517, Juan de Grijalva in 1518, and Fernando Cortés in 1519 and later combined to reveal to Velásquez and to the Spaniards in general the long stretch of shore from the eastern side of Yucatan up to the Pánuco River where the great oil-port of Tampico now stands. The three explorers named and their followers, as well as their patron Velásquez, brought about a momentous westward stride of Spanish power.[5]

Environmentally these coastal regions were no more propitious to Spaniards than the Islands had been; indeed, if anything, they were rather less so. Nevertheless there were compensations, albeit they did not in some cases appear to be such at first. For one thing it soon became painfully clear to the Spaniards that they had now come up against people of altogether sterner stuff than were any of the islanders, even the Caribs. Not only was their fighting mettle greater, but also—and in this lay the exciting element in the matter— they were obviously better disciplined and subject to a far more fully developed political and military control than any existing on the islands. In the battles which took place along the shore of Yucatan and of Mexico the invaders were far from being uniformly victorious; indeed, several times, they had to retreat and to seek safety in departure elsewhere. At the same time, as they nursed their wounds and considered the encounters sustained, they drew solace and encouragement from the now obvious fact that they had come among advanced people who had both wealth and strength. Everything proved it: The fine and stately buildings of stone, the populous villages, the ornately arrayed chieftains, the plentiful trinkets of gold and of strange, precious-seeming stones. Nor was there a total lack of more or less friendly contact with some of these alluring natives. In the conversations which interspersed the more martial events the Spaniards received thrilling accounts of an even more civilized and splendid empire inland, beyond the towering mountains which frowningly guard the hinterland behind the steaming coast.

There followed the epochal and epic march of Cortés and his men into the heart of the Aztec dominions, a march dear to all lovers of high adventure. Between 1519 and 1524 Cortés, who soon cast from him his dependence upon Velásquez and placed himself in direct relations with King Charles, conquered the grandiose empire whose centre was the brilliant lake-city of Tenochtitlán (now Mexico City). By a happy chance he captured the person of Moctezuma, the native emperor, and thereby possessed himself of the entire governmental machinery of that realm.

From the point of view of the more reflective Spaniards the conquest of Mexico meant more than the acquisition of vast treasure in the form of gold, native jewels, superb feather-work, and a great variety of Indian art; it meant also that, in the highlands of Mexico, they had found at last a country suitable to them, a country whose landscape, climate, and other natural features were pleasingly similar to their own Extremadura or to their own Andalucía. Not only that but also they here found a disciplined people practising with skill an advanced type of intensive agriculture equal in worth

and in yield to that of the choicest parts of Spain. The native
society, too, was highly organized along lines roughly similar
to the feudal system to which, by tradition, the Spaniards
were accustomed. All in all, the Conquerors could congratu-
late themselves on having found, after years of disappoint-
ment in unsympathetic islands, a land and a people which
could, by dint of a well-considered policy of adjustment, be
made into a Spanish realm in which institutions of native
origin, overlaid with others brought in from Spain, would
uphold a solid and productive colonial kingdom.[6]

Mexico was by no means the only centre of high native
civilization found and conquered and settled by Spaniards at
this period. In Yucatan there had been, up to about 1450, a
strongly organized empire or league of city-states under the
domination of Mexican rulers who, originally, had been
brought in as allies but who had become commanders. At
about the time mentioned, however, the Mayas had risen in
rebellion against their foreign rulers and thereafter each one
of a score or so of cities became the centre of a small, self-
sufficient state not greatly different in character from those
of ancient Greece. In its general outward aspects civilization
did not decline to any marked extent, albeit the imperial and
collective strength was gone. Handsome, pyramid-studded
cities in whose squares and streets a large population thronged
were scattered over the peninsula, making it an alluring land
for Spaniards.

This was the situation in Yucatan when, in 1526, Francisco
de Montejo the Elder began the arduous task of bringing the
warlike and civilized Mayas under Spanish and Christian
rule. He, aided by his son of the same name and by many
stout Spaniards, had to go through with a terrible series of
campaigns in the course of which, more than once, it looked
as though the Spaniards were doomed to failure. At last,
however, in 1542, Montejo the Younger succeeded in founding two Spanish cities in northern Yucatan, namely, Mérida,
near the northwest corner of the peninsula, and Valladolid,
behind the northeast coast. From those and lesser Spanish

settlements a systematic pushing of Spanish power in all directions followed. It was a slow, painful process replete with both reverses and triumphs. Not until 1696 was the last independent remnant of the Maya people, the Itzas of Lake Peten far in the south of the peninsula, reduced to Spanish rule.[7] To this we shall return in Chapter X.

South of Yucatan, in what is now the highland part of Guatemala, there were various civilized native states whose people spoke dialects akin to the Maya tongue or else, as in the case of certain tribes, a variety of the Nahuatl language spoken by the Aztecs. Although there was not here any great imperial organization, there were many sightly cities, each one the centre of a small and compact state. Warfare was habitual to them, and their armies were both large and well disciplined. Nevertheless, in 1523 and 1524, that skilful and courageous commander, Pedro de Alvarado, who had been second only to Cortés himself in the conquest of Mexico, succeeded by a blend of military astuteness and of diplomacy in reducing the whole of central highland Guatemala to Spanish rule. In July 1524 Alvarado founded the Spanish city of Santiago de los Caballeros de Guatemala, thereby signalizing the completion of his task.[8]

Thus we see that, between 1517 and 1542, the Spanish rule was established in the parts of mainland America adjacent to the northern half of the Caribbean. It was in the regions then won that the highest native civilizations were found by the invaders, and it was in those same regions that Spanish power afterwards entrenched itself most deeply, most completely, and most profitably. An effect of the conquests in Mexico, Yucatan, and Guatemala was the rapid withdrawal from the Caribbean Islands, and especially from Cuba, Hispaniola, and Puerto Rico, of all the most virile elements in the Spanish population there. The monotonous and comparatively unremunerative labor of agriculture and of animal husbandry could not hold vigorous men to their service when, off to the west, rich and civilized realms fraught with adventure and with chances of quickly gained wealth, were beckoning

with irresistible temptations. So great was the outrush from
the Islands to Mexico that the insular authorities became seriously perturbed, envisioning a complete exodus of their Spanish supporters. Nor could either they or the home government
check the westward drift of all except the laziest and least
enterprising settlers.

2. *Spanish Conquest of the Southern Part of the Caribbean*

So far as the southern part of the Caribbean is concerned
the crucial event was the discovery of the Pacific by Vasco
Núñez de Balboa in 1513. Prior to that time there had been
numerous preliminary explorations and a few settlements.
Columbus, on his third voyage out from Spain, in 1498, had
passed along the southern coast of Trinidad and after exploring the Gulf of Paria between Trinidad and Venezuela had
gone westward along a part of what is now the coast of
Venezuela, eventually arriving at Hispaniola. On his fourth
and last voyage, 1502–1503, the Discoverer not only voyaged
along the southern coast of Hispaniola but also examined
what are now the Atlantic seaboards of Nicaragua, Costa
Rica, and Panama. He did not attempt to make settlements
on any of those shores, partly because he could not then spare
the necessary men, but chiefly because they were intensely
tropical regions unnatural to Spaniards who would require
very special motives if they were to settle in such unwholesome and unpleasant places. Later, between 1506 and 1509,
various explorations were made from the Greater Antilles,
especially from Cuba and from Santo Domingo, southwards
along the Atlantic coast of Nicaragua down to the Gulf of
Urabá at the southernmost part of the Caribbean Sea, just
where the Isthmus of Panama joins South America. This was
the route of Diego de Nicuesa, a courtly and bold adventurer,
in 1509–1510. In the course of his voyage he made the first
Spanish settlement at Nombre de Dios, but it did not flourish
for the reason that there was not, as yet, a sufficiently strong
commercial motive to keep it alive in the face of great natural

disadvantages. At the same time Alonso de Ojeda was exploring the coast eastwards from Urabá along what is now the north coast of Colombia. He also made a settlement, called San Sebastián, somewhat to the east of Urabá, but it also failed to survive under the adverse conditions to which it was subject. Indeed, the only Spanish city to be established in this period and to attain to permanence was Santa María la Antigua del Darién founded on the Atlantic side of the Isthmus on the west side of the Gulf of Urabá in 1509. Its founder was a lawyer-adventurer, the Licentiate Martín Fernández de Enciso, and its first Governor was a redoubtable rascal named Pedro Arias de Ávila who, through his great influence at court, became Governor of Castilla del Oro, known to us as Panama.

It was from Santa María la Antigua del Darién, with which the unsuccessful settlements already mentioned were merged between 1509 and 1511, that explorations were conducted in several directions. Also from there it was that, in late September, 1513, Balboa made his memorable discovery of the Pacific, second in importance only to that of the New World itself.[9]

Here we must pause briefly in order to consider the nature and meaning of the work done by the Spaniards in the southern part of the Caribbean down to 1513. Only a few of the leading voyages have been specifically mentioned, but all those of this period were of the same character: preliminary studies. Men of diverse qualities took part in them, heroic soldiers such as Nicuesa, Ojeda, and Núñez de Balboa who combined with unsurpassed personal valor a gift for leadership and for devotion to the best interests of their followers; utter villains and mere slave-hunters; avaricious and oppressive tyrants such as Arias de Ávila. All of them, however, whatever their personal attributes, had physical courage. They needed it. Not only was the climate utterly unwholesome for them but also the land reeked with diseases which they could not well resist, and the woodlands along and behind the shore were full of Indians determined to repel their unwanted visitors with deadly poisoned arrows and with all the darting, hiding, springing tactics which their natural ingenuity in warfare could suggest. As has been said, Darién was the sole settlement of permanent sort to begin in this period. In the case of that city a special effort was made to establish a base and a distributing-point for Spanish power. All the other settlements faded away, at least temporarily, from want of a motive strong enough to maintain them.

The discovery and conquest of Mexico had greatly reduced the Spanish population of the Greater Antilles and also had deprived them of intrinsic importance, making them mere way-stations on the route from the lately conquered empires on the mainland to Spain. The Lesser Antilles, at the eastern end of the Caribbean proper, were then, as at later times, regarded by the Spaniards as unimportant because of their lack of gold; at most, and only temporarily, they were possible sources of slaves. The entire northern coast of South America, also, was a region where settlement was not as yet either possible or desirable, and the same may be said of the coast from Urabá up to Yucatan. Something was still lacking to make those regions valuable to the Spaniards. That something was richness beyond and behind the coasts thus far seen by them.

3. The Effect of the Discovery of the Pacific Ocean

When, in 1513, Núñez de Balboa discovered the Pacific Ocean the Isthmus of Panama changed from being a barrier to further explorations to being a threshold beyond which lay unconjectured marvels. The effect was felt at once, and with rapidly increasing intensity as rumors of mighty and advanced kingdoms lying far to the south on the shore washed by the new-found sea began to percolate through the taverns, drinking-shops, and plazas of Darién and of the towns on the Antillian islands. When, in late November, 1520, Ferdinand Magellan, great Portuguese navigator in the service of Spain, entered that same South Sea by way of the strait which bears his name Núñez de Balboa's discovery at Panama was underscored in no uncertain manner.

Men bent on gaining wealth, on experiencing thrilling adventures, on winning high place and power flocked to the Isthmus. The city of Panama was founded on its first site, overlooking the mysterious ocean revealed so lately, in 1518 under the direction of Governor Arias de Ávila. Before long it eclipsed the older city of Darién on the Atlantic side, becoming a great place of congregation for eager Spaniards from the Caribbean islands and from Spain. The adjacent mainland of South America, both on the Atlantic and on the Pacific sides, was explored from the new city as a base. Already there was a rising tide of rumor concerning wonders far away to the south.

Such rumors travel far and fast, even without other means of transmission than the unaided tongues of men. All along the western coast of South America, from what is now northern Ecuador down to northern Chile, and from the roaring rollers of the Pacific to the hot, forested lowlands east of the Andes, lay a native Empire greater in extent than that of the Aztecs, richer in gold and other potential forms of wealth, and in some respects even more remarkable as a civilization. True, the Inca Empire, for such it was, lacked hieroglyphic writing akin to that of the Aztecs and of the Mayas; true, also, its art was in general less ornate. But, in point of organization, of habitability, and of disciplined felicity on the part of its people it was greatly superior to the war-torn confederacy centring at Tenochtitlán whose gory altars spread terror far and wide in a manner unknown to the Sun-worshipping subjects of the Inca Emperors.[10]

By sheer weight of wondrousness the renown of the Inca Empire spread hundreds and thousands of miles in all directions among peoples of lower and often of much lower cultural attainments and in regions to a greater or less extent disadvantageous as homes for men. He who is disposed to ask *why* the fame of the Inca Empire spread so far may well fix his attention upon the superiority of its general culture to that of the eastern regions. Take, as a single specific point, the llama and its kin (the alpaca, the guanaco, and the vicuña.) For one thing, the only native people in all America who had beasts of burden were the subjects of the Inca, who had the llama. To be sure, the llama was slow, temperamental, and not given to unduly heavy work, so that, to Europeans accustomed to the far more efficient horse, it was not admirable as an aid to man in his toil. Nevertheless, it *was* a beast of burden, and to the natives of the remainder of South America —who were wont to do all their own carrying—it must have seemed prodigious, even stimulating some of them, especially those who dwelt in the upper parts of the Plata drainage, to adopt and to use these helpful quadrupeds. Even the earliest Europeans in South America, used to a New World wherein man was the sole pack-animal, were impressed by the llama when they heard of it and saw it.

Direct evidence of the impression made on Europeans by the llama, and also a hint that this animal was once ridden by men although modern llamas will not carry more than 100 pounds, are provided by two early writers: Hulderich Schmidel and Antonio Galvano. The former was a German soldier and explorer who was in the River Plate country between 1531 and 1555 under the leadership of Pedro de Mendoza. He tells us that, in a region not far from the frontier of the Inca realm, he rode a "sheep," *i.e.*, a llama, some forty miles because he was suffering from a wounded foot.[11] Even more graphic is what Antonio Galvano, a noted Portuguese historian who wrote prior to 1555, tells us on this point, as follows:

There are certaine beastes which those of the countrey call Xacos, and the Spanyards sheepe, because they beare wooll like vnto a sheepe, but are made much like vnto a deere, hauing a saddle backe like vnto a camell. They will carrie the burden of 100 weight. The Spanyards ride vpon them, and when they be wearie they will turne their heads backward, and void out of their mouthes a woonderful stinking water.[12]

The llama, however, was far from being the sole cause of the wide distribution of the Incas' fame. The late Baron Nordenskiöld has shown scientifically that many elements derived from the culture of the Inca Empire spread eastwards and southwards, among them being: Spades, war-clubs, wooden spoons, shirts and girdles, sandals, shell-bead spangles, tassels, woven head-bands, and the arts of weaving and pottery-making.[13]

Moreover, the wide areas lying along the eastern slopes of the Andes contain the headwaters of innumerable streams which are the upper parts of either the Amazonian drainage system or of the Paraguay-Paraná-La Plata drainage system. In those areas, of which the Chaco (between the Paraguay River and the highlands of what is now Bolivia) is typical, dwell great numbers of Indian tribes whose culture is now and always has been much lower than that of the Inca Empire. Not only did these riverine tribes, and particularly those of the Chaco, make a practice of raiding the outlying parts of the Empire in quest of women, but also they were wont to migrate into the highlands when periodical droughts and famines were devastating their own country. Movements of this kind were facilitated by the various rivers, such as the southeastward-flowing Pilcomayo and Bermejo, which, rising well within the highlands and therefore within the Inca Empire, flowed into one or the other of the two great drainages mentioned and so formed a natural highway between the highlands and the eastern regions along which ideas and cultural influences passed back and forth.[14]

In short, the fame of the Inca Empire and of its splendors and marvels spread all the way to the Atlantic Ocean by following the downward course of the Amazon in the north and of the Paraguay-La Plata in the south. Between the mouths of those two rivers, both of which lay west of the Papal Line of Demarcation and so were within the Spanish sphere of possession, stretched the coast of Brazil which, by the terms of the Pope's award and of the Treaty of Tordesillas, belonged to Portugal. The rumors of Incaic greatness first reached the Atlantic at the mouths of the Amazon and of the La Plata, but later it spread along the Brazilian coast between the two. Portuguese exploration of that seaboard began as early as 1500–1501, when Pedro Alvares Cabral made the first careful examination of the Brazilian littoral.[15] It is to be doubted however, that the vague reports of the powerful Andean empire of the Incas had reached the Brazilian coast as early as that, albeit they did arrive there within fifteen years afterwards.

4. The Race to Find the Inca Empire.

In a word, the reputation of the great Inca Empire, at its greatest development from 1450 to 1526, spread eastwardly to the Atlantic by way of the Amazon and southeastwardly by way of the River Plate. Better known than this spread is the contemporaneous northward dissemination of the Incas' fame along the northwestern highlands and coasts of South America, to at least as far north as Panama. It was a rumor of the Inca realm which, being current on the Isthmus in 1513, led Vasco Núñez de Balboa to discover the Pacific in September of that year. This event made it imperative for Spain to find a strait that would lead into the hitherto unsuspected South Sea (Pacific Ocean). As we all know, Magellan found the Strait in 1520, albeit too far south to be of much practical use. This fact, however, is less important for us than is the voyage of Juan Díaz de Solís in 1515–1516. Passing along the coast of Brazil in a southerly direction with his fleet of three small ships and about 100 followers (including both Spaniards and Portuguese), Díaz de Solís properly picked up the first faint hints of tidings to the effect that, somewhere far away to the west, there lay a mysterious civilized realm. We cannot, of course, be certain that Díaz de Solís himself ever heard such whispers. In any case they did him no good, for, in March, 1516, he was murdered by fierce Indians on the Plate River estuary, and those of his men who were not killed with him either got home as best they could or else were cast away along the shores of the river and of the Atlantic north from that point.[16]

If Díaz de Solís did not hear whispers concerning the western empire, his survivors, while living among the Indians at various points in eastern South America, certainly collected from their hosts a great variety of exciting hints. One of the men who had escaped with his life from the disaster suffered in 1516 was a Portuguese soldier named Alejo (or rather Aleixo) García. He, with three or four other men, found a refuge on the island which was afterwards called Santa Catharina (off the Brazilian coast at about 27° 30′ S.), and there they heard alluring tales about an enigmatic potentate far away who was called, by the wild Indians of that part, Great White King. With amazing courage this little band of white men, accompanied part of the way by a large number of Indian auxiliaries, made their way westward across immensely difficult country amid every sort of natural and human peril until at last they entered what is now south-central Bolivia, well within the dominions of the Inca. Thus, at some time between 1520 and 1526, they were the first Europeans to enter that great native Empire. Unfortunately, on the return journey, their native allies turned on them and massacred them.[17]

As different as possible from the humble little band of adventurers who were led by Alejo García and who served only their own interests was the next expedition which approached and in part entered the realm of the Inca from its eastern side. It was a grandiose international expedition headed by Sebastian Cabot under the patronage of King Charles I of Castile. The international character of the undertaking is attested by the fact that when it was begun in 1525 it received financial support not only from Spanish merchants and from the King but also from various Genoese bankers and from Robert Thorne, of Bristol, an associate of some of them. The personnel of the expedition, also, was international. Besides an unusually brilliant series of Spanish gentlemen-adventurers, many of whom had been on the Magellan expedition, there was a German merchant and there were two Englishmen the more important of whom was Roger Barlow, of Bristol, a backer of the expedition and an associate of the Thorne interest.[18]

With a fleet of three good ships and over 200 men of more than usual general excellence, Sebastian Cabot sailed from southern Spain on April 3rd, 1526. The ostensible purpose of the expedition was to pass through the Strait of Magellan and to proceed thence to the East Indies; there was, however, a hidden purpose as well, and it was the special interest of the King. This second purpose was that an exploration be made from the Strait northwards along the west coast of South America as far as Panama. Had this plan been carried out, Peru and the Inca Empire would have been discovered by sea, but from a southerly direction. The documents presented by the modern scholars cited above make it seem likely, however, that Cabot, when he reached Pernambuco in July, 1526, already had some idea about seeking for the Inca Empire by way of the Plate River and its tributaries. At any rate this was his intention at the time of his arrival in the Plate River estuary in mid-February, 1527. By then he had met with various survivors of the Díaz de Solís expedition and, especially, with two men who had accompanied Alejo García and who, because he had sent them eastward from the region of Paraguay in search of aid, had escaped the general massacre of his party.[19]

To make the long story as short as may be it is necessary only to point out that, although Sebastian Cabot himself and also Roger Barlow got no nearer to the Inca Empire than a point close to the present city of Asunción, on the Paraguay River, they there received from the low-cultured Indians around them definite tidings of the Inca Empire. They were even shown and given certain finely fashioned trinkets of silver and gold, as well as a few living llamas.[20]

In July 1528, Cabot sent one of his ships back to Spain for the purpose of making a report to the King and to his backers. In the ship went Roger Barlow, Hernando Calderón, and other members of the expedition. They carried with them some of the llamas and a variety of trinkets and other show-pieces as well as letters, reports, etc. It was, truth to tell, a rather pathetic showing.

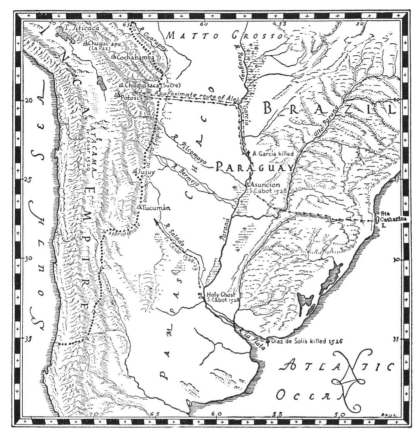

Map to illustrate expeditions towards the Inca Empire from
the southeast.

Alejo García and his followers travelled from the coast of Brazil across country to the
Paraguay River and thence onwards into the Inca Empire. They did so between 1520 and
1526, probably in 1522 or in 1524. In 1528–29 Francisco César and a few followers journeyed from Sebastian Cabot's fort at Holy Ghost into the southern part of the Inca
Empire. The routes indicated on the map are frankly conjectural.

While waiting for results from this embassy to Spain, Cabot and the less than 100 men who now remained with him (many having been killed in skirmishes with the fierce riverine Indians) established themselves at a little post which they had formed and which was called Holy Ghost, at about 32° 30' S., midway between the modern Argentine cities of Rosario and Santa Fé, on the west side of the Paraná River. From this point Cabot, in an effort to acquire more solid results than any yet obtained, sent forth, in the latter half of November, 1528, the audacious young Captain Francisco César and a party of fifteen men to discover the route into the Inca Empire. After leaving Holy Ghost, César divided his small squad into three groups each of which took a separate, but presumably roughly parallel, route towards the west or northwest. Their conduct and manners appear to have been more tactful and urbane than those of Alejo García's party had been, for, having struggled across the Cordillera, they entered the Atacama region, definitely a part of the Inca Empire. There they had pleasant dealings with a native lord who treated them with cordial hospitality, and gave them opportunity to behold how well his land was peopled, how carefully cultivated, and how well provided with flocks of llamas and vicuñas from whose wool fine fabrics were woven. They saw also numerous handicrafts—pottery, metal-working, and so on—that must have convinced them that they had entered the realm which they were seeking. Putting themselves under the protection of the ruling lord—doubtless some high-ranking official of the Incaic hierarchy—they sought his friendship for their own King, whose greatness they did not sing small. After many days of courteous intercourse with their host, César and his companions departed for Holy Ghost in order to report to Cabot on all that they had seen and heard. Their host gave them Indians to carry the many and various presents which he had showered upon them, and he caused guides to conduct them to the frontier. Something calamitous—but perchance nothing worse than a decision by some of the men to remain in the land—must have happened during the return journey; for, when César arrived at Holy Ghost in mid-February, 1529, only seven of the original fifteen men remained with him.[21]

Having shown the salient features of the approach to and entry of the Inca Empire from the eastern side, we must now consider the fact that that realm was being approached simultaneously from the direction of Panama. This is the approach which most historians have studied to the almost complete exclusion of the other. In reality, however, during the decade between 1520 and 1530, Peru was the goal of a race from two directions, by sea from the north and overland from the southeast. Don Enrique de Gandía thinks, correctly, that rumors of the Inca Empire had reached Europe, prior to Cabot's departure, *both* from Panama and from the Plata region, and that the quest for the Mountains of Silver from the latter side was carried on not only by Alejo García—an accidental offshoot as it were of Díaz de Solís's expedition— but also by Sebastian Cabot, acting upon what had become, at any rate for the moment, a policy of King Charles I.[22]

In order fully to understand the significance of this race for the silver and golden realm of the Inca from two directions we must now return to Hernando Calderón and Roger Barlow, who arrived in Spain in November, 1528. They went to the Court, then at Toledo, taking with them specimens of Incaic art in metals and in textiles, and also three of the llamas which they had obtained from the Indians on the Paraguay. It is to be hoped that the llamas, when introduced into the Royal presence, behaved prettily and refrained from untimely expectoration.[23] At any rate, the two emissaries of Cabot succeeded in stimulating the sympathy of the King to such a point that lavish promises of aid poured from his lips. They came to naught, however, for the reason that Francisco Pizarro, who had arrived at Court in the spring of 1528 after a memorable voyage down the coast from Panama, had already sold the King the project of conquering Peru from the northern side. Poor Sebastian Cabot, therefore, was left to struggle home as best he could, and, with only a small remnant of his original personnel, he arrived at Seville in the *Santa María del Espinar* on July 22nd, 1530, to find himself immediately buried under an avalanche of lawsuits into which we need not go.[24]

The King was not alone in his neglect of Cabot, who suffered also as a result of the report which Roger Barlow must have made to Thorne and other backers of the expedition. This does not mean that Barlow acted treacherously towards his leader, for he appears never to have done anything resembling that; rather, it means that the merchants of Seville and of Italy and of England were not in the least interested in risking their money to finance an expedition into a wild and terrible land such as that which, perforce, Barlow described in his report.

5. The Effect of the Discovery of Peru upon the Spanish Main

Panama having become the official portal of the Pacific and an important station on the route to Peru, the opening up of that incredibly rich empire to Spanish exploitation and settlement had an immediate effect upon the Caribbean and upon the countries around it. As, twelve years earlier, the conquest of Mexico had made Cuba, Hispaniola, and to a less extent Puerto Rico important as stations on the maritime highway between New Spain (Mexico) and old Spain, so now did Peru cause the Isthmus of Panama and the northern coast of South America to take on a significance and a value which they had not previously had for Spaniards.

On the Pacific side of the Isthmus the city of Panama, at the site which it occupied from 1518 until its destruction in 1671 by the pirate Henry Morgan (as to which see Chapter IX), was an admirable port for ships sailing to and returning from southern points. It was urgently necessary, however, that a route be made across the Isthmus and that a port or ports be established on the Atlantic side. The places selected for the Atlantic ports were Nombre de Dios and

Puerto Bello which, although founded some twenty years earlier, had languished from inanition. Standing close together almost due north of Panama city, they were linked to it, from about 1530 onwards, by a carefully planned highway which went overland to Venta de Cruces and thence down the Chagres River to Nombre de Dios. This, the celebrated Gold Road, was for more than 200 years the chief artery of commerce for goods and treasure passing from western South America across the Isthmus on the way to Spain. There was likewise an overland road, close to and roughly parallel with the Chagres River route, which was used in the dry season.[25]

The Isthmus was not alone in feeling the results of exploration in South America. Santa Marta, at about 74° 10′ W., hard by the mouth of the Magdalena River which flows northwards from the interior of what is now Colombia, was founded by a brave and generous man named Rodrigo de Bastidas in 1525. Like most of the Spanish cities along the Caribbean shores founded in the last three-fourths of the sixteenth century it became a focus of Spanish culture in very un-Spanish surroundings. Not only was it a centre for missionary effort by churchmen, but also it became a place of considerable trade. Moreover, between 1535 and 1539, it became the entry-port for the expedition of Gonzalo Jiménez de Quesada, vanquisher of the Chibcha nation in the highlands of Bogotá and founder of the rich Spanish realm of New Granada.

Cartagena, about 100 miles to the southwest, and on one of the finest natural harbors in all northern South America, was founded in 1533 by Pedro de Heredia. It rapidly became a city of greatest beauty and wealth by reason of the rich agricultural and mining country behind it, and also because it soon achieved the first importance as a station on the main commercial highway between Spain and the Pacific kingdoms of the Spanish colonial empire.[26]

Thus, little by little as the Spanish power was carried further and further southward along the Pacific, the western end of the north coast of South America became the seat of intensive Spanish occupation. The port-towns were enriched with fine buildings and sightly churches, and rich colonists lived there with all the amenity they could have had at home. Waterworks, docks, and drainage did much to improve the conditions of life. All this sprang, more or less directly, from the development of Spanish rule both in Peru and what is now the highland part of Colombia.[27]

That part of northern South America which lies to the east of Santa Marta was comparatively slow in developing. Adverse conditions along the coast, and a formidable barrier of lofty mountains inland, in what is now Venezuela, combined with a lack of advanced native civilization and of conspicuous amounts of gold or silver to retard the infiltration there of Spanish rule and settlement. Such places as were founded in those parts were established later, and on a small scale.

6. Conclusion

By about 1545, all the richest native civilizations having been conquered, and having begun a long career as producers of bullion wealth for Spain, the Caribbean islands lost much of their original importance. True, Havana and Santo Domingo remained ports where the Spanish shipping congregated as it did in Puerto Bello, Nombre de Dios, Cartagena, Santa Marta and a few lesser points. On the whole, however, the islands themselves were of slight and decreasing interest to the Spanish government and to colonists. At best, on the Greater Antilles—Cuba, Hispaniola, Puerto Rico, and Jamaica—there were a few Spanish planters and herders who raised food-crops and bred cattle and horses. They depended for labor upon slave labor imported from Africa in large and increasing numbers, as a result of which the pure white population was reduced almost to the vanishing-point.

It was, therefore, because the ports in and around the Spanish Main were so many emporiums for a majestic flow of riches from far-flung interior points on the mainland to Seville, chief port of Spain, that the Spanish Main became, by 1525, a focus of foreign envy—and remained so for 275 years.

It was there, principally, that Spain had to fight with her enemies who, naturally enough, were eager to sever her trade-routes and to capture for themselves her laboriously collected wealth.

If Roger Barlow, after his return to England soon after 1530, had had his way, England would have attacked Peru by way of the Amazon with an army of 4,000 men travelling in a great fleet of river-craft. This was a scheme which he tried to foster between 1550 and 1553. It came to naught, however, because political conditions in England forbade and because the plan was impractical in any case.[28]

Still, had the daring scheme of Barlow and his associates gone through, the Amazon and not the Caribbean might have been the area upon which, in later chapters, we would have to concentrate our attention in studying the long and implacable struggle between Spain and her rivals.

Notes to Chapter II

[1] For valuable and detailed studies of these points see: Bourne, 1904, Chs. xiv–xvii. Hanke, 1935, Chs. ii, iv, and v.

[2] Bourne, 1904, Ch. xviii. Scelle, 1906, Vol. I, Bk. I, Chs. i–iii. Newton, 1933, Ch. v.

[3] Historical data, usually but not always reliable, on the cities mentioned in these pages will be found under the several pertinent headings in Alcedo, 1812–1815. For Puerto Rico see: Brau, 1904, Chs. i–xiii, and 1930, entire. Coll y Toste, 1893, especially pp. 118–150, and Abbad y Lasierra, 1866, Chs. i–xiv. I am much indebted to Professor Richard Pattee, of the University of Puerto Rico, for help with the history of Puerto Rico. See: Blanco, 1935.

[4] For Cuba see: Wright, 1916, Bk. I, Chs. i–vi, pp. 5–100. Also the articles on Havana and Santiago de Cuba and Cuba in Alcedo, 1812–1815.

[5] Diaz del Castillo, 1908–1916, Vol. I, Chs. i–xxxiii, where this prince of early chroniclers imperishably sets forth the stirring story. Also: Prescott's *Mexico*. Bourne, 1904, Ch. x. Means, 1917, pp. 24–26. Brebner, 1933, Chs. ii and iii.

[6] Diaz del Castillo, 1908–1916, Bk. III and onwards. Cortés, 1908. Prescott, *Mexico*, 1843, entire. Bourne, 1904, Ch. xi. Brebner, 1933, Chs. iii and iv. Kirkpatrick, 1934, Chs. v–viii.

[7] Means, 1917, Chs. iii, iv, and x, and source materials cited there.

[8] Fuentes y Guzmán, 1882, *passim*. Means, 1917, pp. 84–85, and sources cited there. Bourne, 1904, Ch. xi. Kirkpatrick, 1934, Ch. ix. An excellent idea of the conquest of Guatemala is conveyed by that fine novel, *Maria Paluna*, by Blair Niles.

9 Jane, 1930–1933, *passim* in Vol. II, for third and fourth voyages of Columbus. For the later voyages here mentioned see: Bourne, 1904, pp. 104–111. Wilgus, 1931, pp. 67–69. Means, 1932, pp. 15–16. Chapman, 1933, Ch. i. Kirkpatrick, 1934, pp. 47–54, Medina, 1913–1920.

10 For data on the Incaic civilization of Peru and on its history see: Means, 1931 and 1932, in which many source materials are cited.

11 Schmidel, in L. L. Domínguez, 1891, p. 63. The exact form of the German explorer's name is uncertain. On the title-page of his first edition he is called Ulrich Schmid. Señor Domínguez used for his edition (published by the Hakluyt Society) the text appearing in the first German edition, brought out at Frankfort in 1567, of which a copy exists in The John Carter Brown Library, Providence, R. I. Various other editions are described in the *Manual del librero hispano-americano* of Antonio Palau y Dulcet, Barcelona and London, 1923–1927, 7 vols. See also the Catalogue of The John Carter Brown Library, vol. I.

12 Galvano, 1862, p. 220. This is Vice-Admiral Bethune's edition for the Hakluyt Society of Richard Hakluyt's 1601 translation of Galvano's book, *The Discoveries of the World from their first original unto the year of our Lord 1555.* The English version is here accompanied by the Portuguese text taken from the Lisbon 1653 edition in The John Carter Brown Library. Being spat upon by a llama is an unforgettable, if also a very unpleasant, experience. It sets one apart for a time from one's fellows, as I found when it happened to me while on the Yale University Expedition to Peru in 1914. As stated in the text, modern llamas—who may have formed a labor union—will not carry more than 100 lbs. at any price. If they formerly carried men —as here indicated—they were either more liberal in this respect or else men were less heavy than they are now. The former guess seems the more likely.

13 Nordenskiöld, 1919, especially Ch. xxix.

14 M. Domínguez, 1904, especially pp. 14–16. Data on the *chacu* or Chaco, parts of which were used by the Incas as a vast hunting-ground (*chacu* being the Quechua word for hunt), will be found in: Baudin, 1928, p. 147. Gandía, 1929a, pp. 7–12. Means, 1931, pp. 349–350. Alcedo, 1812–1815, article on Chaco.

15 For early voyages along the coast of Brazil see: Bourne, 1904, Chs. vii-ix. Prestage, 1933, pp. 277–291.

16 Bourne, 1904, Ch. viii, especially pp. 112–114. Chapman, 1933, pp. 63–64. Kirkpatrick, 1934, Ch. x.

17 This account of Alejo García's journey is based upon the following materials, ancient and modern: Díaz de Guzmán, in the Angelis edition, Buenos Aires, 1835. Cabeza de Vaca, in L. L. Domínguez, 1889, pp. 188–233. Nordenskiöld, 1917, and 1919a, pp. 46–54. Means, 1917a, where the age of belicose contact between the Inca Empire and the Guaranís is emphasized, on the basis of materials in Montesinos, 1920, Chs. xxiii and xviv, also, Means, 1931, p. 265. An exceedingly stupid and incorrect mention of Alejo García will be found in: Means, 1932, pp. 253–254. Of the highest importance are: M. Domínguez, 1904, pp. 25–34, and Bishop, 1933, pp. 175–178. Thanks to Mr. Stetson Conn, who has so often aided my studies, I have been able to learn of the content of a modern but little-known biography, amply documented, of Alejo García. This is Mon-

teiro, 1923, especially pp. 24–36, where he dates García's journey 1524. Equally important for the study of Chiriguana history and of Alejo García's raid is: Métraux, 1930, pp. 300–332, where he cites Sarmiento de Gamboa (1907, Ch. lxi) on the wars between the Incas and the Chiriguanas, and where he gives many other data consonant with the material presented in the present text. For an exciting account of an auto-raid across country not greatly different from that traversed further south by García, see: Roger Courteville, *La première traversée de l'Amérique du Sud en automobile. De Rio de Janeiro à La Paz et Lima. Paris* (Librairie Plon), 1930. (The bones of the gallant chariot that made this epochal journey now rest in a back patio of the Museo Bolivariano, at Magdalena la Vieja, near Lima. They should be more properly enshrined!)

[18] The most accessible and reliable of modern authorities on the Sebastian Cabot expedition of 1526–1530 are: Harrisse, 1896; Medina, 1908; Errara, 1895; Tarducci, 1893; E. G. R. Taylor, in her introduction to Barlow, 1932. In all these works many original sources are cited and quoted, most of which the present writer has carefully checked over.

[19] Monteiro, 1923, p. 32. M. Domínguez, 1904, pp. 31–34. Harrisse, 1896, pp. 205–210. Errara, 1895, pp. 25–34. Medina, 1908, I, pp. 144–156. Nordenskiöld, 1919a, pp. 52–53. Gandía, 1929, p. 42, footnote. Taylor, in Barlow, 1932, pp.xxxvi–xxxviii.

[20] Medina, 1908, I, pp. 165–170 and 181–187. Harrisse, 1896, pp. 210–218. Errara, 1895, pp. 35–43. Taylor, in Barlow, 1932, pp. xxxviii–xl.

[21] This is the story of César as set forth, with annotations, in Medina, 1908, I, pp. 191–196, where the narrative of Ruy Díaz de Guzmán is presented and analyzed.

[22] Gandía, 1929, Ch. viii, especially pp. 163–175. See also: M. Domínguez, 1904, pp. 25–43. Taylor, in Barlow, 1932, pp. xxix–xxx and xxxiii–xxxviii. On p. xxxiii she cites Wotton MSS., Appendix III where Peru is said to be the real objective of Cabot's voyage.

[23] See Casimir of Nuremberg's deposition of July, 1530, when he described the things taken home by Barlow. (Barlow, 1932, p. xli.)

[24] Medina, 1908, I, pp. 181–189, 207–208. Harrisse, 1896, pp. 222–226, and 256. Taylor, in Barlow, pp. xl–xliii.

[25] Haring, 1918, Ch. viii. Bourne, 1904, Ch. xix. Means, 1932, Ch. viii, pp. 218–221, and citations in all these works.

[26] Markham, 1912, Chs. viii–xii. Articles on Santa Marta and Cartagena in Alcedo, 1812–1815.

[27] Wilgus, 1931, pp. 107–109. Chapman, 1933, pp. 56–57. Kirkpatrick, 1934, pp. 313–327.

[28] Harrisse, 1896, pp. 365–366. Beazley, 1898, pp. 195–198. Williamson, 1929, pp. 235 and 281–282. Taylor, in Barlow, 1932, pp. liii–lv. Barlow's work was not published until Miss Taylor brought out her admirable edition of it. See also Taylor, 1929.

CHAPTER III

THE EARLIEST ENGLISH AND FRENCH INTRUSIONS IN THE SPANISH MAIN

1. Envy of Spain Begins

HITHERTO we have been examining the work of Spain and, incidentally, of Portugal in creating American empires for their respective sovereigns. We have seen how, with daring and persistence, subjects of those sovereigns explored vast stretches of greatly varied and often immensely difficult territory, and how, as time went by, they settled in and carefully organized those sections of the countries visited which seemed to them suitable for the purpose. In some localities, naturally enough, the processes of settlement and of setting up governmental structure and commercial machinery were slower than in others. In the Spanish Main it was the southern shore of the Caribbean which was most tardy in being brought definitely under Spanish rule. Even there, however, the work was done in time. On the island of Cubagua, close to the Venezuela shore, a little city called Nueva Cadiz was founded by Jacome Castellón in 1547 and rapidly became famous for its pearl-fisheries as did also the larger island of Margarita nearby to the northward. Again, the city of Caracas, now capital of Venezuela, although near the sea is really a highland town difficult to reach from the water. Nevertheless, it was established in 1566 by Diego de Losada, one of the ablest of colonial officials, in order to make a centre of Spanish power in this part of South America and, through its port at La Guayra, a centre of commercial activity also.[1]

The sum of all the work done by Spaniards, and indicated on foregoing pages, was the gradual piecing-together of a great colonial empire. Throughout it was painstakingly organized,

51

the units being towns, officially called cities in many cases, which had their *cabildos* or councils, their local administrators, and likewise their religious functionaries. Over these, in ascending scale, were the governors, captains-general, and viceroys who constituted the fabric of a colonial government which, at least in theory, was bound as closely as possible to the absolute power of the King of Castile, in Spain. The degree to which that government was centralized, the minuteness with which every aspect of administration was supervised by the King, either in person or through the members of his Council of the Indies who accompanied the Court wherever it went, cannot be overemphasized.

The result of all this was that the King of the Spains, in his character of King of Castile, came to possess and to rule a huge transoceanic dominion made up of a series of kingdoms all intimately attached to his personal authority. It was something altogether new in the political experience of Europeans, new both as to kind and as to dimension. Moreover, the wealth steadily pouring from the New World into the coffers of the King of Castile very speedily made him a veritable giant among the sovereigns of Europe, filling with envious wonderment and with growing apprehension all his brother monarchs. Truth to tell, the attitude of the King of Castile was, after 1525 or so, that of an over-zealous game-preserving landlord, with the inevitable result that poachers thronged about in endless efforts to get at the dainty morsels within the ring-fence. Poachers may be illegal, ruffianly, etc., but at any rate they are perfectly natural manifestations of the universal wish to better one's self.

As we have seen in the preceding chapter, King Charles I of Castile, as patron of the Sebastian Cabot expedition in 1526–1530, favored an undertaking of international character. At first glance this might seem to be a sign of a certain liberality on the part of Charles, but a little reflection causes one to see that, in reality, the great expense involved rather than a spirit of generosity was the explanation of the foreigners' participation in that venture. In general, and as a rule, from the time of Columbus onwards, the policy of the Crown of Castile with regard to its American possessions was essentially monopolistic and exclusive, and as time wore on, attack following attack, that policy became more and more intensified.

There was also the question of title. To most Spaniards the Papal Donation, supplemented by the Treaty of Tordesillas, was sufficient to justify the ownership by the Crown of Castile of all America except that portion which belonged to Portugal. More thoughtful Spaniards, of the type represented by Friar Francisco de Victoria (see pp. 17–18), questioned the validity of the Pope's award and held that Castile's real title to the American realms arose from benefits conferred upon the native peoples whose lands were involved. Of those benefits the chief was the boon, considered to be beyond all price, of Catholic Christianity, and to it were added others, such as improved ways of living brought in by the Spaniards and, at least theoretically, superior methods of government. All this, however, was academic as far as the general public in those days was concerned. To most men the important thing was the Pope's award.

As might be expected, the Pope's demarcation of the New World was far from being universally accepted; even France, a Catholic power, questioned it. Consequently, rivals and foes of the two Iberian powers came to maintain that the sole authentic title to lands in the Americas claimed by European states was that conferred by "effective occupation." Precisely what was meant by this formula it is hard to say. One interpretation might be the stark one that a given place belonged to a given European power only until a second power managed to wrest it from the first; and, in fact, this interpretation was the one frequently in force among the rival powers. On the other hand, the enemies of Spain, in the sixteenth century and even afterwards down to our own time, often claimed that little or nothing was being done by the Spanish government and people to explore, settle, and administer the gigantic territories over which they pretended to have a sole right to rule. The falsity of this claim will be frequently demonstrated in this book, and already, in Chapter II, we have seen how ably the Spaniards penetrated wildernesses which later became their firmly held dominions.

2. *The First Attacks upon the Spanish Monopoly*

The earliest attacks on the Spanish monopoly took place, not in American, but in European waters. As early as 1498 Columbus, outward-bound on his third voyage, was obliged to take a new route to Madeira in order to avoid a French fleet lying in wait for him off Cape St. Vincent. At that time France and Spain had lately gone to war, so that the attack would have been an act of legitimate warfare, not, as so many later events, an aggression in peacetime.[2]

It is well to make here a brief digression in order to consider the various kinds of interlopers who presently became active in American waters against the exclusive ownership by Spain. It is fruitless to attempt to draw hard-and-fast lines of distinction; but at any rate we may say that there pirates, called also corsairs, freebooters, buccaneers, and marauders, who were bold bad men of the sea given to preying, for their own profit usually, upon ships of any nation, but preferably upon Spanish vessels, these being the richest prizes and belonging to the enemy-in-chief. There were also contrabandists, ranging from small-scale smugglers, slave-runners, and so on up to great and rich adventurers who, either with or without some form of sanction from their home governments, carried on commercial enterprises in Spain's America in direct contravention of Spanish laws against them. Finally, there were privateers holding letters of marque from their own governments which empowered them to harry Spanish places and commerce to the fullest possible extent.

Although, as will readily be understood, the moral character and the general significance of these groups of men varied enormously, they were all considered by the Spanish government to be intruders, and the term "pirate" was the one generally applied to all alike by Spanish authority. The chief reasons why the three classes are not as sharply defined as one could wish are, in the first place, that some men sometimes belonged to one group and at other times to another, and, in the second place, that sometimes foreign monarchs used both pirates and contrabandists as pawns in their game of assault upon Spanish power, with the result that one is frequently in doubt as to their proper classification.

One more point should here be made clear. The phrase, "No peace beyond the Line," is often heard and almost as often misunderstood, some people even thinking that the Line in question was the Equator! In fact, however, the Line meant was a right angle made up of the meridian passing through the Island of Ferro in the Azores and of that part of the Tropic of Cancer which ran eastward from that meridian. It was a dogma of international politics, perhaps as early as the reign of Francis I of France (d. 1547), and certainly from the Treaty of Cateau-Cambrésis (1559) onwards, that any assaults which took place beyond this demarcation could have no bearing upon diplomatic arrangements in Europe. Spain, naturally, was untiring in her efforts to win recognition for her exclusive rights, but as neither France nor England would give in to her she was fain to accept, at least tacitly, the principle of "No peace beyond the Line." Therefore, treaties down to and including the Treaty of Vervins (1598) maintain a studied silence on questions regarding the Indies. As a practical result, therefore, foreign aggressions in Spanish America were not held to be causes of war in Europe.[3] This did not at all mean that Spain refrained from diplomatic protests to this or that sovereign concerning depredations within her overseas territory; on the contrary, such protests were often made, their results varying in accordance with the general situation at the moment.

It is not clear who was the first intruder actually to enter Spanish America, nor is his nationality surely known. One of the earliest, certainly, was an Englishman whose raid, in 1527, was quaintly prophetic.

At that time the rival houses of Valois and Hapsburg were

carrying on an interminable wrangle in Europe, with Henry VIII as a make-weight between them on their see-saw, favoring now the one, now the other. In 1527, Henry shifted his alliance to the Valois side and, as a small part in his new policy, he sent forth a navigator named John Rut in command of the *Mary of Gilford* and the *Samson* on an exploration which, like that of the contemporary Sebastian Cabot, had both a visible and a hidden purpose. The former was that of seeking a northwest passage to the realm of the Grand Khan of Tartary; the second was to harry the Spaniards in their American waters. Thus, both Cabot and Rut had for their ostensible objective the Far East, to be reached, Columbuswise, by going west; both had a secret purpose, namely that of studying countries nearer at hand and trading with their people. The parallel ends there, however, for Cabot's expedition was an international affair under Spanish auspices and was directed against the interests of no European power; Rut's expedition, on the other hand, was a strictly English enterprise whose hidden purpose was a direct thrust by England at the supremacy of Spain in America. Rut himself gives us a very clear indication, in a letter sent home from Newfoundland on August 3rd, 1527, that he had received secondary instructions which he was then planning to obey.[4]

It is by no means certain as yet whether it was Rut in the *Mary of Gilford,* or Rut in the *Samson,* or some as yet unidentified English captain in some other ship, who, in November, 1527, made a great stir by arriving in Santo Domingo harbor.[5] Whoever the bold voyager was, and whether his ship was a warship of the King of England or a merchantman sailing with that King's orders, the advent in Santo Domingo was both unprecedented and epochal.

We may now examine the English visit to Santo Domingo in November, 1527, in the light of the contemporary documents presented by Miss Wright. The first of them is dated at Santo Domingo on Tuesday, November 26th, 1527. From this paper it appears that on the afternoon of the day before a large three-master belonging to the King of England put into that port and that its skipper, with ten or twelve seamen, came ashore. They stated to the authorities that they had left England nine months before (namely, in February, 1527) and that they had visited Newfoundland and Labrador and had gone as far north as 50° in quest of a strait leading to Tartary, at which part of the cruise they had had another ship with them. In the north the expedition had suffered grievously from cold and many deaths had resulted therefrom; also the other vessel and its pilot had been lost.

Apparently the Judges of the Audiencia received the visiting ship with kindness and sent out to her the High Sheriff and two pilots in order to warp the ship into the harbor. While the English vessel was still at the mouth of the harbor those on board her showed to the Spaniards various linens, woollens, and other merchandise which they had with them for barter. Afterwards, Englishmen and Spaniards sat down to dinner in a spirit of joviality.[6]

At this point, however, the urbanity of the proceedings was sadly ruffled by a stone shot fired from a small lombard in the fortress, which shot passed so near the ship that the English, in spite of the assurances of their Spanish guests, hastily sent the visitors ashore in a boat and immediately afterwards sailed out of the harbor.[7]

In a later letter which is dated at Santo Domingo on December 9th, 1527, and which reached Madrid on March 11th, 1528, we are told that, three or four days after its first departure, the English ship came back into Santo Domingo harbor. On this second occasion there was none of the former urbanity. A landing-party of 30–40 men, armed with archery-tackle, small firearms and a cannon, went ashore at a point some little distance from the town. First attempting to purchase from the people on a private estate a supply of meat and of other food, they afterwards, on the flat refusal of the people to sell, resorted to less pacific means. Indeed, they stole all the hens, eggs, vegetables, and other provender that they could find, and they also forcibly took the clothing of sundry poor colonists with whom they met. By way of culmination to their raid, the English, at last making off to their ship, shouted out all manner of insults to the resentful islanders, promising to come back to attack them again and in larger force.[8]

The effect of this unprecedented visitation can be imagined. The Dons at Santo Domingo charge one another with malfeasance in office, dereliction from duty, and all the other accusations to which flustered officials are liable under such unwonted stress. The King, too, became not unnaturally excited about the affair. In a letter from Madrid dated March 27th, 1528, very soon after he had received the unpalatable news, the King roundly blames his servants at Santo Domingo for their laxity and confusion, and he bids them to be more observant of his laws in future. Three days after the Royal letter was written in Madrid the authorities at Santo Domingo, wishing to bolster up their weak position as much as might be, wrote again to the King, expressing fear lest the English come back, and wailing piteously about the poor state of the defenses of Santo Domingo.[9]

It is difficult to classify this first invasion by Englishmen of Spain's American *mare clausum*. If the ship were indeed a warship of the King of England her advent might be interpreted as an act of legitimate warfare. Yet, from the presence on board of various merchandise, one would gather that the original purpose of the raid had been that of contraband trading. Finally, as we have seen, the conduct of the English degenerated to the level of mere piracy, and the Spaniards regarded their visitors as pirates.

3. *French and English Interlopers, 1527–1567*

Unfortunately for the Spanish government's attempts to enforce its monopolistic policy, foreigners were by no means the only foes of that policy. In the period between 1527 and about 1567 the menace of foreign corsairs was present and increasing. There were many French raids in American waters and even into the territories around them. The year 1537 was particularly bad for the Spanish government in this respect. Not only did French pirates take Chagres on the Isthmus of Panama and invade Honduras, but also the house of Ango, of Dieppe, organized an attack on the fleet bearing treasure from Peru and succeeded in taking nine of the ships so that the remainder brought into Seville for the coffers of Charles a paltry 280,000,000 maravedis (£1,960,000).[10]

In order to maintain the now crystallized official policy of exclusivism, the Spanish government gradually worked out the system of convoyed fleets, supplemented by Coast Guard ships for police-work, which is so well known that it requires no special comment here.[11] This system, whose inception in very modest form may be traced back to 1501, was led from step to step by successive attacks. Thus we find that the use of semi-annual convoyed fleets was begun in 1543 as a direct result of a newly opened war with France which had led to an intensification of French aggressions. In the normal course of legitimate warfare the French attacked the island of Cubagua in July, 1543, with a fleet of six ships, and burned the chief settlement there. To the credit of the French it must be said, however, that, when the Treaty of Crespy was made in 1544, Francis I behaved well, not only ordering his subjects to quit Spanish waters but also acknowledging the paramountcy of Spain. This, of course, did not rid the Caribbean of French corsairs, and still less did it drive forth pirates of other nations —including Mohammedan raiders from Algiers or from Salé. Still, it showed that the French tended to fight fairly.

Again, when France and Spain went to war in 1552, France sent François le Clerc, called Pié de Palo (Peg-Leg) by the Spaniards, with a royal French squadron of ten ships to wage war on the Dons. Puerto Rico and Hispaniola saw all too much of Peg-Leg in those days, and his Protestant lieutenant, Jacques de Sores, pillaged Santiago de Cuba in 1554, winning 80,000 pesos of booty, and utterly destroyed Havana in July, 1555, having wrung every possible jewel and coin from its people. But this was war. It came to an end, as far as the French government's countenance was concerned, with the Truce of Vaucelles in 1556, albeit for only two years or so. Charles's reaction to this French war was his effort to improve the fleet-system and the supplementary maritime police in 1553–1555.[12] Thus the game of offense and defense went on.

In all this period there were few, if any, English intruders in Spanish American waters. The already hinted-at Spanish foes of Spain's monopoly, that is, a large part of the Spanish population of the Caribbean islands, were, however, preparing the way for English contrabandists during these years. They did so not from inherent disloyalty to the King but rather from dire necessity. In the period after 1527 the West Indian commerce in hides and other produce had rapidly outgrown the legal shipping facilities; moreover, slaves had become a crying need. Without them the plantations and such mines as there were could not be worked. Slavery, of white men (Jews and Moors) as well as of Negroes, was an established institution in Spain at the end of the fourteenth century. As a result, the first Negro slaves brought to the Antilles, in 1502 or so, were brought from Spain. It is necessary to distinguish here between these "domestic" slaves and the Bozal Negro slaves, captured in their native Africa and dragged off to servitude in America. The former category was of but evanescent importance, soon giving place to the Bozal element direct from Africa.

The significance of all this for us is that, from 1518 onwards, the King of Castile had to foster the carrying of Negroes from freedom in Africa to slavery in America. The lugubrious business—then and long afterwards regarded as completely righteous—was carried on under contracts and licenses called *asientos,* which the Crown allotted to favored persons and which these usually rented out on lucrative terms to the actual slave-carrying agencies.[13]

Having set up a legal business in slave-snaring and slave-vending which was intended to be no less monopolistic in spirit and in practice than the trade in other articles of commerce, the Spanish government became in this particular no less the victim of illegal procedure than in the other kinds of commerce which it sought to monopolize. Men of many nations worked diligently to snatch, through contrabandist methods, profits which Spain considered to be rightly hers.

This process was aided by Spain's own subjects in America. There was, among the colonists of the second and later generations, a spirit of recalcitrance regarding the Royal laws about commerce of all sorts, particularly when the fundamental needs of the settlers were concerned. This was natural enough. It was also, at least in part, the fault of the Crown, not only because of the inadequate provisions for carrying on legal trade and for defending it, but also because the Crown unquestionably overburdened lawful business with imposts of sundry sorts which colonists avoided if they could.

Smuggling, consequently, received popular sanction, partly due to a weakening of the bonds of discipline and of the sentiment of obedient loyalty which set the colonists in sharp contrast with the more faithful and zealous of the Spanish officials fresh from the homeland. It may have been this contrast which gave rise to the tragic distinction between *chapetones* (Spaniards born in Spain) and *criollos* (persons of Spanish blood born in the Indies) from which, ultimately, the revolution against Spain partly took its rise. Thus it came about that colonials readily connived at illicit trade in slaves and goods whenever it suited them. True, hypocritical officials often abetted in contraband dealings, as we shall see; but the more honest among them tried to repress illegal business.[14]

It is sad, but true, that the first important appearance of Englishmen in the Caribbean after 1527 was in the rôle of slave-smugglers. In March, 1563, came John Hawkins with four ships laden with Guinea slaves, and with banned silks and other goods, in quest of trade. Like his father before him, he had made slaving trips to Guinea and Brazil for years past, and he had powerful friends in the Canary Islands where, as a young man, he learned "that Negroes were very good merchandise in Hispaniola, and that they might easily be had upon the coast of Guinea."[15] What is to us a horrible traffic in human woe was merely good business then. He was, in short, the slave-dealer type of contrabandist.

Arrived at Puerto de Plata on the north shore of Hispaniola in March, 1563, Hawkins at once put himself into touch with the local Spanish authorities and, in collusion with them, speedily disposed of his slaves and his merchandise, to good advantage. Thereby he infringed Spanish law on at least three counts: by being a foreign intruder in Spanish waters; by bringing in unmanifested goods and selling them; and by landing without the requisite Royal license therefore.[16] To these counts may well be added a fourth: he induced Spanish officials to depart from the path of duty and to traffic with him in violation of their oaths of office.

Hawkins's visit to Puerto de Plata is described in documents presented by Miss Wright. One is a letter to the King (Philip II) from the President of the Audiencia of Santo Domingo, the Licentiate Alonso Arias de Herrera, dated at Santo Domingo on May 20th, 1563. He tells us that a Lutheran Englishman with four handsome vessels came into Puerto de Plata and that, in spite of efforts to drive the foreigner away, he, Arias, and other officials had to allow Hawkins to trade in order to secure his departure.[17]

Miss Wright correctly interprets the situation thus: In 1527 the Hawkins party would probably have been hanged by colonial officials had there then been laws providing for such a course. In 1563 there was plenty of law, but not much will among either the colonists or the officials to enforce it because of the growth of imperious economic need to carry on trade whenever opportunity, no matter how illegal, arose. Neither the heretic religion nor the foreign nationality of the Hawkins party weighed much with the colonists or with the officials, albeit efforts were made to give a law-abiding appearance to the transactions with the heretic contrabandist whose coming coincided so nicely with their necessities. The English attitude in all this was that Spain and her Indies were all one kingdom and that, as they had long enjoyed the privilege of trade with Spain, they automatically had it for trade with the

Indies, too; and, in any case, in the quality of heretics, they denied all authoritativeness to the Pope's demarcation and allotment of the New World. The commerce carried on was successful. Hawkins sold his 105 slaves in such a way that the Crown received 350,646 *reales* in customs duties, which sum was duly turned over to the Treasurer of the Crown.[18]

Leaving Puerto de Plata Hawkins, on this his first trip to America, visited one or two other islands and then went home. It seems probable that Hawkins, even thus early, was something more than a contrabandist seeking business wherever he could find it. Mr. Newton thinks that, from 1558 to 1562, he was trying to get permission to help Spain against the French intruders in return for a legal part in the American trade which part England longed to have.[19] This, it must be confessed, puts Hawkins in a better light than he would be in if he were only a contrabandist; instead, he seems to have been a man with a sanely constructive policy.

Hawkins's second voyage, 1564–65, had a *quasi*-official character by virtue of the secret backing which it received from Queen Elizabeth and her ministers. That it had such backing is certain because of a statement made by Hawkins to the Governor of Venezuela, Licentiate Alonso Bernaldez, at Borburata, April 16th, 1565, in which these words occur: "Whereas by order of Elizabeth, queen of England, my mistress, *whose fleet this is* . . ." (italics mine).[20]

As on the previous voyage, there was active trade from which, although it was contraband, the Crown received substantial customs duties. The fact that Hawkins paid those duties—but not the thirty-ducat tax on slaves—indicates that he was anxious to show the Spanish government how very desirable was the sort of trade which he wished to foster between England and Spanish America. Also, there was on the second trip further rather comical chicanery with the Spanish officials. We see Hawkins roaring threats with mock rage and the Dons pretending to be frightened into trading with him in order to escape greater evils.[21]

Hawkins also visited the Río de la Hacha, a minor port

some 90 miles east of Santa Marta on the Venezuelan coast. There he pursued his usual course, but with distinct improvement in his technique, for, on May 21st, 1565, he obtained from six local officials a paper in which they, "in so far as they were authorized to do so," gave him license to trade in their port, and to deal in "slaves, cloths, linens, wines, arms, and other merchandise," with the proviso that customs duties to 7½ per cent be paid on the goods thus sold. The cream of the jest is, of course, that the signatories had no faintest shadow of authority to make any such concession—as both they and Hawkins knew perfectly well. Furthermore, at Río de la Hacha, the English contrabandist booked large orders for future deliveries, which were subsequently made by the Lovell expedition of 1566–1567. Finally, he obtained, for display at home in England, a notarial certificate of good conduct in which it is stated that ". . . the said captain and the men of his fleet have traded and transacted business with all the people of this town in the slaves and merchandise which their vessels brought, maintaining the peace and without disturbing it, and working no harm to any person whatsoever of any quality or description."[22]

It is but just to observe that, aside from the fundamental illegality of his doings, Hawkins behaved well on this occasion. Not only did he provide the people visited with goods sorely needed, but also he paid, or caused to be paid, substantial sums of money to the Royal treasury in the form of customs duties, and all this was done without disorderly conduct.

Hawkins arrived home from his second voyage on September 20th, 1565, and with characteristic energy began preparations for a third expedition. At this point, however, the now thoroughly outraged Spanish government tardily made itself felt. On October 10th, 1566, Ambassador Guzmán de Silva served a sharp notice on Queen Elizabeth to the effect that she would better check such depredations forthwith. The royal lady was seriously alarmed, to judge by what followed. First she forbade Hawkins to go to the Indies at all or to make a further nuisance of himself. Conceivably this was done with a sly wink of the royal eye; but more likely not, because on October 17th, 1566, the port authorities of Plymouth were ordered to stay Hawkins's ships in harbor and on October 30th the Admiralty put Hawkins under bond not to sail to the Indies nor to send ships thither.[23]

Nevertheless, on November 9th, 1566, Hawkins's ships slipped out of Plymouth under command of John Lovell, believed by the Spaniards to be a kinsman of Hawkins. The course followed by Lovell was what Hawkins's would have been, going first to Guinea for a load of slaves, and sailing thence to the island of Margarita, off the north shore of Venezuela and not far west of Trinidad, arriving there about Easter, 1567. At roughly the same time there arrived also a French fleet of contrabandists under Jean Bontemps and the two forces joined for purposes of trade, albeit the French seem to have been much less well disciplined and more riotous than were the English. Having transacted business at Margarita, Lovell went on to the Río de la Hacha, reaching there on May 18th. A new Governor, Don Pedro Ponce de León, now ruled Venezuela, an altogether more strict and upright man than the venal and pliant Bernaldez had been. Governor Ponce de León took a severe line with Lovell as a result of which the English smuggler had to dump ninety slaves at Río de la Hacha in order to prevent their perishing of thirst, the Spanish governor having shut off all supplies to the fleet.[24]

France, at this period, was seething with civil war between her Catholic government and the Huguenot element in her population. We have already noted how the Truce of Vaucelles (1556) between France and Spain had put a temporary stop to official French raids into the West Indies. Nevertheless, French pirates, acting on their own initiative, continued operations, and with a success so noteworthy that, in 1558 or 1559, the ministers of Henri II presented to their master a grand plan for a general and enormous onslaught against the Spanish possessions in the Caribbean, a plan which included not only formidable attacks on the fleets of Spain but also the capture of such capital places as Santo Domingo, Nombre de Dios (and also Panama on the Pacific), and Havana. In short, Henri II's plan was the forerunner of the later ones of Piet Hein and of Cromwell to be discussed in another chapter. It is probable that it grew from the brain of the greatest of French Huguenots, Admiral Gaspar de Coligny. At first glance it may seem strange that a heretic should be so influential with the Catholic government of France that he could induce it to consider such an onslaught on Catholic Spain; but, when it is remembered that the long-lasting enmity between the houses of Valois and Hapsburg was not ended until the Treaty of Cateau-Cambrésis in April, 1559, the situation becomes clear. After that date the Huguenot party was increasingly out of favor with the French government and also the latter tended more and more to link itself with the Spanish government as a measure of defense against the French Protestant element.

Coligny, meanwhile, was endeavoring to establish refuges for his co-religionists in America. Unfortunately for them the places chosen for this purpose were first Portuguese Brazil and later Spanish Florida, in both of which they were trespassers. Although the Treaty of Cateau-Cambrésis put a stop to the Coligny plan for a big-scale attack on Spanish America, it did not prevent the founding by Coligny of a pitiful little Huguenot colony in Florida under René de Laudonnière in 1562.

Concurrently with these events there was not only the strengthening of ties between the French and Spanish governments but also the progressive intensification by the latter of its maritime defences, both on the sea and on the shore. The moving genius in this process was the Admiral Pedro Menéndez de Avilés who, ever since 1555, had labored indefatigably to provide his master, Philip II, with a perfected fleet-system to be defended by adequate convoys and by swift-sailing *armadillas* for the policing of the Caribbean, and also by impregnable land fortifications at such crucial points as the Isthmus, Nombre de Dios, Havana, Santo Domingo, and

Florida. This last was particularly important in Menéndez's scheme because it commanded the Florida or Bahama Channel through which the Spain-bound fleets were wont to take their way.

Unfortunately for them it was on Florida that the Huguenots had pitched as the site for their Protestant colony. Naturally, neither the Spanish government nor Admiral Menéndez could calmly tolerate their presence on the peninsula. As is well known, Menéndez, after prolonged campaigning, managed to defeat the French in September, 1565, with a bloody vengefulness arising from the religious bitterness so common in that day, and also from the wrath occasioned by the bold invasion by these foreign pirates of Spain's possession. In all truth, the fate of the Huguenot colony was deplorable; but it was partly, at least, the fault of the settlers themselves because, while homeward bound in 1565, shortly before the catastrophe, Hawkins had offered to take the unfortunate people home. This offer was partly inspired, no doubt, by a wish to curry favor with Spain by removing the French Huguenots from the country in which they were trespassing; nevertheless, it was an offer which the French would have been wise to accept. The treatment which they soon afterwards got from Menéndez, and the foundation by him of St. Augustine, not only mark the "effective possession" of Florida by Spain, but also form a part of the Admiral's great work in building up Spain's defenses in the Caribbean.[25]

4. Hawkins at San Juan de Ulúa: 1568

This brings us to the culmination of Hawkins's attempt to win for England legal participation in the trade of Spanish America. It is obvious that, in view of the new alignment between Spain and France in Europe, his schemes were destined to failure. Now that Spain had no more to fear from France—at any rate so far as the French government was concerned—King Philip II was able to intensify indefinitely his policy of exclusion, which is exactly what he did. As for

England, not yet were her people filled with that unutterable hatred of Spain and of her Faith which afterwards moved them so profoundly; Hawkins was fated to be a factor in an enormous and sudden increase of popular loathing for Spain on the part of Elizabethan England.

Hawkins's third voyage was even more definitely a venture approved by the Queen of England than the second had been. This is shown by the fact that his two chief ships were her property, provided for his use for the precise purpose of invading the preserves of the Queen's brother-in-law, Philip II. The ships in question were: H.M.S. *Jesus of Lubeck,* 700 tons, 180 men, 22 guns and 42 secondary pieces of armament; this ship being the flagship was in command of Captain John Hawkins; H.M.S. *Minion,* between 300 and 350 tons; the *William and John,* 150 tons; the *Swallow,* 100 tons; the *Judith,* 50 tons, under the command of a young man named Francis Drake; the *Angel,* 32 tons; and two or three smaller vessels.[26] With this formidable fleet Hawkins sailed in October, 1567, and shaped his usual course for Guinea for the customary dolorous purpose. Having done so, he began his wonted round of visits in the ports of the Spanish Main, but he found a wholly new spirit of increased resistance on the part of officials with the result that business dealings were both more difficult and less lucrative than on former occasions. Trade was also hampered, to some extent, by the growth of brawling and tumultuousness among the English crews while on shore, apparently as a result of the influence of certain rowdy Frenchmen who were with them.[27]

With profits much less satisfactory than formerly, Hawkins tried to sail for home in August, 1568. In the Florida Channel he ran into fearfully tempestuous weather and had to turn westward in order to save his fleet. Scudding before the gale the English squadron went further west than any of their nation had ever gone, and mid-September found them off San Juan de Ulúa, on an island opposite to Vera Cruz, the port of Mexico. By this time the ships were much strained by the buffeting they had received, the venerable *Jesus of*

Lubeck being in a particularly bad condition. Hawkins induced the port authorities to admit him to the harbor between San Juan de Ulúa and Vera Cruz on the plea that, unless shelter was afforded him, the ships of his Queen, a friend and ally of Philip of Spain, would be wrecked along the coast by the hurricane which was still raging. It was well known to Hawkins that a great Spanish fleet was hourly expected, and on September 17th, 1568, it hove in sight—tall galleons bearing not only a Spanish Captain-General, Don Francisco de Luxán, but also the new Spanish Viceroy of New Spain, Don Martín Enríquez de Almansa. Apparently Hawkins was already in the harbor at that time, for on the following day Viceroy Enríquez, from his flagship riding uncomfortably on the rough sea without the harbor, accepted terms which Hawkins had sent to him concerning the entry of the Spanish fleet into its own harbor. In this letter of acceptance the Viceroy gave his word to maintain peaceful relations and arranged for an exchange of hostages.[28]

When, on Tuesday September 21st, 1568, Viceroy Enríquez and Captain-General Luxán brought their Royal fleet into the harbor they discovered that Hawkins had possessed himself of the fortress of San Juan de Ulúa. This, it seems to me, afforded the Viceroy a legitimate excuse for changing swiftly from a peaceable to a warlike policy towards Hawkins, for the taking of the fortress was certainly a breach of his own terms. It is, of course, quite possible that Viceroy Enríquez intended, in any case, to break his promise given under compulsion to the Lutheran interloper. The somewhat intricate code of honor accepted in those days by Catholic gentlemen of Spain may well have led him to believe that a forced undertaking with one whom he could not regard as other than a heretic house-breaker did not engage his honor in any way.

However all that may have been, Viceroy Enríquez caused a grand attack to be begun against the English on the morning of Thursday, September 23rd, 1568. The battle lasted for hours and was a magnificent fight in which cannonading and fireships and all manner of warfare took their part. The victory of the Spaniards was complete. Only the *Jesus,* the *Minion* and the *Judith* (commanded by Francis Drake), got away from the battle, and of these three the *Jesus* had to be abandoned outside the port on account of her unseaworthy condition. When that was done the Spaniards boarded her and took away whatever she held, including their hostages whom the English, to their credit, had not harmed. The two remaining ships were so terribly overcrowded with fugitive Englishmen that some 100 of the 200 on the *Minion* had to be abandoned on the mainland afterwards. There they were taken by Spanish authority and sent inland. After two years or three, during which they were not greatly molested by the government of New Spain, they were taken in charge by the newly arrived Holy Inquisition which gave them severe treatment. The aforementioned young man named Francis Drake did not, on this occasion, behave heroically in deserting his commander. After setting ashore another hundred men, he sailed away in the *Judith* on his own course and finally reached Plymouth on January 16th, 1569. Nine days later arrived Hawkins in the *Minion* with only fifteen men left out of the 100 who had stayed with him. For both vessels the homeward journey was sad, starvation-ridden, and utterly desolate.[29]

5. Conclusion

The thrashing received by the English at San Juan de Ulúa taught those ambitious islanders that they were offending a power considerably greater than they were as yet, and it filled them with a perfectly natural rage. Also, perhaps, the glimpse which Hawkins, Drake, and the rest had of New Spain—one of the particularly rutilant jewels in the Crown of Castile—heightened their already mounting commercial covetousness by displaying before them the vast wealth of Spain's colonies. Anger caused by the defeat of 1568, coupled with envy arising from increased knowledge of what riches were waiting to be snatched, engendered the implacable hatred of Spain which thereafter burned in English breasts. To it were added from time to time new elements such as the clash between religions, and the belief, long current in England, that by attacking the Spaniards, the English would be aiding the poor Indians to escape from destruction. This last factor was largely due to Bartolomé de las Casas, who, to use Fernández Duro's words, "was called the Apostle of the Indians, but who might much better have been called their Lawyer,"[30] who, with unbalanced eloquence and vehement exaggeration, won a degree of publicity in his own time and for many generations afterwards which was largely the cause of the highly unpleasant reputation borne by Spaniards in the rest of Europe.[31]

The effect wrought by the victory of San Juan de Ulúa on continental minds was considerable, and varied in kind according to the sympathies of those concerned. An indication of all this comes to us through the Fugger News-Letters. The Fugger family, originally of Augsburg, owned one of those great banking houses which had its branches and its informants all over Europe, with the result that everything worth knowing was known to them as soon as it was known to any one. Thus, in a News-Letter dated from Seville January 21st, 1569, we have a rather garbled account, quoted from English letters via Vigo, of the affair at "San Juan de Lua near Vera Cruz," but without mention of Hawkins by name.[32] In another Letter, dated from Seville February 11th, 1569, we have an account of English piracy along the Spanish Main— but still without mention of Hawkins by name—where as much as 600,000 ducats are thought to have been collected by the contrabandists, albeit the writer of the Letter doubts if it were more than 400,000 ducats.[33] In other Letters we have other indications of the interest taken in these matters in Europe. One Letter, after relating, from Seville December 7th, 1569, how Hawkins, in a rage because of his late defeat, has challenged Menéndez, Luxán, or any other Spanish captain, to meet him at Havana and fight it out, goes on to say that Drake is hunting for the treasure-fleet from New Spain, and that both Hawkins and Drake have Queen Elizabeth's support and secret backing in spite of her agreement with the King of Spain. The Letter says: "It is the nature and habit of this nation not to keep faith, so the Queen pretends that all has been done without her knowledge and desire."[34]

From the modern standpoint King Philip II made a great mistake in not falling in with Hawkins's plans and hopes for a legitimate trade between England and Spanish America. From such a trade great benefits would have arisen, for the Spanish Crown, for its subjects on both sides of the water, and for the English traders. But it is not by modern standards that such a matter can be justly judged. Judged by those of his own day Philip's course was the inevitable and the right one. He, a Catholic and absolute sovereign committed to a definitely exclusive and monopolistic policy long in preparation, could not suddenly allow himself to be swayed away therefrom merely because a heretic subject of a heretic Queen wished him to do so. Consequently, the illicit trade remained illicit; Spanish America remained Catholic and so bound to repel invaders, particularly non-Catholics. Nevertheless, human creatures being then very similar to what they are now, prohibitions did not prohibit and so, often with the connivance of the more venal colonial officials, contrabandists continued to flourish, largely because the settlers in Spanish America sorely needed the goods and the slaves which they provided.[35]

Notes for Chapter III

[1] See the articles on the places named in Alcedo, 1812–1815. Of special importance for this region is: Rionegro, 1914, especially Chs. iv–xxv.

[2] Marcel, 1902, pp. 6–7. Jane, 1930–1933, II, pp. 8–11, where the letter from Columbus to the Catholic Sovereigns, dated October 18th, 1498, from Hispaniola, describes the matter.

[3] Marcel, 1902, pp. 9–10, where he shows that Francis I, far from accepting the Papal line of demarcation and the Treaty of Tordesillas, allowed his subjects to do what they liked beyond the Line defined in the text, sometimes called the Line of Amity. Also see: Newton, 1933, pp. 121–123.

[4] Rut's letter will be found in Williamson, 1929, pp. 104–105. It was addressed to Henry VIII and clearly shows that secondary instructions about explorations southwards had been received. See also: Newton, 1933, pp. 49–50; Wright, 1928, p. 1.

[5] Materials for the study of this complicated question include: **Herrera,**

Decade II, Bk. V, Ch. iii; Wright, 1928, p. 1; H. P. Biggar, *An English Expedition to America in 1527*, in *Mélanges d'Histoire offerts à M. Charles Bémont*, Paris, 1913; Biggar, *The Precursors of Jacques Cartier*, Ottawa, 1911, p. xxix (these two works being cited by Miss Wright); F. A. Kirkpatrick, *The First Recorded English Voyage to the West Indies*, in *Eng. Hist. Rev.*, Vol. XX (1905), pp. 115–124; Williamson, 1929, pp. 104–111, 256–261; Beazley, 1898, p. 181; (Messrs. Kirkpatrick and Williamson seem to think that it may have been Rut in the *Samson* which was later lost, but Williamson admits that the point is not proven); Brebner, 1933, p. 114, thinks that the voyager was Rut; Newton, 1933, pp. 49–50, is neutral as between Rut and some other not known. This seems to be the safest position to take; for us the point is one of no great moment.

⁶ Here Miss Wright cites Fernández de Oviedo, 1851–1855, I, p. 611 and Herrera, Dec. II, Lib. V, Cap. iii, as showing that the goods were probably being offered in payment for supplies needed by the English.

⁷ All this is set forth in Document 1 A, Wright, 1928, pp. 29–34, being a letter or report written at Santo Domingo, November 26th–December 9th, 1527.

⁸ Wright, 1928, pp. 35–56.

⁹ Wright, 1928, pp. 57–59. Needless to say, the King's letter of March 27th, 1528, and the letter of March 30th from Santo Domingo "crossed in the post." See also: Fernández Duro, 1895–1903, I, Ch. xv.

¹⁰ For the divers sorts of French raids at this period see: Marcel, 1902, pp. 10–20, where he cites many source-materials. Of general importance is Alcedo y Herrera, 1740, upon which is based Justo Zaragoza's *Piraterías y agresiones de los Ingleses y de otros pueblos de Europa en la América española desde el siglo XVI al XVIII*, Madrid, 1883. Also of the highest importance for habitual consultation on all points having to do with shipping and so forth is: Haring, 1918. Reference to the Ango affair of 1537 is in Newton, 1933, pp. 51–52.

¹¹ See: Haring, 1918, Chs. v, vi, and ix.

¹² Newton, 1933, pp. 52–59. Marcel, 1902, pp. 8–9, 15–20. Haring, 1918, Ch. ix. For the Spanish commercial system in general see: Means, 1932, pp. 218–221; Fernández Duro, 1895–1903, I, Ch. xv and xxii.

¹³ The standard work on the slave-trade is Scelle, 1906.

¹⁴ Wright, 1928, pp. 6–7.

¹⁵ Quoted from DNB article on Hawkins, cited below.

¹⁶ Wright, 1928, pp. 7–8, where she cites specific laws broken by Hawkins.

¹⁷ This is document 5 in Miss Wright's series, pp. 61–63. She tells us that Hawkins had left Plymouth in October, 1562, citing Hakluyt, X, pp. 7–8, in her note 3 at p. 61.

¹⁸ Wright, 1928, pp. 9–13, and Documents, 6, pp. 64–66, and 7, pp. 67–71, and 8, pp. 72–75, being three letters to the King from officials who referred to the Hawkins incident of 1563.

¹⁹ Newton, 1933, pp. 67–69, where he shows that Hawkins's first voyage was backed by a syndicate of London merchants, and that Hawkins was interested not only in slaving but also in building up an English participation in legal West Indian trade in such commodities as hides, sugar, gold, silver, and pearls.

[20] Wright, 1928, pp. 82–83.

[21] See documents revealing this side of the matter in: Wright, 1928, pp. 75–86. For accounts of corsair activities in northern Venezuela see: Rionegro, 1914, pp. 140–152.

[22] The documents here referred to are: The licence to trade (May 21st), Wright, 1928, pp. 92–93; and the certificate of good conduct, covering the time between Saturday morning May 19th to 4 P.M. on Wednesday May 30th, 1565, Wright, 1928, p. 94. See also her p. 15. After his return from his second voyage Hawkins, who brought home great wealth in pearls, jewels, silver, and gold, was granted his first armorial bearings. His crest was "a demi-Moor, proper, in chains," wherein we see a direct reference to his slaving activities. DNB article on Hawkins, p. 214.

[23] Wright, 1928, pp. 15–16. See also: Article on Sir John Hawkins by J. K. L.(aughton), in DNB, XXV, 1891, pp. 212–219.

[24] Wright, 1928, pp. 15–18. Williamson, 1927, pp. 122–123. Corbett, 1898, I, Ch. ii, pp. 72–98.

[25] Winsor, II, pp. 260–270. Fernández Duro, 1895–1903, II, Ch. xiii, especially, pp. 209–214, 220–228. Newton, 1933, pp. 58–60, 72–76. Chapman, 1933, p. 105. Wilgus, 1931, p. 99. Dau, 1934. Laudonnière, 1586.

[26] Corbett, 1898, I, p. 99, note. Williamson, 1927, pp. 145–148. Wilkinson, 1933, p. 11, note, where he remarks that the *Jesus of Lubeck* was the last foreign-built ship ever to be used by the English navy.

[27] Wright, 1928, pp. 19 and 116–127, where she gives Spanish accounts from Río de la Hacha and from Cartagena in September, 1568, describing Hawkins's latest visits to those places.

[28] Wright, 1928, pp. 20–26, and Document 25, p. 128, which is the Viceroy's acceptance of Hawkins's terms and is dated on the Spanish flagship, off San Juan de Ulúa on September 18th, 1568. Document 26 is an account of matters from Luis Zegri to and of Mexico, from Vera Cruz September 18th, 1568, pp. 129–130.

[29] For accounts of the attitude of Hawkins towards Drake see: Wright, 1932, pp. xx–xxii; Corbett, 1898, I, pp. 420–421. For the San Juan de Ulúa affair, see: Corbett, 1898, I, Chs. ii and iii; Williamson, 1927, pp. 184–202; Wright, 1928, pp. 24–26 and pp. 131–152, which last is Viceroy Enrique's account of the matter and those of various witnesses, dated 27–30 September 1568; Fernández Duro, 1895–1903, II, Ch. xii, pp. 197–208; Hart, 1922, Ch. ii; Rogers, 1927, Chs. i and ii; Beer, 1908, Ch. iv.

[30] Fernández Duro, 1895–1903, II, pp. 228–229.

[31] On these points see: Means, 1932, pp. 229–232 and 253, and the sources cited there.

[32] Fugger News-Letters, Series I, No. 4.

[33] Fugger News-Letters, Series II, No. 4, where it is stated that, by way of reprisal for all this, English merchants at San Lucar, Cadiz, and Seville were seized, but were released on bail, next day.

[34] Fugger News-Letters, Series II, No. 11. An epigram of Francis I of France on the English is here quoted:

> Anglicus, Anglicus est cui nunquam credere fas est,
> Tum tibi dicit ave, tanquam ab hoste cave.

(He is an Englishman to whom it is never right to give credence, when he says Hail to you, be on your guard against him as against an enemy.) I am indebted to Mr. Mark Kiley for this translation.

[35] A good idea of the political organization of Spanish America under Philip II can be gained by consulting Beltrán y Rózpide, 1927, and López de Velasco, 1894.

CHAPTER IV

DRAKE AND OTHER DESPOILERS, 1570–1600

1. French and Netherlands Corsairs on the Spanish Main

THE defeat at San Juan de Ulúa, although serious, was only a temporary set-back for Englishmen intent upon wringing wealth from the Spanish Main. In the meanwhile, Frenchmen and Netherlanders were likewise active, and to them we now must turn.

With the French, as we have noted, the tradition of prodding the Dons was at least as ancient as it was among the English, and it was nearly as constantly maintained in activity. There is a curious point in connection with the French attitude towards Spain and her overseas empire which seems not to have been emphasized as much as it should be. It is this: Catholic Frenchmen, including the French government, deeply resented the Papal donation to Spain and to Portugal of the entire New World. Catholic Frenchmen, holding themselves to be no less sons of the Church than were their southern neighbors, found themselves excluded by His Holiness from all part in the new and grandiose task of bringing to the Faith the millions of infidels dwelling in America. This, quite as much as political and economic considerations, filled them with envy and stirred them to aggressive action. As time wore on, Protestantism arose in once wholly Catholic France and, in the Huguenot party, came to assume a large place in the general scheme of things. To Huguenots, no less than to English Protestants, the Papal donation was intrinsically absurd, and the manner in which Catholic Spain and Portugal allocated to themselves, by virtue of that donation, all rights and privileges in the New World was nothing short of abominable. Thus it came about that all Frenchmen, whether

Catholic or Huguenot, were desirous of doing all that they could to break down the Spanish-Portuguese monopoly.

The French corsairs who operated in the Spanish Main were, for a time, the chief outward manifestation of the national attitude. One of the most picturesque of French buccaneers was François le Clerc, otherwise called Peg-Leg (Jambe-de-bois, Pié de palo). In him the common attitude of Catholic and of Huguenot Frenchmen is summed up. Not only was he a man whom the Admiral Gaspar de Coligny, chief of the Huguenots, was pleased to invite to his table, but also he was one whom King Henry II, in September, 1555, was delighted to honor with a patent of nobility in which le Clerc is described by the King as "our dear and well-beloved François le Clerc, one of the captains of our navy." Further on in the same patent the King feelingly describes how his pirate friend had lost a leg and had received grave injury to an arm, in spite of which misfortunes of war he had continued to assault the Spaniards.[1]

Although le Clerc has been mentioned in the preceding chapter (pages 59–60), it is necessary to recur to him here in order to illustrate a point very important for all periods in the history of French-Spanish relations. It is this: The French government tended to be appreciably more scrupulous with regard to the observance of treaties than was the English. In spite of the then accepted principle of "no peace beyond the Line" (see page 55), the rulers of France withheld their countenance from corsairs during the times when treaties were in force. On the other hand, when war was on, they fought with all their might. This honorable policy is shown forth with great nicety by the career of le Clerc and by that of his associate, Jacques de Sores, also mentioned in the preceding chapter. For the most part such as they harried the Spaniards only during wartime, albeit other hardy spirits, most of them obscure, continued their activities even against the prohibition of their own government. The scrupulousness of the French rulers, however, was a fact. It was in a period of war, between 1558 and 1559 and just prior to the Treaty of Cateau-Cambrésis, that the French government, probably in consultation with Admiral Coligny, planned operations on an immense scale against Spanish power in America. A strong fleet of twelve or more ships was to capture the treasure from Peru at Nombre de Dios, ruining Santo Domingo and Puerto Rico on the way out, and then it was to seize the fleet of New Spain at Vera Cruz, ending up by a great attack on Havana while on the way home. It was a plan on unprecedented scale, and, incidentally, it anticipated by almost a century the Western Design of Oliver Cromwell, described on pages 189-196. The point important for us is that, immediately after the signing of the Treaty of Cateau-Cambrésis in April, 1559, the whole thing was given up.[2] We must not lose sight of the fact that there was a sharp contrast between the official policy of the French government and the conduct in America of many corsairs of that nation. The latter gave no thought or weight to the solemn agreements of governments.

French incursions in the Caribbean were numerous from 1570 onwards, many of them being of the frankly outlaw sort, but none the less dangerous for all that. Sometimes the French mariners acted by themselves, but often they made alliances with pirates of other nations. Thus Francis Drake, following the example set him, but not with much emphasis, by John Hawkins, had at least two French pirates as colleagues. One was Captain Paul Blondel, called "Bland" by the English; another, and more important one was Guillaume le Testu who, as we shall see, served him well as an aide in his doings.[3]

Guillaume le Testu, it should be noted in passing, was not only a buccaneer of unusually wide experience in assaulting Spanish ships and places, but also he was a great map-maker. In this more respectable part of his life-work he drew upon knowledge gained in the course of his voyages hither and yon about the Spanish Main.[4]

Most of the French corsairs of this period and of others were, as is but natural, obscure marine thieves whose chief claim to fame lies in their daring and in the skill with which they darted far and wide over the rolling waters of the Caribbean. We catch a glimpse of their manner of working from a document of 1571 printed by Monsieur Marcel. The author was a man named Vicente Estévez, a native of Jerez de la Frontera, hard by Cadiz. In his report, signed at Madrid in October, 1571, he relates to the President of the Royal Council of the Indies the chief features of his life in the Indies, as a planter in Jamaica, and as the pilot of a frigate which cruised about the Caribbean picking up cargoes from one port to another. This honest man, typical of thousands of hard-working Spanish settlers in the islands and mainlands of Spanish America, was making a voyage from Yucatan, whither he had gone in quest of salt, home to Jamaica when, at dawn on a March morning of 1571, he and his seven companions suddenly saw that a French ship of some seventy tons and a large pinnace were bearing down upon them. Estévez at once changed his course and made all speed for Cartagena where he arrived safely in spite of eager pursuit by the French ships. Having given warning to the Governor of Cartagena that corsairs were in the offing, Estévez managed to return to Yucatan where on May 8th his frigate was surprised and taken by the same French pinnace, which seemed to spring up before them as though by magic, there being a dead calm at the time. There were thirty-seven Frenchmen in the pinnace and only eight Spaniards so that the latter had no chance this time to escape. The corsairs took over the Spanish frigate and helped themselves to the provender which she carried. Finding that Estévez was a pilot by profession and well versed in all those waters, the Frenchmen obliged him to serve them. With great astuteness Pilot Estévez laid a course for the northeast corner of Yucatan where, at his suggestion, twenty-three of the Frenchmen went ashore to hunt for game in the woods. As the Spaniards had expected, the fierce Indians of that region set upon the shore-party and shot them all with their arrows. Those who remained aboard the frigate finally made sail for Normandy, taking their Spanish captives with them. On the journey to Havre, where they arrived at the end of

July, 1571, the French pirates regaled their captive with tales of their deeds. They told him how they and their kind were wont to harry the entire coast, from the island of Margarita all along the northern coast of South America to the Isthmus, and thence onward to Nombre de Dios and to Yucatan. These particular pirates, whose names are not preserved, had had a special method of working. The large ship which they had had with them when Estévez's frigate was first chased by them, but which they had later lost sight of, would stand off shore and the pinnace would go inshore to make the attack, afterwards retreating with the booty to the protection of the bigger vessel. In this way they had successfully taken a merchantman in the very harbor of Chagres (Nombre de Dios) and so had won spoils of silk, linen, and wine, as well as other valuable things. The same procedure was repeated again and again and, on previous piratical campaigns, the big ship would take the plunder across to Havre in Normandy at certain times in order to sell it.[5]

In short, French piracy was not only extensive but well planned. From the point of view of their countrymen, these corsairs were successful business-men of considerable importance. In their treatment of Estévez and his men they were, as one would expect, decidedly rough. But at least they let him go once France was reached, and he made his way home by the help of the Spanish ambassador in Paris.

At this same period the Netherlanders were beginning their struggle to rid themselves of the yoke which Spain had laid upon their unwilling necks. Under the leadership of Prince William of Orange a great nationalist movement was getting into its stride. A part of it was a society called *les Gueux* (the Sea-Beggars), made of hardy spirits directed by the Seigneur of Dolhain. Under a commission from the Prince of Orange these Flemish and Dutch rebels against the rule of Philip II of Spain in their country made a formidable attack upon Spanish power there. Although they never came into American waters, the Sea-Beggars may justly be regarded as the initial step towards corsairing by the Netherlanders. They built up a splendidly equipped and well manned fleet of privateers which, with some English help, very seriously bothered the Duke of Alva and other Spanish authorities in the Low Countries.[6]

2. Spanish Measures for Defense

In view of the increasing attacks upon their monopoly the Spaniards, quite naturally, did all they could to defend their interests in the Indies. For a long time, as we have noted, the Spanish government had been working out a system of convoyed fleets for the carrying on of trade and of administration in the colonies. In 1567 Admiral Menéndez de Avilés completed the defensive system and gave it the form which it continued to have for many years after. The special purpose of the system was to ensure the safe passage to and fro of the great fleets which connected Spain with Cartagena, Puerto Bello, Nombre de Dios—all these being connected also to Peru by routes through the Pacific—and with Havana, which was an important assembly-point for home-bound fleets. The chief weakness of the system had been that the less important island and mainland possessions of Spain in the Caribbean had been largely left to defend themselves as best they could while at the same time local shipping between them had been left practically defenseless.

As perfected by Menéndez in 1567 there was a general improvement and enlargement of the original idea. Not only were all the chief ports and even the secondary ones provided with new fortresses and citadels massively built of masonry and provided with heavy artillery, but also a new kind of ship was evolved for the carrying of specially valuable cargoes such as bullion and pearls. The *galizabra*, as this type of vessel was called, was not very large but it was exceedingly swift for those days, being of the lateen (fore-and-aft) rig traditional in the Mediterranean and being also provided with oars so that it could go even in dead calms which would hold galleons and other entirely sailing ships still. In addition to all this, there was worked out, between 1575 and 1582, a supplementary system of maritime police in the form of two windward fleets, one of which had its home port at Santo Domingo, the other at Cartagena. These police squadrons were, unfortunately, horribly expensive to maintain; nevertheless, they did much to defend local shipping and to protect harbors and coasts.[7]

In short, it is clear that the English were soon to have various competitors in the grand game of Don-badgering; indeed, the French were already in the field, and very active. At the same time Spanish resistance was stiffening, and new ways of maintaining the now sacrosanct monopoly were being perfected by Spain.

3. The Career of Francis Drake in Spanish America

After the disaster at sea to San Juan de Ulúa and his inglorious exit therefrom Francis Drake came, naturally enough, to loathe Spain and Spaniards with all his heart. He differed from John Hawkins, whom he had so gravely wronged by his desertion, in that Hawkins besides being a successful contrabandist was a man moved by a constructive purpose, namely, to induce the Spanish government to allow Englishmen to take part, legally, in the trade of the West Indies. Drake, on the other hand, was altogether destructive, wishing only to destroy Spanish power and not caring in the least for new policies of trade.

There is some doubt as to Drake's whereabouts and as to his doings in 1569 and 1570. If, as is likely, he was in the Caribbean at least part of that time, it is probable that he was associating with various French corsairs such as Blondel and le Testu, whom we have already mentioned in connection with him. Although he may have been smuggling, for the sake of gain, his principal business during this interim was that of studying the Spanish trade-routes, learning about the Cimaroons or renegade Negro slaves who were to be found in all parts of the Caribbean area, and otherwise gaining knowledge which was later to be a firm foundation for his active career of hostility against the Spaniards.[8]

The commercial aspect of Drake's voyages in 1570 and 1571 must not be overlooked. It was not merely that he was a dealer in contraband goods, much as Hawkins had been. He was being backed in a financial way by the injured John Hawkins and by kinsmen of his. It was necessary to keep them in good humor by showing a handsome profit on the venture's trade. At this time Drake was still, in the words of his own nephew, "a meane subject of her Majesties," and was in no way more distinguished or more brilliant than other English captains then engaged in harrying Spanish trade in the Caribbean.[9] In those preliminary voyages, however, Drake laid the foundations for his fame, not by a crescendo of successes against the enemy, but by patient and often dangerously unsuccessful investigations intended to provide knowledge of how best to make a grand attack on the Peruvian silver treasure after it had reached the port of Panama and before it was placed in the strongly guarded armada which was to carry it into Spain. At the same time, probably February, 1571, Drake began to feel his way towards friendly relations with the fierce and Spanish-hating Cimaroons (escaped Negro slaves) and with the unconquered wild Indians who abounded in those parts, greatly endangering the Spanish trade-routes.[10] Finally, at a point on the Isthmus remote from Spanish habitations, Drake, in one of these preliminary voyages, founded a small secret base, "Port Pheasant," for his operations on the Isthmus.

Meanwhile, at home in England, there was a not unreasonable rising ferment of anti-Spanish enthusiasm nurtured by such events as the Pope's excommunication of Elizabeth in 1570 and the Ridolfi plot (March-September, 1571) for the assassination of the Queen in which, disgracefully and unworthily, King Philip had a definite part.[11]

On the whole it cannot be wondered at that the Queen of England, tacitly, and many of her subjects, with open enthusiasm, approved raids against the commerce of Spain in the Caribbean. Loot was plentiful and varied, including not alone gold and silver but also emeralds, pearls, silks, velvets, linens, wines, and oil brought out to the colonies for distribution and sale. Such goods, falling into English hands, might be either taken home at a profit, or else might be sold, contraband-wise, in the Indies, also at a profit. In either case, a corresponding damage was done to the original owners of the merchandise. In all this the French corsairs co-operated, and even led, they being, if anything, more ferocious than the English, who preferred quiet trade when they could get it. Both French and English learned new techniques for up-river work, for landing, for surprise attacks, which made them more often than not the masters of their Spanish victims. The latter never developed the agility and adaptability of the English, and their clumsiness as sailors, in their towering galleons, more than overbalanced their undoubted courage.[12]

Such was the background against which was made Captain Drake's first voyage as an independent commander, his purpose being to capture the Peruvian silver treasure. The expedition was impressive on the score of modesty; for, in his flagship *Pascha,* of only seventy tons, and in the *Swan,* commanded by his brother John Drake, of a mere twenty-five tons, there was a tiny force of seventy-three men and boys, John Oxenham among them. This personnel, though very small in view of the task undertaken, was equipped and provisioned in the most complete manner, and its pitch of enthusiasm was high.[13]

The voyage was a quick one. Leaving Plymouth on May 24th, 1572, and passing within sight of the Madeira and of the Canary Islands on June 3rd, they proceeded to America, sailing some ten leagues off Santa Marta on July 6th. From that point they made for Port Pheasant on the part of the Isthmian coast called Acla, near where the Scots afterwards set up New Edinburgh (see Chapter IX). On arriving there on July 12th they found the place to have been lately occupied—a fire was still smoking—and a letter inscribed on a leaden slab by one John Garret of Plymouth in which he told them that the Spaniards had "bewrayed" the place and had stolen all the goods which Drake had left there, all this being dated only six days earlier, at which time Garret and his men had gone away. In spite of this untoward advertisement, Captain Drake built at Port Pheasant the first English fort to be erected on Caribbean shore, a small affair in the form of an equilateral pentagon made of stout timbers.

That done, three pinnaces brought out in sections from England were put together by the carpenters who worked so expeditiously that the little craft were ready and equipped in a week's time. In them they made for Nombre de Dios which famed emporium and strong-place this miniature army assaulted on the night of July 28th and captured, to the sound of drum and trumpet and the spitting of fire-arms. The entry of the English in these circumstances must have convinced the Spaniards, jerked from their slumbers, that a large force was upon them. They made no defense worthy of the name, and the single gunner who was awake at a battery nearby fled for his life. The market-place was assaulted from two directions at once, Drake leading one party and John Drake and Oxenham the other, so that presently the very heart of Nombre de Dios was in the hands of less than sixty Englishmen. Under the bright flare of firepikes the invaders quickly examined the city which they had so daringly captured, and its inhabitants, stunned by the suddenness of their coming, at first looked on helplessly. When at length the Spanish militiamen did rally to the defense of the town they attacked the English hotly for a space, but the latter were provided with arrows of special type, and with deadly and unusual firepikes so that, when it came to hand-to-hand fighting the English got the better of it in spite of their small numbers; moreover, the skilful use by Drake of swiftly-moving squads of a few men each confused the defenders and caused them presently to break and flee. Afterwards Captain Drake caused three Spanish prisoners to show to him and his men the Governor's palace and the Royal Treasure-House, in the first of which they beheld an astonishing pile of silver bars much too cumbersome to be stolen.

Dawn was now approaching and a tropical deluge was pouring down, to the injury of the bow-strings and the powder. Word was brought that the pinnaces were in danger of capture. Drake acted with characteristic vigor. Though suffering grievously from a wound in his leg, he wished to pillage the town, and only his men's insistence forced him back to the pinnaces while John Drake and John Oxenham and their squad gathered what booty they could by breaking into the King's Treasure-House where the gold and jewels were stored. At daybreak on July 29th they got away in the pinnaces, capturing as they went a ship well laden with wine. They betook themselves to a neighboring island to rest and recuperate, and to feast upon the produce of the gardens there.

No one can deny that the action was heroically gallant. The discipline maintained was perfect, and there were no needless cruelties. This quality of the English under Drake was candidly recognized by the Spaniards themselves, for, the next day, the Governor of Nombre de Dios sent a Spanish gentleman to visit them and to enquire if they needed anything. The meeting was courteous on both sides, Drake assuring his guest that the arrows used had not been poisoned as the Spaniards had feared, and that the only commodity which the English wanted was some of "their Harvest, which they get out of the Earth, and send into Spaine to trouble all the Earth."[14]

The main objective of Drake—the Peruvian silver treasure —was still untaken, and in this sense his expedition was so far a failure. He resolved to try again. Accordingly, from August, 1572, to January, 1573, Drake employed himself in cruising up and down the shore, first with the idea of conducting illicit trade in the tradition of Hawkins, later, when this proved impossible because of the increased strictness of the Spaniards, busying himself with what can only be called piracy. The rainy season was now on, and it was necessary to found a new headquarters on Slaughter Island in the Gulf of San Blas. Leaving part of his men there, Drake raided shipping and ports—Cartagena, Santa Marta and Curaçao all knew him in those days—and he likewise caused some of his men to study the Chagres River and Venta Cruces overland route while he also took measures to enter into alliance with the several bands of Cimaroons. In December, 1572, he returned to Slaughter Island where he found that his brother John had died, and soon after came a plague, probably of yellow fever or of typhoid, which carried off Joseph Drake and various others.

On January 5th, 1573, there arrived at Nombre de Dios the Admiral Diego Flores de Valdés and the fleet intended to carry home the silver treasure from Peru. This was the moment to attack the longed-for wealth before it could be placed in safety on the fleet. Aided by the Cimaroons and by Guillaume le Testu who now once more appears as an associate of the English, Drake, Oxenham and their men made determined attacks on Venta Cruces and on the Gold Road near Nombre de Dios. In the fighting which befell between the end of January and early April, 1573, Guillaume le Testu met a violent death.[15]

In this period also took place the picturesque and yet entirely probable incident of the birth of Drake's ambition to carry his depredations into the Pacific at which ocean he and Oxenham, as every school child is told, gazed from a treetop at some point on the Isthmian divide. His courage, fed by his undying hatred, was undaunted by the many losses among his followers, nor was it checked by such trifling obstacles as a continent that barred the way to new scenes of endeavor. With rich booty won from the ill-defended pack train near Nombre de Dios—in the vanquishing of which his French and Cimaroon allies had been invaluable to him—Drake sailed away for England, and after considerable further successes, reached Plymouth on Sunday, August 9th, 1573.[16]

Drake, on his return to England, was not only a successful but also a celebrated man. True, he had to go through the motions of obtaining a pardon for having made so momentous a raid into a friendly realm without permission from his Queen so to do; but it cannot be supposed that he ran any serious danger of punishment. Thereafter, for twelve years, Drake saw the Caribbean no more. It remained, however, the scene of piratical incursions by other Englishmen of less note who differed from him only in point of subsequent fame. In the interim, Drake's life was a crescendo of anti-Spanish activity which lies beyond the scope of the present study.

Conspicuous in this period of Drake's life is his justly celebrated circumnavigation in the *Golden Hind,* 1577–1580,[17] in the course of which he led the first Englishmen who passed through the Strait of Magellan, thus fulfilling his tree-top vow to sail an English ship upon the hitherto inviolate Pacific. His ravaging of the coasts of Chile and Peru and his spectacular, as well as extremely lucrative, capture of the great treasure-ship, *Nuestra Señora de la Inmaculada Concepción* are as well known today as they were sensational in his own time. The voyage around the world was, indeed, a long series of bold depredations which gave to Drake, aside from great wealth, enormous reputation and a great renown among his own people and among the Spaniards. It was all done, however, with remarkable decency in that no wanton violations of persons were permitted. Drake maintained perfect discipline, and if he was a thief, he was also capable of gallantry; nor was he a murderer of the helpless. Having what he held to be a duty to perform, he did it in masterly style which commands one's admiration even against one's sympathies.[18]

In the period between 1573 and 1585 both Spain and England were the scenes of events tending towards an ultimate show-down. The underlying nature of the struggle has been briefly indicated above on pages 83–84. The superficial manifestations of the conflict include a continuance of piracy and of privateering—a *quasi*-legal variation of the former—together with intricate diplomatic developments and an unceasing ferment of rumor which spread all over Europe by means of news conveyed in official dispatches and in business communications. The Fugger News-Letters of this period are replete with references to Drake: In one dated from Cologne, October 20th, 1580, Drake, described as "a pirate who has been away for three years," is said to have returned with 2,000,000 ducats' worth of booty stolen in Spanish America; and in one dated at Antwerp December 3rd, 1580, he is said to have presented to Queen Elizabeth several horse-loads of silver and gold stolen in Peru.[19] Yet, in spite of all that Drake and other despoilers could do, Spain's overseas realms continued to spout forth untold wealth. In one Fugger News-Letter, undated but of this period, it is stated that from Peru and the Main have come 1,500,000 ducats for the King and 4,500,000 ducats for merchants, as well as 600,000 ducats for the King from New Spain and 1,100,000 for merchants, not to mention rich cargoes of hides, cochineal, and cinnamon. Again, a News-Letter of September 26th, 1583, from Madrid, records the arrival at Seville three days before of 15,000,000 ducats' worth of treasure.[20] In other words, Spain was far from being beaten.

In the meanwhile, Queen Elizabeth and Lord Burghley were still resisting the urgings of Grenville, Walsingham and their party that an open rupture with Spain be made. There had long been plentiful excuse for such a break, as, for instance, the Spanish plan of 1573–74 to capture the Scilly Isles and convert them into a base for a heavy-armed Spanish squadron which could effectively bottle up the shipping of England, Netherlands, and the French Huguenots. This plan, originated by Admiral Pedro Menéndez de Avilés and accepted by Philip II, was brought to naught by the death of the admiral from an epidemic which ravaged his fleet in September, 1574.[21]

It was not until 1584, however, that the Queen, knowing open hostility to be very near, began seriously to consider using Drake as a powerful weapon against Spain. She well knew that to do so would be to make the portentous step from tacit approval of piracy and of privateering to open and official warfare. In July, 1585, however, the step became inevitable in view of Philip's high-handed action in seizing all the English ships in Spanish ports—an action not without good cause from his point of view.[22] This was followed in August, 1585, by the Queen's alliance with the revolted Netherlands whose former leader, Prince William of Orange, had been assassinated, with Philip's complicity, a year before.[23] Such events were among the numerous factors which created the general situation in which Drake's next American exploits were a part. Long delays arising from lingering timidity—or from wise cautiousness, as you prefer—ensued before Drake was commissioned by his Queen to fare forth and do his worst. The issue was decided by the receipt in England of tidings from Sir Walter Ralegh's emissaries, Ralph Lane and Richard Grenville, concerning the defencelessness of such places as Puerto Rico and large parts of the Island of Hispaniola. Spurred on by this evidence of the enemy's unpreparedness, the Queen issued the commission, and on September 14th, 1585, Drake and his fleet of thirty vessels (twenty-eight privately owned fighting ships and two belonging to the Queen) set off from Plymouth.

On the way to America Drake raided the Spaniards at Bayonne south of Bordeaux and violated Vigo; afterwards he sacked and burned Santiago in the Cape Verde Islands, being driven thence only by a plague which carried off some 300 of his 2,300 men. Frightened by this disaster, which threatened the success of his carefully pondered scheme for crippling Spain in her Indies, Drake sailed westward intent on taking Santo Domingo, still a city of the first importance although by now many parts of Hispaniola and other islands were fallen into great neglect. Following his former policy, Sir Francis made friends with sundry groups of savage Caribs and with the Cimaroon bands who infested the interior of Hispaniola. Thus strengthened, he delivered, on January 1st, 1586, his attack against Santo Domingo, using for the first time a stratagem afterwards destined to be employed often with varying success. While the fleet engaged the attention of the chief fort from the water, a small landing party made its way from the point where it had come ashore to the rear of the town from which quarter no attack was expected. The city, caught as though in a pair of pincers, quickly fell, and it was occupied by the English for a full month until, on the payment of a ransom of 25,000 ducats, the invaders decamped. The smallness of the ransom was incommensurate with the deadliness of the blow to Philip's prestige.[24] It is the opinion of the writer of a Fugger News-Letter, dated from Madrid April 5th, 1586, that King Philip himself was largely responsible for the disaster. This writer, friendly to Spain be it noted, asserts that, although the King had had plentiful advance information about Drake's plans and movements, he had taken no measures for defending his possessions in America against the enemy. The writer adds that only now is the King bestirring himself.[25] Another News-Letter, from Antwerp, May 3rd, 1586, contains a hint that Drake's fleet may have been far stronger than is indicated above. According to this document the Prince of Parma, Philip's Governor of Brussels, had heard that Drake's ships numbered thirty-six belonging to Queen Elizabeth, twenty French ships, and enough vessels belonging to Don Antonio (pretender to the Portuguese throne) to bring the total to eighty. It is further stated that Drake has liberated and armed the blacks and that he has ravaged the island.[26] It is fairly certain that there was considerable truth in the opinion expressed in the first of these two letters and that King Philip's multiplicity of duties and cares prevented his making his American cities as strong as they should have been. As to the second letter, although it probably exaggerates the size of the fleet, it at least illustrates the reputation to which Drake had attained.[27]

Cartagena, chief city of the Spanish Main and an emporium of the first class, particularly famed for its pearls as well as for gold and silver, was Drake's next objective. In spite of the earnest and devoted efforts of Don Pedro Vicque Manrique, General of the Coastal Guard-Fleet, Cartagena was taken by a variation of the twofold attack technique already described. It was an action daringly conceived and brilliantly executed—in short, it was good, clean fighting which shows both sides at their best. At that time Cartagena was not so heavily fortified as it was later, and this fact, coupled with the cleverness with which the twofold, pincer-like attack was managed, explains why it fell before a force of not more than 1,200 or so English.

Sir Francis Drake's original plan had looked to the permanent conversion of Cartagena to English uses. He envisioned a powerful port and fortress there which should serve his Queen as a veritable lance-head wherewith to prod her foeman's vitals and to prod again. From an Englished Cartagena would be spread English commerce and English rule; the trade routes of Spain conveniently near at hand would have been endangered in an unheard-of degree, and might even have been utterly broken. Although born of hate and of envy it was a vision which did a certain amount of credit to Sir Francis Drake if only because it was far ahead of its time. In fact, of course, the grand project came to naught; a bare 800 ablebodied men were left to Drake after the fall of Cartagena, the fighting and recurrence of epidemic having carried off or disabled all the rest. With so small a force it was obviously impossible to hold the place. Thus was he bereft of the honor of founding the first permanent English colony in tropical America.[28]

So, inevitably, Drake had to take the part more usual with him, and immeasurably more ignoble, namely, that of wringing from the humbled city a ransom, and then departing. By dint of destroying one by one the fairest and most sacred buildings until the wretched authorities and burghers would pay an acceptable sum, a fund of 110,000 ducats was at length obtained. The remainder of Drake's stay in America on this occasion was an anti-climax; the projected raids on Panama and on Havana had to be abandoned, and the attempt to capture the home-bound fleet of Spain also failed.

Drake and his fleet left Cartagena at the end of March, 1586, and on the way home had the solace of ravaging St. Augustine in Florida. Afterwards, in Virginia, he picked up the miserable little colony sent thither by Ralegh and languishing now amid a howling wilderness. He took them home in the same ships which carried his plunder of nearly $2,000,-000 and the 240 pieces of artillery which constituted the solid fruits of his venture. Plymouth was reached on July 28th, 1586.[29]

4. Conclusion

Neither with the minor depredations of the English in American waters at this period and just after nor with the epochal events in Europe—the all-too-vincible Armada affair of 1588 among the rest—need we concern ourselves beyond remarking that that stupendous defeat, which marked the arrival of England at the beginning of maritime supremacy, was the product, at least in part, of pig-headed pride on the side of that most imprudent King Don Felipe de Hapsburgo. Against all common sense he insisted that the crucial enterprise be led by the Duke of Medina Sidonia, a grandee sufficiently candid and patriotic to urge his master to appoint some leader more expert than he in things marine. To blue-blooded but inept Medina were entrusted the fleet of 131 ships and the 25,000 men upon whom Philip relied to make him master of that noxious heretic northern isle. The result, in which Drake played the leading rôle, is known to all.[30] The defeat did not ruin Spain, but it made manifest to the world at large that the colossal Philip was but a fallible human being after all.[31]

Following the Armada affair came an abortive attempt by Drake to capture Lisbon in 1589, and after that six years of idleness and disgrace. The ageing Queen of Pirates loved not the unsuccessful, no matter what their services to her in the past. In 1593–1595, however, her coast of Cornwall was harried by the Dons, and at last she summoned to her aid the man whom her foes feared far more than they did the Evil One. In August, 1595, a well-fitted fleet of 27 sail, commanded by Drake and by Hawkins, carrying 2,500 sailors and artillerymen and from 2,500 to 3,000 foot-soldiers (under the command of Sir Thomas Baskerville), sailed forth to attack Panama. At the Canary Islands the English had their first taste of a renewed Spanish vigilance, and they were driven off with heavy losses when they attempted an assault.

In the Indies, too, defenses had been greatly strengthened, and 1,500 picked troops under Don Pedro Tello de Guzmán gave the invaders a fiery welcome from the splendid new fortifications of San Juan de Puerto Rico. Entry into the port was made impossible by the purposeful sinking of two large ships in the entrance, so that the English ships had to ride uncomfortably outside. In that position they received a withering fire from the shore-batteries. As the attack went on Sir John Hawkins, who had been ailing for some time, died, and various other officers were killed by a shot which entered the stern cabin where they were supping. This was in November, 1595.[32]

The repulse from San Juan de Puerto Rico, and the death of Hawkins were but the beginning of a long series of frustrations; for, neither by sea nor by land, could Drake and Baskerville make real headway against the enemy. Having been rebuffed at Havana, by strong forces under Pedro Menéndez Márquez, worthy son of the great admiral, Drake retreated westward in a feint at Nicaragua and, while off the terrible fever-haunted shore of Veragua, where a plague of malaria and dysentery swept through the fleet with high mortality, Sir Francis died, in January, 1596. Could an ocean grave bear an epitaph, the most fitting one for the resting place of this man would be the words of Lord Burghley, uttered after his return from the Indies in 1586: "Truly, Sir Francis Drake is a fearful man to the King of Spain." [33]

With the deaths of Hawkins and of Drake most of the fire and all the heroism passed out of the Elizabethan warfare against Spain in America. The giants being gone to Neptune only the pygmies remained to jab at Philip II with envenomed pins for lances. Among them was one George Clifford, Earl of Cumberland, a prominent corsair who, since 1587, had led at his own expense, but with the Queen's commission, no less than eleven private naval expeditions into Spanish American waters.[34] His success had fluctuated.

Between April and July, 1598, corsair Cumberland ravaged the Caribbean with a fleet of 18 sail and over 1,000 soldiers. In June, by using the method of attack already worked out by Drake—assault from two sides at once—he managed to capture San Juan de Puerto Rico. An epidemic was at that time working great mischief among the Spaniards on the island, and the able commander Tello de Guzmán was not present to direct the defense as he had done three years earlier. By June 19th, Cumberland was master of San Juan, even of the Morro, but his reward was meager, no gold being available, only hides, ginger, and other merchandise; moreover, the Governor flatly refused to pay a ransom, so that the victory was somewhat of the hollow sort, all the more so that the English were presently ravaged by the same epidemic as that which had done so much harm on the island before their coming.

Nevertheless, the capture and the retention during some six weeks of San Juan was a grievous blow to the prestige of Spain. Tidings of it, reaching Philip II early in September, 1598, hastened that monarch's death. On September 13th, in that small and far from luxurious chamber in the Escorial whence, with his eyes upon the altar in the adjacent church, he had so long striven to rule the whole New World and much of Europe as well, Philip II passed to his reward. Another giant was gone, an imprudent and self-deluded giant who cherished impossible-to-be-realized ambitions, but a giant none the less.[35]

In that same year France, long wracked by internecine war, regained national unity and, at Vervins, May 2nd, 1598, her new master, Henry IV, made his peace with Philip. The two Protestant nations, England and the Netherlands, were thus left alone to fight the Catholic Spain of Philip III.[36] In fact, the *dramatis personæ* were changing fast, and no less rapidly new projects, new alignments, new policies, and new methods were taking the places of old. Soon the great lady, perchance the greatest giant of them all, the immortal and undefeated Elizabeth, was to pass also, leaving behind her an England more expert on the seas than ever before, but one whose people thenceforward lacked much of the grandeur of vision and of daring which those who preceded them had had.

NOTES TO CHAPTER IV

[1] Marcel, 1902, pp. 19–20.

[2] Newton, 1933, pp. 58–60. Altamira y Crevea, III, section 632.

[3] Wright, 1932, pp. xviii, xxii–xxiii, xxxii–xxxiii.

[4] Wright, 1932, pp. xvi–xviii, xxxi. Marcel, 1902, pp. 23–24, where he tells us that a "magnificent atlas" by le Testu, of le Havre, is conserved in the Ministry of War, in Paris, and another map in the Ministry of Foreign Affairs.

[5] Marcel, 1902, pp. 26–31, where he reproduces the relation of Estévez entire and in Spanish.

[6] Fugger News-Letters, Series II, pp. 13–14, No. 26, dated from Antwerp, June 4th, 1573. Williamson, 1927, pp. 218–223, 257–260, 263–267. Newton, 1933, pp. 81–82. Other data on this subject will be found in Kervyn de Lettenhove, 1882–1891, Vol. VI.

[7] Newton, 1933, pp. 82–84. Fernández Duro, 1895–1903, II, Chs. xx–xxiii. Williamson, 1927, pp. 457–458. Haring, 1918, pp. 251–255. Means, 1932, pp. 219–221. Chapman, 1933, pp. 160–166. See also Philip II's regulations of 1590 regarding the fleet system as set forth in Ordenanzas, 1619.

[8] Wright, 1932, pp. xxii–xxix.

[9] Wright, 1932, pp. xxvi–xxix, where she emphasizes the trading aspects of these voyages, and also the probability that business was done in association with the Hawkins interests. On pp. xxviii–xxix Miss Wright gives important details of the Spanish overland trade-route from Panama on the Pacific to Venta Cruces and thence, partly by the River Chagres and partly by road, to Nombre de Dios.

[10] On p. xix (1932), Miss Wright cites contemporary Spanish documents which show how formidable an element were the Cimaroons—300 out of every 1,000 slaves becoming such—with their lawlessness and their hatred of Spain, conducing to co-operation with foreign interlopers. Miss Wright thinks, p. xxxvi, that Drake's real acquaintance with the Cimaroons did not begin until *after* his 1571 trip. See: Corbett, 1898, I, pp. 176–177, where he makes it clear that Drake was at least thinking about the Cimaroons before 1571.

[11] Newton, 1933, p. 88. Wright, 1932, pp. xxxv–xxxvi. Mariéjol, 1933, pp. 181–182. Article on Roberto di Ridolfi, in DNB, XLVIII, 1896, pp. 290–292. Hume, 1908, pp. 306–311 and 318, where the Ridolfi plot is carefully described.

[12] Wright, 1932, pp. xxvii–xxxv. The documents presented by Miss Wright show very clearly what effect the foreign raids had on the Spaniards at various parts of the Isthmus.

[13] Miss Wright, 1932, p. 254, note, shows that the *Pascha* was probably owned by the Hawkins brothers. Their interests now as before were primarily commercial rather than warlike; nevertheless, John Hawkins was, at this time, being detained by the Queen for service in home waters—or at any rate his ships were being so employed—as a defence against Alva in the Netherlands

and Catholic rebels in Britain. Newton, 1933, pp. 84–91. Corbett, 1898, I, Chs. v and vi, Hart, 1922, pp. 26–27. Rogers, 1927, Chs. iii and iv. Benson, 1927, Ch. iv. From this point onwards to page 87 the narrative is based upon that superbly scholarly volume already cited, Wright, 1932. As it is accessible in any really good library, specific citations are spared the reader as much as possible. The materials therein are a beautiful series of contemporary Spanish documents—which no one but Miss Wright, resident in Seville and deeply expert withal, could have assembled. Likewise, there are English documents, of which the most important is *Sir Francis Drake Revived,* written by Philip Nichols, Preacher, from materials provided by Christopher Ceely, Ellis Hixom, and other members of Drake's following. The book was reviewed by Sir Francis Drake himself, and was published long after his death by his nephew, Sir Francis Drake, Baronet, in 1628 at London.

14 *Sir Francis Drake Revived,* at pages 257–268 of Wright, 1932. Quotation from p. 268. Also pp. xxxvii–xxxviii.

15 Wright, 1932, pp. xliii–xliv.

16 Wright, 1932, pp. xl–xlv, in the course of which she cites and quotes many Spanish documents pertinent to the theme, including a refutation, by Don Ernesto Restrepo Tirado of Fernández Duro's claim that the sight-of-the-Pacific-from-a-treetop incident was impossible. Señor Restrepo, an important Colombian historian, wrote to Miss Wright in June, 1931, about how he himself had viewed both oceans from a treetop on the Isthmian watershed. (See Miss Wright's note at pp. xli–xlii, where she quotes Señor Restrepo's letter to her and cites Fernández Duro, 1895–1903, II, p. 343, note 1, in order to rebut his skepticism. See also pp. 268–238, being the pertinent part of *Sir Francis Drake Revived.* Newton, 1933, pp. 91–94. Williamson, 1927, p. 75.

17 According to Fernández Duro, 1895–1903, II, p. 345, Queen Elizabeth personally invested 1,000 crowns in this venture.

18 The rich ship referred to by her correct name in the text is better known as the *Cacafuego*—which I decline to translate in these pure pages (it is usually rendered "Spitfire" by English-speaking editors). The value of her cargo is variously stated to have been from $240,000 to $12,600,000. After the capture, the Spanish sailors, with wry humor, dubbed her *Cacaplata,* "Spitsilver." On this part of Drake's career see: Corbett, 1898, I, Ch. ix; Nuttall, 1914, pp. 134–210; Rogers, 1927, Ch. vi; Benson, 1927, Ch. viii; Fernández Duro, 1895–1903, II, pp. 340–352; Means, 1932, pp. 132–133, 232. An amusing manifestation of the fear in which Drake came to be held in Spain is a story, the source of which escapes me, to the effect that Philip II once invited a lady of his court to accompany him upon his barge on the Lake of Segovia, and the lady held back, in terror lest "el Draque" capture them! The complete absence of a lake at Segovia makes this yarn all the more entertaining!

19 Fugger News-Letters, Series II, nos. 86 and 90. On April 4th, 1581, upon the deck of the *Golden Hind* at Greenwich, Queen Elizabeth knighted Drake, thus signalizing her esteem for him and the fact that he was no longer her "meane subject," but one most highly prized. Citations for knighting of Drake. Corbett, 1898, I, Ch. xi. Fernández Duro, 1895–1903, II, Ch. xx, III, Ch. i.

20 Fugger News-Letters, Series II, no. 87, and Series I, no. 56.

[21] Newton, 1933, pp. 95–97.

[22] Newton, 1933, p. 98.

[23] Waldman, 1933, pp. 241–244.

[24] Newton, 1933, pp. 99–103. Rogers, 1927, Ch. x. Corbett, 1898, II, Ch. ii.

[25] Fugger News-Letters, Series II, no. 207.

[26] Fugger News-Letters, Series II, no. 212.

[27] See: Newton, 1933, pp. 101–103. Rogers, 1927, Ch. x. Benson, 1927, Ch. xvi. Fernández Duro, 1895–1903, III, pp. 106–115. Corbett, 1898, II, Ch. i.

[28] Newton, 1933, pp. 103–105. Benson, 1927, Ch. xi. Corbett, 1898, II, Ch. ii.

[29] Newton, 1933, pp. 105–107. Benson, 1927, pp. 200–203. Corbett, II, Ch. vi. Hart, 1922, pp. 33–39. Wright, 1916, Ch. xxi. Various of the Fugger News-Letters refer, rather inaccurately, to the 1585–1586 journey of Drake. One of them contains the incomprehensible assertion that Queen Elizabeth had declared that Drake's raids were not backed by her but were being carried on at the behest of Don Antonio of Portugal. (Series II, no. 221, Antwerp, July 5th, 1586.) Another says that Drake has arrived at London with 50–60 ships and a vast booty. (Series II, no. 233, Antwerp, September 6th, 1586.) Laudonnière, 1586.

[30] Chapman, 1918, pp. 254–256. Corbett, 1898, II, Chs. v and vi. Benson, 1927, Chs. xiii and xiv. Rogers, 1927, Ch. viii. Fernández Duro, 1895–1903, III, Ch. ii.

[31] A quaint sidelight is thrown on the Armada by one of the Fugger News-Letters. It relates that the Duke of Medina Sidonia, finding 600 women in the fleet, ordered them all ashore. The soldiers and sailors whose doxies they were did not like this strictness, "but were comforted with the report that there were comely wenches in England." (Series I, no. 84, Madrid, May 18th, 1588.) Another Letter, a report from England via Hamburg, gives a vivid account of the terrible disaster to Spain's dearest hopes. (Series I, no. 92, Augsburg, November 19th, 1588.)

[32] The date is given as November 12th, 1595 by: Newton, 1933, p. 111; Williamson, 1927; Corbett, 1898; DNB. The date of the battle of San Juan de Puerto Rico in which the English were driven off from that stronghold, and the date of Hawkins's death appear in a contemporary Spanish document as of November 22d, 1595. See: Bertram T. Lee, *Una relación desconocida sobre Sir Francis Drake,* in Revista Histórica, IX, pp. 88–93, Lima, 1928. The document published by Mr. Lee is in the National Library, in Lima.

[33] Corbett, 1898, I, pp. 61 and 122–123, note. See also: Rogers, 1927, p. 196; Newton, 1933, pp. 109–114; Fernández Duro, 1895–1903, II, pp. 499–514, III, pp. 106–115. Artíñano, 1917, Pt. III, Ch. vi, sections 1 and 2; Hart, 1922, Ch. ii.

[34] Newton, 1914, pp. 37–38, where he shows that the Queen's commission to Cumberland became a model for later grants of a similar purpose. See also: Corbett, 1900, Ch. x.

[35] Mariéjol, 1933, pp. 336–340, 356–357. Loth, 1932, pp. 284–289.

[36] Newton, 1933, pp. 114–120.

CHAPTER V

EL DORADO: THAT MYTH OF EASY MONEY

1. *The Great Conquests in North-Western South America*

ON pages 45–48 some reference was made to the effect of the conquest of Peru upon certain parts of the Spanish Main. In the present chapter we are to trace that effect further and to that end we shall examine some of the more typical journeys which were made by Spaniards and others either from the Spanish Main into the interior of northern South America or else from that interior to or towards the Spanish Main. In particular we shall study two very important trans-continental voyages from Peru into the Caribbean, those of Francisco de Orellana and of Lope de Aguirre, the Traitor. It will thus be shown that the Spanish Main was the very centre of Spanish power in America no less than the focus of envy for the enemies of Spain.

In general terms it may be said that the conquest of Peru took place between 1525 and 1535. The first of these two dates is that of the first voyage of Francisco Pizarro southwards in a definite hope of finding the great realm said to lie in that direction; the second is the date of the founding of Lima as the capital of Spain in Peru and in South America generally. In those days, we must remember, Peru was a name of wider application than it is at present. It was then used as a synonym for what had been the Inca Empire so that it included all the territory now occupied by the republics of Ecuador, Peru, and Bolivia, together with northern Chile and northwestern Argentina. Indeed, the Spaniards sometimes applied the name Peru to the whole of Spanish South America. As a rule, however, in the colonial period, Peru meant the Viceroyalty of Peru, having its capital at Lima and spreading over all the wide area formerly ruled by the Incas and even into regions which they never saw.

During the decade between 1525 and 1535 the Inca Empire was brought under Spanish rule by Francisco Pizarro, Diego de Almagro, and their followers who, as did conquerors elsewhere, varied greatly in point of character and quality. In the years between 1535 and 1569 there followed a period of tumults and of internecine strife between sundry factions among the conquerors, and, concurrently, between the servants of the King of Castile and those who would resist or even throw off his authority. The period of turmoil was brought to an end by the great but stern Viceroy Toledo, who ruled Peru from 1569 to 1581 in such a way that the Royal authority was firmly established in the realm at last.

These momentous events were accompanied by a steady flow of Spaniards into Peru. Soldiers, priests, administrators, lawyers, adventurers—men of many sorts and many natures— spread throughout the country and gave rise to a new upper class which took the place of the deposed caste of the Incas. In time something like a saturation point was approached; that is, as the best lands and the best parts of the Indian population were taken under the control of the Spaniards there came to be more and more Spaniards who, if they were to win fame, riches, and power, must go further and further afield. They were chiefly recent arrivals, many of them being men of unruly disposition who made much trouble for their more early established compatriots and, especially, for the viceregal government. To rid the settled parts of Peru of these explosive elements various governors and viceroys encouraged explorations into the unknown interior of the continent, that is, into the vast wilds east of the Andes where lay the enormous drainage-basins of the Amazon and of the River Plate.[1]

Processes similar to those here indicated were at work in other parts of South America also. For us the area now occupied by Ecuador, Colombia, and Venezuela are specially important. In general terms it may be said that Ecuador was conquered from the south, from Peru proper, in which the Spaniards were but following in the footsteps of the Incas. Thus, in 1533 and 1534, Sebastián Moyano, better known as Sebastián Benalcazar, founded Riobamba (in the southern highlands of Ecuador) and Quito (almost on the Equator), acting therein as the agent of Pizarro and Almagro, the conquerors of Peru. Colombia and Venezuela, on the other hand, were conquered from the north, that is, from the Spanish Main. A glance at the map will show why this was inevitable. True, the country which we call Colombia touches the Pacific as well as the Caribbean; but its Pacific coast is a damp, unwholesome, impenetrable forest area in which even the doughty Spaniards could make but little headway. The Caribbean shore, although of course tropical likewise, is altogether better as a base for exploring-parties and for conquering armies. For one thing the great Magdalena River empties itself into the Caribbean near its southwestern corner, and, by flowing from mysterious regions in the interior, inevitably drew the attention of Spaniards in that direction, at the same time affording them a natural route for explorations. Further east, Venezuela faces towards the Caribbean. Its long coastal belt is for the most part narrow and is hemmed in by steep and lofty mountains beyond which, to the south, lie the *Llanos* (Plains) whose rivers are tributaries of the great Orinoco which flows into the Atlantic south of the island of Trinidad through an extensive delta. Only at the western end of the north coast of Venezuela is there a seeming waterway leading to the hinterland in the south. This is the so-called Lake of Maracaibo, in reality an arm of the sea, which runs southwards some 200 miles. In truth it is not a natural pathway to the interior because, at its southern end, the Maracaibo lagoon comes close to a wall of high mountains which can be penetrated only with difficulty. The coast of Venezuela, being less alluring than that of Colombia, was settled relatively late and with comparative slowness. The city of Maracaibo, founded in 1571, was never of the first importance; Caracas and its port of La Guayra date from 1566; Cumaná, near the eastern end of the coast, though founded as early as 1520, was but slight in importance then and afterwards, and that largely in connection with the pearl islands of Cubagua and Margarita to the north of it in the Caribbean.[2]

Venezuela, as it chanced, had a unique history in the sense that it was opened up to European influences largely by Germans rather than by Spaniards. In this we see a result of the multiplicity of crowns worn by the Spanish monarch who, besides being King Charles I of Castile, was also Holy Roman Emperor Charles V. At Augsburg, in his German dominions, there was the rich and powerful banking-house of the Welsers to whom the Emperor was under rather uncomfortable monetary obligations. Having advanced to Charles large sums of money wherewith he convinced certain electors that he would be an excellent Emperor, the Welsers not unnaturally looked to the successful candidate for a substantial token of his regard for them. Thus it came about that, in 1528, Charles made the Welsers perpetual lords proprietors of Venezuela and awarded them a grant which, it was expected, would bring to the Augsburgers heavy profits from gold, slaves, and whatever other commodities might be found. In order to put their Venezuelan province to the fullest possible use the Welsers sent out 300 or more German colonists and appointed Ambrose Ehinger, usually known as Ambrose Alfinger, as Governor. He established himself at Coro, on the eastern side of the Gulf of Venezuela which leads southward into the Lake of Maracaibo, in February, 1529, thus establishing German control. It lasted only down to about 1550, but in that period many explorations led by Germans penetrated the southern portions of Venezuela, across the mountains from Coro and onwards into the upper drainage of the Orinoco. It is worth while to note in passing that the Germans varied in character precisely as did the Spaniards, the English and all other conquerors of America, people being then, as now, much the same from nation to nation.[3]

In the sharpest contrast to all this was the contemporary history of what is now Colombia. Here everything done was the work of Spaniards. As we have seen, Santa Marta, slightly to the east of the mouth of the Magdalena, was founded in 1525, and Cartagena, some 100 miles to the southwest, in 1533. It was the older city that served as a base for the conquest of the Chibcha kingdoms in the highlands around Bogotá, the capital city of modern Colombia. As Cortés was to Mexico and Pizarro was to Peru so was Gonzalo Jiménez de Quesada to Colombia. In April, 1536, the Captain-General of Santa Marta appointed Jiménez de Quesada to lead a large and well-fitted expedition in five good ships southwards up the Magdalena.

The march southwards from the point where the ships had to be abandoned, and onwards into the Chibcha highlands east of the upper Magdalena, was skilfully carried out. Jiménez de Quesada, a man of good birth and of splendid education, was not only an unsurpassed leader of men but also a person far less cruel and rapacious than were all too many in those days. Nevertheless, the march was fraught with danger, from the Indians, from diseases, and from other mischance. In spite of this, Jiménez de Quesada succeeded in reaching the cool and beautiful tableland of Bogotá with 166 men and 59 horses. The Chibcha kingdoms, though somewhat simpler in organization and in culture than the realm of the Inca, managed to put up a considerable resistance against the invaders; but, as happened so often, knights in armor, cavalry, and above all firearms, were not to be resisted by any equipment which the natives could oppose to them. By the end of January, 1538, the conquest of the Chibchas was an accomplished fact. Although plunder, chiefly in the form of gold and of emeralds, had been taken, to the value of about $550,-000, there had been little or none of that wanton savagery which so often stained the conquest of Peru. Jiménez de Quesada would not permit it, except on one occasion when he yielded to a great temptation and allowed a native king to be tortured in an effort to extract from him news of buried treasure. He, too, was a victim of the deadly evil of gold-lust, as so many others were.

On August 6th, 1538, Jiménez de Quesada founded the Spanish city of Santa Fé de Bogotá, thereby signalizing the commencement of Spanish rule. Shortly afterwards there came from the direction of Quito a party of Spaniards led by Sebastián de Benalcazar and, from the direction of Venezuela, Nicolás Federmann, an employe of the Welsers, with other Spaniards. These two parties merged with the original conquerors and so consolidated Spanish power in Colombia.[4]

For us the significance of the events here briefly recounted is this: The western and northern sides of South America were, by 1540, definitely under Spanish rule. True, there were many regions of more or less extent where there was no intensive Spanish occupation. Such were the more damp and jungly parts of the Pacific coast of Colombia which, even today, are almost without inhabitants of Spanish descent; such, also, were various regions along the low-lying rivers where the humid heat, the dense vegetation, and the fierce Indians, not to mention the total lack of cultivable lands, of gold mines, and of other natural attractions, made it impossible for Spaniards to settle with benefit to themselves. All the higher-lying areas, however, became centres of Spanish occupation, with cities and towns, with churches, government, and the usual Spanish political organization. It was from these centres as bases that the exploration of the interior of the southern continent was carried on. In a sense the process was a continuation of the draining to which, as already noted, the Greater Antilles were subject after the discovery of Mexico and, more especially, after the conquest of Peru. This was true not only because a good many of the investigations of the interior came from and worked back to the Caribbean but also because the Spanish settlement of Peru and the subsequent penetration eastwards therefrom were largely performed by men who had once been settlers in the Caribbean area and who might have remained there had they not been lured southwards to the newer fields of endeavor.

2. The Rise of the El Dorado Myth

A curious feature of many explorations which were made from the relatively stable settlements along the northern and western margins of South America towards the interior of the continent was their will-o'-the-wisp quality. From an early date, persistent rumors of mysterious kingdoms of fabulous wealth and power lurking far within the continent hypnotized adventurers and led them through huge wildernesses and innumerable dangers. Sometimes, as in the case of the whispers about the Inca Empire, which lured Alejo García, Cabot, Barlow, César, and others onward, these tales rested on fact; others were compounded of facts misinterpreted or otherwise deformed by Europeans desirous of winning quickly untold riches; still others were the merest dream-stuff, product of an inordinate craving for gold.

The truth of the El Dorado matter was that the Chibcha chieftain of Guatabita in the highland of Colombia was wont to make, prior to his accession or, as some say, annually, a sacrifice to the gods by throwing gold and other precious objects into a lake in his small dominion. He then performed an impressive lustral rite in the course of which he was anointed with a sticky substance over which was scattered finely powdered gold, so that he glistened like a Golden Man —El Dorado. At the proper moment, from a ceremonial raft, he plunged into the water and ritualistically washed from his person the gold-dust upon it.[5]

Simple enough is the basis in fact of the El Dorado legend; but the fantastic proportions to which it grew, not only among the Spaniards but also among the Germans in Venezuela and later the English in Guiana, pass all bournes of sense. From a charming and simple lustral ceremony on the water of a little tarn in the highlands of Bogotá arose a glittering dream in which the reality, a Gilded Man, became transformed by the gold-seeking imaginations of men into a Golden Kingdom.[6]

The very numerous journeys which were made in quest of

El Dorado have not, as a rule, direct connection with the history of the Spanish Main. Their effect was to make known, little by little, and at the cost of immense toil, daring, and sacrifice of lives, the interior regions lying in the drainage of the Orinoco, or in that of the Amazon. Some of these journeys were from Quito towards the east; others, largely led by Germans connected with the Welser interests in Venezuela, were towards the south. Of them all only a few have direct bearing upon the theme treated in this book, and these we shall now study.

3. Francisco de Orellana's Journey from the Andes to the Caribbean

Beyond doubt Gonzalo Pizarro, younger brother of the Marquis Francisco Pizarro, conqueror of Peru, was one of those who had it in mind to discover and to vanquish the supposed Golden Kingdom said to lie somewhere in the eastern wildernesses far beyond the already conquered Andean highlands. In 1539 the Marquis Pizarro appointed Gonzalo to be his Governor at Quito, and in so doing he laid upon him the special duty of exploring the unknown country beyond and eastwards from that city.[7]

We may safely assume that, after taking possession of his post, Gonzalo talked freely with the Spanish settlers at Quito and with the Indians there. In this way he soon became filled with a conviction that, in the east, there was a powerful lord or monarch who was wont to go about with his body covered by a finely ground gold-dust which was renewed every day after his bath. This Indian potentate, so it was said, deemed it a vulgar and common thing to wear richly wrought golden armor such as that which satisfied the lesser chiefs about him; neither would he deign to wear any sort of raiment which might abate the splendor of his person.[8] We can easily imagine that Gonzalo Pizarro and other Spaniards at Quito must have found the tales of this legendary gold-powdered chieftain most alluring.

In order to obey his brother's instructions and, incidentally, to seek out the Golden King, Gonzalo Pizarro made his preparations for his venture between December 1st, 1540, and February 18th, 1541. In addition to nearly 4,000 highland Indians (who had to be chained to keep them from running away) there were more than 200 Spaniards in the expedition most of whom were gentlemen-adventurers of high rank drawn from the cream of the conquering element in Peru. The equipment assembled by Gonzalo was worthy of the quality of his followers and of the goal which he hoped to reach. There were nearly as many horses as men, and huge numbers of llamas to carry burdens and to serve as food. There were great packs of dogs for hunting and for assaulting Indian attackers, as well as thousands of hogs driven on the hoof. Besides all this there were lavish supplies of arquebuses, cross-bows, and ammunition for them. In short, it was an expedition organized on a very grand scale for those times.[9]

To the original force, which left Quito at the end of February, 1541, there was presently added another contingent under the leadership of Francisco de Orellana who, as he was busy with affairs of moment at Guayaquil (now the chief port of Ecuador), was delayed in starting. As soon as he could, however, Orellana with his twenty-three men went up to Quito and, finding that the main body of the expedition had already departed eastwards, he quickly pushed onwards, finally joining Gonzalo and the main army late in March at a place called Sumaco about sixty-five miles east from Quito.[10]

Even thus early in the course of the journey tremendous difficulties had been encountered. The expedition had already passed beyond the eastern side of the Andes and had gone down into the thick, moist, gloomy forest-region which the Incas had never succeeded in adding to their realm and which the Spaniards found most unwholesome. The highland Indians died by dozens and scores, those who remained being overburdened and driven onwards; the llamas likewise perished in the heat and the hogs which were not eaten succumbed to exhaustion. Added to these trials were the natives of the region who, darting about in the shadows of the great trees, and flitting from ambush to ambush, discharged their poisoned darts against the invaders while keeping themselves from harm. The raiment of the Spaniards, soaked in sweat and by rains, rotted on their bodies, and their armor, firearms and other metal things rusted apace. Worst of all, as they pressed onward, was the ever-growing menace of hunger which presently became a grim reality; for, strangely enough, in this country of all-too-abundant vegetation, there was very little food that the Spaniards could find, either because they were poor in woodcraft or else because it was not there.

Thus, month after month, matters progressed with a steady increase of peril and of deprivations. Towards the end of 1541, the expedition, lacking many of its white members and practically all its highland Indian servants, was on the bank of the Coca River. A temporary surcease from misfortune then permitted Gonzalo Pizarro to reflect upon the desperate situation. Taking, very likely, a hint from the canoe-using river Indians among whom his party had long been travelling, he decided to build a boat of sorts in which the most sick of his men and all the impedimenta could descend by the river while the horses and the more healthy soldiers followed along the shore.

This plan was a good one in several respects. The marchers by land would be relieved of heavy packs; the boat, even if a modest affair by European standards, would at any rate be larger and more imposing than the biggest of the Indian dug-out canoes, so that, in case of need, it could serve as a refuge in case of attack by the Indians in their own craft. Finally, if worst came to worst, the whole party could get into the boat and in her make their way to the Atlantic. This was the significance of the proposed boat as seen by Gonzalo Pizarro himself.[11]

The leader's suggestion about building a boat was not hailed with unanimous delight. Francisco de Orellana, second in command, was one of those who opposed it at first. Apparently the chief reason why he did so was that he was then of the opinion that the entire force ought to turn back towards the Andes in quest of Pasto or of Popayán in the highlands between Quito and Bogotá rather than to plunge themselves further in the wilds which had treated them so ill.[12]

Before long, however, Orellana accepted his chief's decision and, once he had done so, he eagerly joined in the arduous toil of building the brigantine. To create, in the midst of a wilderness, a boat capable of carrying a hundred men or so is no easy matter, particularly when only green timber is available for planks and such oddments as old horseshoes and castaway bits of armor are the materials from which nails are wrought. However, at a place some twelve miles down the Coca from Guema, they did it. The Indian village where the work was done received the name of El Barco, the Bark. In a short time, perhaps a fortnight or less, they constructed a boat described as "watertight and strong, but not very large."

After the building of the bark they went onwards down the Coca River towards its junction with the Napo. Their hopes were now high; for, although the marchers along the shore encountered continuous hardships in the form of swamps where some of the party and a number of horses were drowned, they now had received from the Indians with whom they had been friendly while the boat was building, a quantity of fresh maize and other good victuals. Moreover, they were repeatedly told of great and powerful kingdoms downstream. Surely these must be the realms of the Golden King of whom, back in Quito, they had heard so much.

In this manner, passing painfully across the mouths of many rivers which flow into the very wide main stream, they went beyond the confluence of the Coca and the Napo and onwards down the latter stream to a little beyond its junction with the Aguarico. At that point, about 175 miles eastwardly in a straight line from Quito, they arrived about December 23rd, 1541.[13]

At this point, a little below the confluence of the Napo and the Aguarico and considerably above the junction of the Napo with the Curaray (the next big river to flow into the

Napo), took place the most crucial events in the whole history of the expedition.[14] The situation was again acutely serious, food running low, many deaths from fever, drowning, and other causes, a general feeling of gravest anxiety all abroad among both leaders and men. In these circumstances tidings were received that there was a good land, well provided with food and inhabited by powerful tribes of advanced culture, some distance downstream near the confluence of the next great river (the Curaray).

A bold plan was now presented by Orellana to his chief. He offered to take sixty men, the brigantine and some canoes, and to go downstream in quest of the rumored supplies in order to obtain some of them and to bring them back to Pizarro's camp. It was understood between the two leaders that, if no food was found, or if Orellana failed to return to the camp after a reasonable length of time, Pizarro was to make shift as best he could, taking no more account of Orellana and his men. It was equally understood that, in the case that food was found, Orellana was to come back with it to the camp of his chief in order to bring succor to the men waiting there. It was specifically decided that, *on no account*, was Orellana to pass beyond the next river, *i.e.*, the Curaray.[15]

All this being agreed upon, Orellana and the men who were to accompany him departed in the brigantine on December 26th, 1541, almost a year after the setting forth from Quito. Pizarro never saw Orellana or any of his companions again. After waiting disconsolately for many days, Pizarro and those with him turned back towards Quito. After a journey even more horrible than the going out, a journey during which the food became so scarce that herbs stewed in the blood of the few horses which they had left was a positive delicacy, the unfortunate creatures at last struggled up the eastern side of the Andes at a point further north than that at which they had entered. When at last they crawled out of the woods into the highlands near Quito they were practically naked, their clothes having long since rotted and their useless armor having been thrown away as too heavy for feeble skeletons such as they to carry. Compassionate people came to them in wonderment at seeing their pitiful state and they covered the shivering forms of the unhappy wanderers with their own cloaks. In this manner Gonzalo Pizarro reached Quito with only eighty of his original force in June, 1542.[16]

Orellana having departed from Pizarro on December 26th, 1541, made progress downstream at an infinitely greater rate than any that had been made before. The Napo was very broad, a mile or two, and growing wider as it received confluents. Its current was strong, but not so strong that a boat could not have gone against it had the will been there. On January 3rd, 1542, the Orellana party having already passed the Curaray, arrived at an Indian village which they named Aparia the Lesser. There they remained until February 2nd, 1542. At this place they made 2,000 nails from such odds and ends of iron as they could find. More sinister, they also made an elaborate series of documents designed to exonerate Orellana and his men from all unfaithfulness to their commander, Gonzalo Pizarro. True, the documents were pseudo-legal rather than legal by reason of the fact that the notary whom Orellana appointed to draw them up had no proper qualifications for his post and was, in fact, merely an expeditioner selected by Orellana for the purpose. Likewise at Aparia the Lesser Orellana acted out a solemn farce of wishing to try to go back upstream to Pizarro—which as eye-witnesses afterwards said under oath could have been done perfectly well—and of allowing his men to "require" him to lead them downstream to the Atlantic. The length of the stay at Aparia the Lesser was partly due to a feigned belief that Pizarro might catch up with them. How this was to be done, they having the boat with them, no one seemed to know. The whole thing was a tissue of deceitfulness.

Leaving Aparia the Lesser on February 2nd, 1542, they went down the Napo so rapidly that they reached the junction of the Marañon on February 12th. They were now nearly 500 miles from Quito in a straight line roughly southeastwardly.

Not yet had they caught a glimpse of the Golden King whom they were seeking. Where was he?

From this point onwards they were travelling the main stream of the mighty Amazon. On February 26th, 1542, they arrived at Aparia the Greater, named after a powerful Indian chief in whose principal village they stayed until April 24th. During that time they built a new brigantine which they called *San Pedro*. The original boat had rotted badly, as was but natural considering the conditions under which it was built. Now, at Aparia the Greater, and with the aid of the chief Aparia and of his people whom the wily Orellana had filled with yarns about the Spaniards being children of the Sun, a fine new brigantine was constructed in forty-one days. Later, at a place further down the river, a third and larger brigantine, the *Victoria,* was built; it was in these two ships, *San Pedro* and *Victoria,* that the last part of the journey of Orellana was performed.[17]

On April 24th, 1542, Orellana and his followers made their departure from Aparia the Greater with the blessing of the Chief Aparia, who provided them with abundant food and other supplies. The travellers, at that moment, were some 600 miles southeast from Quito and some 450 miles from the place where they had left Pizarro four months before.

Still they had not found the Gilded King. Possibly they had ceased to think about him and had turned their thoughts to the Atlantic towards which they were headed. Immediately after leaving the domain of Aparia they passed into a great belt of forested wilderness through which they journeyed until May 12th. On that day they came within sight of several large villages which, as they afterwards learned, were part of the domain of a great chief named Machiparo.

This realm was the first of a long series of river kingdoms. True, it was not Golden, nor had it a Gilded King. Nevertheless, these kingdoms were well worthy of admiration. They belonged to people of the great Guaraní-Carib stock which was so widely distributed both in South America and in the Antilles. The general name of these river-folk was

Omagua, the domain of the Omagua proper lying downstream from that of Machiparo and extending along the river for a distance of 200 miles. Still other domains lay further down. In point of culture all these realms were in a high degree noteworthy. Although not of the high civilization found in the Andes or in Mexico, they were admirable in that, on an intermediate plane of development, they had fine pottery, good agriculture, well-built houses arranged in orderly villages, and a firm rule by powerful chiefs each one with lesser chiefs under him. In short, they were societies which were perfectly adjusted to their special environment, as was made evident by their skill in using the products of their land and, particularly, in their dexterity in river-navigation with their fine, large dug-out canoes.

Moreover, the inhabitants of Machiparo's domain were warlike. They attacked the Spaniards so fiercely and in such numbers that they gravely imperilled the lives of the wanderers. Only a timely arquebuse-shot which killed one of the Indian leaders and threw his men into a confusion of astonishment saved the Spaniards' lives and allowed them to slip past their attackers. Thereafter they kept in mid-stream and dared make no landing. At the end of the first day of travel through Omagua-land the Spaniards came to a village small enough to capture, and therein they found, among other notable things, certain very large jars made of fine porcelain as were also various plates, bowls, and candelabra. This fine ceramic ware greatly astonished the travellers, and no wonder, if, as Father Carvajal avers, it really was not only beautifully painted but also glazed so that it was better than the ware of Málaga and as good as the Roman. The Indians told the Spanish explorers that inland similar objects were made of gold and silver, and the visitors saw that there were various well-made roads leading from the village into the country away from the river in a northerly direction; but, because of their small number, they dared not follow the highways.[18]

Throughout the remainder of the journey of the Spaniards down the great river they had many fights with the natives

through whose lands they passed. In one such battle, on
June 24th, Orellana was shot in an eye and otherwise very
badly wounded. Soon after that they made their way into
the realm of a great chieftainess, Coñorí, who, with her war-
rior-women, fought the invaders fiercely. So impressed were
the Spaniards by this tribe of embattled women that they
added the name "Amazons" to the others by which the river
was then designated, and today it is the most usual designa-
tion of this greatest of streams.[19]

At last, on August 24th, 1542, the *San Pedro* and the *Victoria* came out upon the open sea. For some 300 miles they
had been feeling the effects of the tide, which had told them
that they were approaching their goal. Prows were turned
towards the Spanish Main, and, although the two brigantines
became separated from one another in transit, they both
reached the pearl island of Cubagua in safety, the *San Pedro*
on September 9th, and the *Victoria* two days later.[20]

Thus was completed one of the greatest voyages of all time.
From Quito to the mouth of the Amazon is 2,000 miles in a
straight eastwardly line, and of course much more by the
winding river. From the mouth of the Amazon to Cubagua
is more than 1,200 miles more. In the face of stupendous
difficulties arising from the nature of the country traversed
and from the great native populations encountered, this little
band of men, sixty at most, and tragically less as war, accident, and disease slew some of them, covered a distance of
over 3,200 miles in ten months. However one may view the
manner in which they left their chief, Gonzalo Pizarro, and
his companions, to their fate, one must frankly give honor
to Orellana and his followers for their masterly accomplishment of a grand Odyssey rarely equalled and never surpassed.
Moreover, in one point, at least, Orellana appears in a favorable light as regards Pizarro: in the various "acts of possession" which he officially drew up from time to time as he
proceeded he scrupulously mentioned his leader immediately
after the King, taking possession of the realms in question in
the names of both.[21]

The life of Orellana, after his epic journey from Quito to Cubagua in the Spanish Main, by the Amazon and by the open sea in two not large ships, was an anti-climax. As quickly as he could he went to Spain and laid before the King all the vast and varied information which he had collected, at the same time asking for the governorship of New Andalusia, which would include the whole of the Amazonian country traversed by him. The King and his Council of the Indies accepted the proposition, and an expedition was fitted out in Spain for its accomplishment. Orellana stopped at the island of Margarita, off the coast of Venezuela and just north of Cubagua, on his way to the Amazon, and then, in December, 1546, proceeded to the river of rivers. At the mouth thereof he had a sharp battle with the Indians in which seventeen of his men were slain. At the time Orellana was a sick man, and this catastrophe broke his heart so that he died. Appropriately he was buried at the foot of a mighty tree close to the waters of the majestic stream whose waters his keels had so daringly furrowed.[22]

4. The Journey of Lope de Aguirre from Peru to the Spanish Main by Way of the Amazon

Orellana had found neither a Gilded Man nor a Golden Kingdom. Nevertheless the search for one or the other of them continued, and it produced a second trans-continental journey, this time from Peru to the mouth of the Amazon, and thence to the coast-country of Venezuela. The moving spirits in it, and some of the events in its course, stand in sharp contrast to the Pizarro-Orellana venture.

As Pizarro faded from the picture in the case of the earlier journey, having been, to begin with, the leader in it, so also did the original commander of the next great Amazonian voyage. This was a young nobleman of many good qualities but of a weak will whose name was Pedro de Ursúa. After a brilliant and varied career in the Spanish colonies he arrived in Peru, where, in 1559, and under the personal patronage of the Viceroy Marquis of Cañete, he fitted out an expedition for the purpose of tracing to their source the prevalent rumors about El Dorado, which was then believed to be somewhere in the Amazon country, possibly among the Omaguas; and this belief persisted in spite of Orellana's failure to find any Gilded King in that region.

During 1559 and 1560 Ursúa was busy between Lima and the banks of the Huallaga, which, lying east of the continental divide, is one of the great streams of northeastern Peru, flowing northwardly into the Marañón-Amazon main river. A shipyard was set up on the Huallaga and work went ahead fairly steadily on several boats suitable for river-navigation. At the same time men for the expedition were recruited from Lima, Cuzco, and other parts of Peru. They were, for the most part, as different as possible from the select group of high-born cavaliers who had gone with Pizarro and Orellana; indeed, on the whole they were a rowdy and turbulent lot, the very scum of the Spanish element in Peru. Of them all by far the worst, as well as the most dynamic, was Lope de Aguirre, a man of bad repute who had been mixed up in every unseemly broil that had taken place in Peru since 1538.[23] He it was who became second in command to Ursúa.

From the very beginning, even while the boats were still building, Aguirre made gravest trouble for Don Pedro de Ursúa and the other decent members of the expedition. He was a specialist in brawls and indiscipline. At length, however, on September 26th, 1560, the main body of the expedition started down the Huallaga under Ursúa. With them went Doña Inés de Atienza, a lovely *mestiza* widow from Trujillo who had sold all her possessions in order to follow Don Pedro by whom she was greatly loved; present also were one or two tirewomen of hers and the daughter of Aguirre, with a waiting woman or nurse.

All the vicissitudes of fluvial travel were experienced, and they were rendered all the more dreadful by the incessant plotting and bickering that went on among the expeditionaries. At the end of November they reached Machiparo and remained there for five or six weeks. Aguirre and others were now definitely conspiring to murder Ursúa, partly because he was too mild to suit them as a leader, but chiefly because of their wish to get at Doña Inés. On the night of January 1st, 1561, at a little village somewhat below Machiparo, Ursúa was assassinated in circumstances of the utmost barbarity.[24]

After the death of Ursúa and the assumption of leadership by Aguirre the expedition degenerated into a gory vortex of murder, rape, and madness, touched here and there with crazy comedy. Not having found a Gilded King, Aguirre proceeded to confect a king of sorts by his own act, choosing for the royal rôle a weak-kneed fellow named Fernando de Guzmán, whom he dubbed "Lord and Prince of Peru," in the stead of Philip II, formally "dethroned." This farce was gone through with at Machiparo, on the Amazon, where Orellana had been nearly twenty years before, the date of the "crowning" of Guzmán being March 23rd, 1561. There was much wild talk of how an independent kingdom of Peru was to be created, and the new "king" was surrounded by a rigmarole of madmen's pomp and etiquette. In the meanwhile, Doña Inés, gracious and ill-fated lady, was tossed from villain to villain until she, too, was slain by the furious beasts around her.[25]

The remainder of Aguirre's story is a crescendo of maniac carnage. As were so many others, Don Fernando, who had now become "Prince of Peru, Tierra Firme, and Chile," was slain. The journey, however, continued. Aguirre and his *Marañones* (as they styled themselves) followed exactly the same route that Orellana had taken, encountering the same tribes, fighting with them in the same way, and, early in July, 1561, issuing upon the Atlantic at or near the same place where their predecessors had done so. They, too, built ships and sailed up the coast, reaching Margarita Island on July 21st, 1561. After a final whirl of hideous deeds there and on the adjacent mainland of Venezuela, Aguirre met his end, near Barquisemeto, on October 26th, 1561. On that day, after he had slain his own daughter so that she should not live to be called a traitor's child (the one kind act of his life), he was captured by the authorities, and promptly executed.[26]

5. Conclusion

The two trans-continental voyages here described had points in common and as many points of divergence. The original purpose of both expeditions was to find the Gilded King and his realm; to a large extent the route followed was the same in both cases; in each instance the original leader was replaced by another; and the two journeys linked the interior of South America to the Spanish Main in an extraordinary way. There, however, the parallel stops. Whatever his failings may have been, Orellana was certainly not a lecher and a murderer, and his men were of a quality far superior in all respects to most of the *Marañones* who followed the mad traitor Aguirre.

With the numerous expeditions which were sent into the Orinoco and Amazon drainages from the Andean highlands during the period between 1561 and 1600 we need not long concern ourselves. They were much alike, and some of them partook of the nature of El Dorado hunting only in a limited degree. That is, after the pursuit, capture, and judicial murder, at Cuzco, of the Inca Tupac Amaru I, 1571–1572, stories grew up, to some extent on bases of truth, to the effect that some of his attendants and subjects had made good their escape downstream so that in time they were able to re-create, after a fashion, the Inca realm. If it were done, it must necessarily have been amid environmental conditions sharply different from those prevailing in the original Inca Empire; still, given the special circumstances, a people so highly developed and organized and so proudly imperial in temperament as were the Inca family would not find the requisite adjustment too difficult. The wish to escape from the strangers who had taken their homeland and who oppressed the dwellers therein with unwonted exactions would supply an irresistible motive for the change.

At any rate, El Dorado, towards the end of the sixteenth century, became a Golden Kingdom rather than a Gilded Man. There grew up lustrous legends about mysterious civilized states—Paititi, Enim, and others—said to be hidden away in the tangled wilds of Amazonia.

As to the supposed site of the El Dorado kingdom—with which the Omaguas and a mythical Inca city of Manoa came to be mixed up—it may be said that it tended to skid eastwards down the Amazon until it came to rest in the unexplored wilderness behind Guiana. The skidding process was helped by the expeditions from the kingdoms of New Granada, Quito, and Peru, during this period (after 1570), and by explorations southwards from Venezuela, which, not finding El Dorado in the regions seen by them, resulted in the assumption that it was farther on.

During the decades when the Spaniards were making good their hold on Venezuela, New Granada, Quito, and Peru, and were penetrating southwards and eastwards from those bases towards the middle of the continent, there were also interesting developments along the northeastern and eastern coasts of South America. The Island of Margarita appears to have been the easternmost of the important and continuously occupied Spanish settlements on the north coast of the continent, and the fact that the two trans-continental-down-the-Amazon cruises (Orellana and Aguirre) made for it when they issued from the Amazon-mouth indicates that they both looked upon it as the nearest Spanish place. The Island of Trinidad, forming the eastern side of the Gulf of Paria (whose other sides are Venezuela on the west and the Orinoco delta—also part of Venezuela—on the south), was settled by the Spaniards under Governor Don Antonio de Sedeño in 1532. After that, although definitely a Spanish possession, Trinidad fell into a state of neglect similar to that suffered by other goldless islands. True, there are numerous Spanish names to be found on Trinidad, but it is probable that most of them, if not all, date from a period subsequent to that now under consideration. Carib names, on the other hand, almost equally plentiful, may well antedate the Spanish period. Such place-names as Arima, Cunupia, Chaguanas, Guayaguayare, Charuma, and Caroni suggest that there was once a strong Carib element in the population of this island and that through it passed the migrant Caribs who are known to have made their way into the semi-lunar northward-stretching archipelago of the Lesser Antilles. Mixed with them, in a manner which only long and painstaking analysis will ever definitely unravel and explain, were the Arawak folk, both on the mainland and on the islands, and these last were the older element, having later been overrun by the more dynamic Caribs.[27]

Southeastwardly from Trinidad lay a stretch of coast which had the delta of the Orinoco at one end and the mouths of the Amazon at the other. Between those great river-systems lay the vast region which we know as the Guianas, British, Dutch and French. The nature of the country and the character of its inhabitants were such that, although several attempts were made by Spain to win and hold this part of South America, she never succeeded in establishing there a truly effective occupation. In the valleys of the Orinoco and of the Amazon her claim was good, but not in the Guianas between them. Portugal, at this time, was a mere appanage of Spain, and consequently Brazil likewise belonged to the Crown of Castile. Here, however, we are concerned rather with the history of events in the Orinoco country and in the country immediately to the south of it, now part of the republic of Venezuela, where the mythical kingdom of El Dorado finally took up its supposed site. Still, we must at least mention the fact that the Spaniards made strenuous efforts, between 1542 and 1576, to acquire a grip upon the Guianas. The expeditions which sought to penetrate those wilds and to establish Spanish rule thereover encountered overwhelming obstacles without compensating advantages of the kind they desired. At least two of the explorers lost their own lives and those of many companions at the hands of the intractable and resentful Caribs.[28]

Notes to Chapter V

1 All this is described with more detail in: Means, 1932, Chs. ii–v, where many authorities, ancient and modern, are cited. See also, Urteaga and Romero, 1926; Urteaga, 1933; Valcárcel, 1933; and Cúneo-Vidal, 1925, and 1925a.

2 See articles on the various places named in Alcedo, 1812–1815. Chapman, 1933, pp. 54, 57–58. Wilgus, 1931, pp. 64–65, 107–109. Kirkpatrick, 1934, Ch. xxiv.

3 Kirkpatrick, 1934, pp. 303–309. Chapman, 1933, pp. 57–58.

4 Markham, 1912, Chs. ix–xii. Kirkpatrick, 1934, Ch. xxv. Wilgus, 1931, pp. 107–109.

5 The two best source materials for the truth about the Gilded Man are: Rodríguez Fresle, 1890, Ch. ii, pp. 6–9, written about 1636 by a son of one of the conquerors of New Granada; and Juan de Castellanos, in his *Elegias de varones ilustres,* especially the Elegy on Sebastián de Benalcazar. The John Carter Brown Library has a copy of the 1st edition (1589) of this work. Good modern accounts of the matter include: Restrepo, 1895, pp. 83–87; Markham, 1912, pp. 24–27; Gandía, 1929, Ch. vii; Liborio Zerda, *El Dorado, estudio histórico, etnográfico, y arqueológico de los Chibchas,* Bogotá, 1885; Adolph Bandelier, *The Gilded Man,* New York (Appleton), 1893, with various later editions.

6 Restrepo, 1895, pp. 84–87, where he refers to the old writings of Castellanos and of Rodríguez Fresle.

7 Means, 1932, pp. 67–68, citing the narratives of Pedro Pizarro and of Pedro de Cieza de León, both contemporaries of the Marquis and of his brother, Gonzalo.

8 This is the tale as told by some men from Quito to the historian Fernández de Oviedo, at Santo Domingo, not long after the events now to be set forth. See: Fernández de Oviedo, Pt. III, Bk. XI, Ch. ii, quoted in Bertram T. Lee's edition of Medina, 1894. This great piece of historical research will hereafter be cited as Lee-Medina, the date and place of its issue being 1934 at New York, as duly set forth in the Bibliography of the present book. Medina's book, and Mr. Lee's development of it, are based on the contemporary documents which are there set out, so that no source of information could possibly be more authoritative.

9 Lee-Medina, pp. 45–46.

10 Lee-Medina, pp. 46–50.

11 Lee-Medina, pp. 53–54. Pizarro makes this clear in his Letter to the King, written from Tomebamba (in the southern highlands of Ecuador) on September 3rd, 1542. It is printed in Lee-Medina, pp. 245–251. Means, 1934, pp. 278–280.

12 This is the reason given in Lee-Medina, p. 54, note. On p. 169 Friar Gaspar de Carvajal, the chief chronicler of Orellana's journey, who accompanied him all the way, asserts that Orellana had "several good reasons" for opposing the boat-idea, including that given in the text. It is well to note in passing that whereas Carvajal asserts that the locality, Quema or Guema, where all this took place was 130 leagues (390 miles) from Quito, it is in

reality only about 90 miles in a straight line. (See the map at page 49 of Lee-Medina.) Sumaco, about 65 miles from Quito, is about 40 miles southwest from Guema, and Popayán is about 200 miles almost due north from Guema, with Pasto about half way between them. Partly from lack of accurate geographical knowledge, and largely as a result of the impression made upon them by their terrific struggles to advance, the Spaniards very often greatly exaggerated the distances covered. In this early part of the journey they were often pathetically small, considering the cost of making them.

[13] Lee-Medina, pp. 59–62.

[14] Lee-Medina, p. 62. Means, 1934, pp. 280–281, is quite incorrect in supposing that they were still on the Coca above its junction with the Napo. On the contrary, as Medina clearly shows, they were on the Napo between the Aguarico and the Curaray, being nearer to the former.

[15] Carvajal, in Lee-Medina, p. 170. Means, 1934, pp. 280–281.

[16] Pizarro himself describes the return journey to Quito in his already cited Letter to the King, from Tomebamba on September 3rd, 1542. (See Note 11.) See also: Cieza, 1918, pp. 54–77. This just and well-informed chronicler was in Peru at the time and in a position to receive reliable information on these events.

[17] Lee-Medina, pp. 98–100, 105–106, 446–447, and elsewhere.

[18] Lee-Medina, pp. 200–201, quoting Father Carvajal. Rich data on the Omaguas and other Guaraní-Carib peoples of the Amazon will be found in: Bertoni, 1922; Métraux, 1928.

[19] Lee-Medina, pp. 220–222, quoting Father Carvajal.

[20] Lee-Medina, p. 125.

[21] The late José Toribio Medina, one of the greatest historians ever born in the Americas, made, in his 1894 book, reissued with improvements by Lee in 1934, the strongest possible case in favor of Orellana's conduct towards Pizarro. To that work, which I had never seen at the time of my 1932 book, my attention was called by my friend, Mr. William Charles Cooke, of Bishopstown, Ireland, who urged me to study it. He thought that, on page 81 of "Fall of the Inca Empire" (1932), I had been less than just to Orellana. Accordingly, in as nearly an impartial mood as I could achieve, I carefully analyzed the evidence presented in Medina, 1894, and in Lee-Medina, 1934, as a result of which I came, regretfully, to the opinion that Orellana was indeed much less than absolutely faithful to his leader. (See: Means, 1934, for this analysis of the evidence.) Nevertheless, the fact remains that Orellana and his men performed a superlative act of heroism and persistence, and for that they should be given greatest honor.

[22] Lee-Medina, pp. 124–152. A bibliography of the Orellana voyage will be found on pages 294–295 of Means, 1934. See also: Kirkpatrick, 1934, pp. 237–242.

[23] Jos, 1927, pp. 42–52.

[24] Jos, 1927, pp. 63–68. Harlow-Ralegh, 1928, pp. lxi-lxiii. Simón, 1861, pp. 3–45.

[25] Jos, 1927, p. 87.

[26] Don Emiliano Jos, whom we have so often and so profitably consulted, proves beyond doubt that Aguirre followed the Amazon route, not the Cas-

siquiari-Orinoco route so often claimed for him. See: Jos, 1927, Chs. vi, ix–xi. This very scholarly monograph is a model of what historical research should be—and too often is not. See also: Simón, 1861, Chs. xi–li; Baralt and Díaz, 1887, I, Ch. xii; especially pp. 213–219; Southey, 1821; Harlow-Ralegh, 1928, pp. lxii–lxiv, where the Cassiquiari-Orinoco route is supported, the work of Señor Jos not being cited.

[27] Wissler, 1922, pp. 251–257. Bertoni, 1922, pp. 331–336.

[28] Harlow-Ralegh, 1928, pp. lxvii–lxviii.

CHAPTER VI

RALEGH SEEKS EL DORADO IN GUIANA

1. Explanation

To many it will seem that there can be little if any connection between the hunt for El Dorado in the interior of South America and the founding of English colonies by Sir Walter Ralegh and others in tropical America and, particularly, in the Spanish Main. Yet it is quite true that there *was* a connection and that there was a chain of developments which will be described in just proportions in this chapter and the next. For the moment it suffices to say that the various Spanish attempts to find El Dorado, the Gilded King or the Golden Kingdom (in the end, more generally the latter), had gradually concentrated the attention of the hunters on the lower Orinoco drainage, in territory now forming the eastern part of Venezuela. To that same region, as we shall see in this chapter, the attention of Englishmen, particularly of Sir Walter Ralegh, was also drawn—and for the same purpose, namely, the hope of finding a Golden Kingdom. Not only that, but also, as we shall see in the next chapter, the English effort in the Orinoco region led directly to the founding of the earliest English colonies in the Spanish Main.

The sum, therefore, of this dull but necessary explanation is that we have a chain of connected circumstance, made up of the following links: The Eastward search for El Dorado from Peru and from Quito; the two great Amazonian voyages—Orellana and Aguirre—whose effect is to cause the supposed site of El Dorado to slide into the still unknown regions of the lower Orinoco drainage; the attraction thither not only of continued Spanish interest but also of a new element, that is, Ralegh and other Englishmen; and, finally, the founding of the first Caribbean colony of England as an accident aris-

124

ing out of the English voyages to the Orinoco and adjacent regions.

This, it is hoped, will make what follows comprehensible.

2. *Spanish Seekers for El Dorado Arrive in the Lower Orinoco*

To begin with, it is well to remind ourselves of the chief features of the Orinoco drainage. Without being as immense in extent as either the Amazon drainage or the Paraguay-Paraná-Plata drainage, it is still a vast area which, in its upper parts, lies close to the highlands of Colombia, and, in its lower stretches, runs eastwardly immediately to the south of the mountains rising behind the coast of Venezuela. The mouths of the Orinoco, although not giving on the Caribbean, are not far distant therefrom and are immediately south of the island of Trinidad which, in turn, is close to the southern end of the long chain of the Lesser Antilles at the eastern margin of the Caribbean. With all the regions indicated above the Orinoco is connected, both geographically and historically.

On pages 103–104 something was said of the conquest of New Granada in the highlands of Bogotá (now Colombia) by Gonzalo Jiménez de Quesada. That conquest and that conqueror are intimately linked with Spanish penetration of the Orinoco and, especially, of the lower Orinoco, where, at the end of the sixteenth century, El Dorado was supposed to lie hidden.

It befell thus: When Jiménez de Quesada died in 1579, without children, he left all his extensive properties in New Granada to his niece Doña María de Oruña and to her husband Don Antonio de Berrio.[1] The old Conqueror, in his latter years, had spent a great deal of time, money, and nervous energy in hunting for El Dorado in regions far to the east of Bogotá in the upper part of the Orinoco system. Indeed, the hunt had become an obsession with him precisely as it did with so many others. Therefore, knowing that his nephew-in-law, Berrio, aged about sixty in 1579, had had a long and distinguished career in many parts of Europe and in North

Africa, Jiménez de Quesada laid upon him the moral obligation to continue the quest for El Dorado, doing so in the same
will that conferred upon Berrio and his wife the great wealth
which Jiménez de Quesada had amassed.

Doña María de Oruña, Berrio her husband, and their eight
children arrived in Bogotá from Spain in 1580. On learning
of the terms of the will, Berrio gallantly accepted the charge
laid upon him, and, in spite of his age, plunged enthusiastically into his new duties, remaining faithful to them during
the last seventeen years of his life.

Both in 1580 and almost constantly afterwards, Berrio had
to contend against the jealousy and petty-mindedness of many
officials who sought by every possible means to hamper his
activity. In this respect his situation was not unlike that of
Cortés at the beginning of the conquest of Mexico (see pages
30–32), and, like Cortés, he made direct appeal to the King
with such success that he was appointed in 1586 to be Governor of the Province of El Dorado. That term as then used
included the whole upper part of the Orinoco drainage.[2]

Between January, 1584, and September, 1591, Berrio made
three amazing preliminary explorations in the upper Orinoco
country. He always, at this period, worked eastwards from
Bogotá as a base and, in a very thorough manner, travelling
sometimes by land and sometimes by canoes on the rivers,
scoured the region indicated. Some parts thereof had already
been entered from Bogotá or by German expeditions from
Venezuela (see pages 102–106), but Berrio's work was both
more extensive and more carefully done than that of any of
his predecessors.

The third expedition of Berrio, March, 1590, to September,
1591, was particularly important, as well as particularly
arduous. At a convenient point on one of the uppermost
streams of the Orinoco system he assembled a fleet of twenty
canoes, twenty rafts, and very plentiful supplies for his 112
Spaniards, numerous Indian servants, and 220 horses. The
heavy outlays of money necessitated by all this Berrio met
from his private wealth inherited from his uncle whose work

he was continuing. On this journey Berrio came to the junction of the Caroni and the Orinoco main stream. Indian friends told Berrio that the Golden Kingdom which he sought lay 300 miles to the south, far up the Caroni which flows northward into the Orinoco. By that time, however, sickness and skirmishes with the Indians to the east had reduced his force to less than half its original size. Therefore, finding himself thus weakened, he decided not to attempt then to get around the formidable falls of the Caroni near its mouth but rather to go downstream to the Atlantic. There followed a dangerous battle with a chieftain named Morequito, a little below the Caroni, but the Spaniards managed to continue with their plan. Further down the Orinoco they entered the native province of Barquicana whose chief, Carapana, treated the travellers well and even accepted the overlordship of the King of Spain. He also regaled them with heartening tales about the grandeurs of a rich realm far to the southwards which surely must be El Dorado. Finally, Carapana provided them with canoes and guides so that they were able to go down the Orinoco to its delta and to proceed thence to the island of Margarita in the southeastern Caribbean.[3]

Thus, in spite of divers grave obstacles, Berrio completed and duly reported upon a superb achievement in exploration which, in addition to making known a vast range of territory, narrowed down the area supposed to contain the fabled and much longed-for realm of El Dorado. Berrio, in September, 1591, firmly believed that it lay in the country around the upper part of the Caroni, that is some 300 miles south of the Orinoco main stream which he had lately traversed. The basis of his belief was information received from Carapana and other Indians which, from Berrio's point of view, was highly authoritative.

3.   El Dorado Gains a New Name: Manoa

The next development in the story of El Dorado has touches of high comedy. El Dorado, the fabulous kingdom of unimaginable splendor and riches acquired a new name, Manoa, and, later, a new affiliation, namely, a spurious historical connection with the Inca Empire formerly existing in the Andes.

The first of these steps came about in a curious manner. Berrio and his men remained at Margarita from September, 1591, to January, 1593. Sometime during that interval there arrived at Margarita a Spaniard named Juan Martín, who, thirteen years earlier, had been a member of an expedition into the country around the junction of the Caroni with the Orinoco, which expedition had been massacred with the sole exception of Martín. He had then settled down among the Indians, had assumed their way of living, and had at last become a chieftain among them. Finally, after some ten years of life as an Indian potentate, Martín decided that he would, if he could, return to civilization and to Christianity. He managed to make his way from tribe to tribe in an easterly direction from the Caroni, still wearing Indian dress and speaking the Indian tongue. On the Essequibo River, in what is now British Guiana, he fell in with some friendly Arawak Indians by whose aid he was carried up the coast in a canoe and was finally set ashore on Margarita. Brightly if lightly clad in native gauds he rushed to the first church that he saw and there poured forth fervent prayers of thanksgiving uttered in Spanish strongly tinged by an Indian accent. As Margarita was a drowsy little place any such picturesque occurrence was a blessed relief from boredom. Juan Martín became the hero of the hour and, naturally enough, he made the most of his prominence in the public eye.

Increasingly scintillant were the tales which he told of his adventures. Berrio and all others present on the little island listened avidly to Martín's stories of a great golden realm, which he called Manoa, lying far away near the headwaters of the Caroni. To Berrio these yarns were a confirmation of what he had heard at the mouth of the Caroni; to Ralegh, later on, they were all that and much more. Like all other liars who have a receptive audience Martín embroidered and re-embroidered his tissue of mendacity until at last he was telling his hearers that he himself had trod those glittering streets and that he himself had stood blinded in the presence of that shining monarch who ruled in Manoa the Golden and in all its wide-spreading domains. A culmination of the embroidery process was Martín's statement that he had arrived in the city of Manoa at noon and that it was so vast that he had had to walk through its streets all the rest of that day and all the day after before he reached the palace at its centre. It was in this form that the description of El Dorado, henceforth called Manoa, reached Berrio and, through him, as we shall see, Sir Walter Ralegh.[4]

4. Berrio Ponders on Manoa, Otherwise Called El Dorado

Although hampered by the jealousy of the governor of that island Berrio while living at Margarita continued to ponder on the problem of how to reach Manoa or El Dorado. He came to the conclusion that future campaigns could best be conducted from some base near the delta of the Orinoco whence progress upstream to the Caroni and thence onwards up the length of that river could readily be made. For the purpose in view the island of Trinidad, undoubtedly a Spanish possession but then, apparently, deserted, seemed to offer the greatest usefulness. It was not very far from Margarita and it was close to the Orinoco delta; moreover, it had a good natural harbor on the side towards Venezuela, to the west.

At Margarita Berrio met with a man who, from 1591 onwards, was closely associated with him. This was Domingo de Vera Ybargoien.* He was a brilliant, witty, boastful, and persuasive sort of fellow who, in spite of a tendency towards somewhat fantastic theatricality, was extremely useful to Berrio and for a long time sincerely devoted to his interests. The first errand which Vera performed for his new chief was to go to the Governor of Venezuela, Diego Osorio, in quest of

* This name is sometimes given in other forms, as "Domingo de Vera Ibargoien," "Domingo de Ybargoien y Vera," etc. The one used in the text is as correct as any.

soldiers and money for the Manoa enterprise, and in that Vera was successful, promptly returning to Berrio at Margarita.

Then, in May, 1592, Governor Berrio sent his aide, Vera, to take formal possession of the island of Trinidad, where, on May 19th, with suitable official pomp, Vera founded the city of San José de Oruña, named after the family of the Governor's wife. This important step was designed to prepare the way for the new campaign in search of Manoa.[5] Soon after this, from San José on Trinidad as a base, Berrio made special and successful efforts to establish friendly relations with the Indians along the Orinoco as far up as the Caroni. He found it easy enough to bring the mild Arawak tribes into friendship, and he succeeded also in winning over and in Christianizing the intractable and proud Carib tribes, including Morequito, who now seemed forgetful of his ancient resentment against the Spanish invaders.

On December 24th, 1592, a new complication arose in an unexpected way that threatened gravely to endanger all Berrio's preparations. There arrived at Margarita, from Spain, Don Francisco de Vides, armed with a Royal commission as Governor of Cumaná and of a great extent of coastal territory lying from northeastern Venezuela well onwards towards the Amazon. Thus, this grant included the delta of the Orinoco, precisely where Berrio was planning to commence operations, and, still worse for him, the island of Trinidad which Vides was ordered to settle within six months of his arrival in America. In this connection we must remember that Berrio's appointment as Governor of El Dorado, in 1586, had conferred upon him the great inland region in the upper Orinoco (where he had then supposed that El Dorado lay), but it did not give him either the lower Orinoco or Trinidad, a fact which he seems to have overlooked. By granting to Vides the coastal region defined above, Philip II had unconsciously cut the ground from under Berrio's feet, and had also provided him with a new enemy who could be—and very soon was—extremely troublesome to Berrio.[6] This new element, added to the continuous enmity of Governor Sarmiento of Margarita, made a difficult situation for Governor Berrio. The one bright spot was the fact that Governor Osorio of Venezuela was Berrio's friend and helper.

After all efforts to induce Vides to co-operate with him had failed, Berrio determined, pending the arrival of regulating instructions from the King, to proceed with his own plans as speedily as possible.

After settling, or rather re-settling, Trinidad, Governor Berrio sent his aide Vera and thirty-five men, in April, 1593, to the land of the now outwardly friendly and Christian Morequito. The object of this move was to acquire more precise information about Manoa and to prepare the way for the coming of Berrio himself with a larger force. Vera did his work faithfully, and he drew up, in duplicate, a notarial report upon his doings from April 27th to after May 11th, 1593. This paper and various others, also in duplicate, were sent to Spain by different ships. One set, unfortunately, was in a ship which was captured at sea by Captain George Popham, in 1594, and thus the material in the papers came into the knowledge of Ralegh, who in this manner, by an accident, not to say by a theft, became possessed of Berrio's entire scheme and all that pertained to it.[7]

5. Sir Walter Ralegh's Search for Manoa the Golden

The information conveyed in the captured papers included an account of how to reach Manoa, otherwise the New El Dorado. There were also data on dealings with Morequito and with Carapana at the mouth of the Caroni. Finally, there were data on the golden booty which Vera had obtained from the Indians during a journey from which he had returned to Trinidad in late May, 1593.[8]

Ralegh, through these documents, gained possession of all that Berrio knew about El Dorado and Manoa. Much of it was pure fable, the production of Juan Martín's exuberant imagination. At this stage in his career Ralegh, who had made unsuccessful attempts to establish a permanent English colony in Virginia, was in deepest disgrace with Queen Elizabeth on account of his clandestine marriage to Elizabeth Throgmorton. As the Queen was the supreme fount of favors and riches, Ralegh, who dearly loved such things, was eager to regain her regard. To do so, and also to obliterate the fiasco in Virginia, he must do something splendid, dramatic, spectacular which would enable him to enhance the greatness of the English crown and so win for him the smiles of its somewhat difficult wearer.[9]

Ralegh had long been intellectually interested in the great native empires and civilizations conquered by the Spaniards in the New World. Likewise he had read much about the fabled realm of El Dorado. Indeed, considering how few books were then current on these subjects in England, he had covered an amazing amount of ground, both in the Spanish authors and in those of other nationalities. One has the feeling that if he could come back among us he would make an excellent archæologist. His mind, therefore, was eagerly receptive to the information conveyed by the papers captured at sea by Captain Popham. Reflecting upon it, and remembering all that he had read before about the Incas and their splendors, he now came to the conclusion that Manoa—of which he now heard for the first time as synonymous with the older term El Dorado—was nothing less than a re-born Inca Empire. Upon this theme he elaborated in his mind, hunting through his books (which he was wont to take about with him, even on the high seas), and delving into his memories of things read. What could be more logical than that descendants of the Incas of Peru should flee eastwards from the oppression of the Spaniards and should re-create, in the wilds behind the Orinoco and the Guiana coast, their ancient power and state? The idea gripped him hard. No wonder. To reduce such a rich realm, and one with so gloriously picturesque a past, to a mighty province over which Queen Elizabeth would be sovereign would be to do something truly memorable in that lady's honor, and something which she could not fail to reward.

Leaving Sir Walter Ralegh to plan his course of action with

respect to Manoa and its Inca monarch, we must return briefly to Governor Berrio, at San José on Trinidad, between 1592 and 1595. It was a difficult time for him. His friend, Governor Osorio of Venezuela, betrayed him and tried to find Manoa without his aid; Governors Sarmiento of Margarita and Vides of Trinidad continued to pester him until Sarmiento was slain by an English pirate in a fight and Vides was ordered by the King to co-operate with Berrio in spite of the conflict between their claims.[10]

In 1594–1595 Berrio was having still other perplexities. He now had a little advance-garrison in Carapana's country, below the Caroni inflow on the Orinoco. Carapana was a faithful friend and there was no danger from him, but Morequito, the powerful chief upstream near the Caroni, had now thrown off all semblance of good will and was threatening to become troublesome. Moreover, towards the end of 1594 there came to Trinidad a certain Captain Jacob Whiddon, who was an employee of Ralegh and who had been sent thither to see what could be learned. There was a skirmish between Whiddon's men and Berrio's in which eight of the former were slain. Ralegh afterwards claimed that it was "treacherously" done, but one cannot see why, as Berrio's men were but defending their own.[11]

In this situation Berrio took two important measures. First he sent his son, Fernando de Berrio y Oruña, all the long way overland to New Granada in quest of reinforcements. Later some soldiers made their way overland to where Berrio was, travelling through the difficult country between New Granada and the Caroni. Second, in mid-November, 1594, Governor Berrio sent his faithful aide, Vera, to Spain in quest of aid and troops and colonists. Among the reports and papers of information which Vera carried with him was a petition to the King signed by twenty-eight of Berrio's men in which it was prayed that all possible help be given to their enterprise.[12]

The climax of Governor Berrio's career was now at hand. On February 6th, 1595, Sir Walter Ralegh sailed from England in quest of Manoa. He had with him 100 soldiers in four ships, and also some smaller boats for up-river work. Passing by the Canaries, he reached the eastern shore of Trinidad on March 22nd. Twelve days were then spent in spying about without being seen by the Spaniards on the other side of the island. Then, between April 4th and April 8th, Ralegh made his attack on San José, which probably contained not more than fifty Spanish fighting-men, and, after a struggle, succeeded in taking it. The poor little town was then burned to the ground and Governor Berrio, his lieutenant Alvaro Jorge and other officers, were taken as prisoners on board Ralegh's flagship.[13]

During the month of Governor Berrio's detention on Ralegh's ship a game was played by the two. The Englishman was expecting reinforcements from his associate, Amyas Preston, and, equally, but with secrecy, Berrio was looking forward to the arrival from Spain of Vera with a great increase of force. Meanwhile, with varying stratagem, Berrio first sought to frighten off his enemy and captor with horrendous tales of the dangers that lurked along the road to Manoa and, that failing, later he feigned stupidity, doing so with histrionic skill so complete that he quite fooled Ralegh into thinking him an uninformed and ignorant fellow.[14]

Ralegh and his men set forth from Trinidad and travelled up the Orinoco to the Caroni where they were much impressed by the spray-shrouded cataracts whose sonorous roar could be heard for long distance. The Caroni, only some 125 miles from Trinidad in a straight line, was Ralegh's furthest west! Such were the modest proportions of Ralegh's achievement in his much-touted "discouerie" of Guiana.[15]

Turning northwards in June, 1595, Ralegh bethought him that such odds and ends of gold and information as he had managed to collect in Guiana would not be likely to recompense Sir Robert Cecil and others who had backed his venture. So, in June, he attacked Margarita Island whence, with considerable emphasis, he was driven away by an excellent new Governor, Don Pedro de Salazar, and, on June 23rd, he assaulted Cumaná where he met with a sharp defeat and heavy losses. Having thus learned that the mettle of the Dons was too keen for him, Ralegh set Berrio and Alvaro Jorge ashore at Cumaná, where they promptly fell into the hands of vindictive Francisco de Vides. Then he made sail for home.[16]

On the way home and after his arrival in England, Ralegh busied himself with dressing up his plan to add Guiana to the realms of his Queen. In order the better to sell to that lady his grand project he confected his celebrated book, enhancing its allure with apt quotations from works about the Incas, and showing how, by uniting the tribes of Guiana, both the "borderers" and the subjects of the "Inga," under the English standard, the Spaniards could be undermined and supplemented by the subjects of Queen Bess. The sovereign lady was far too astute, however, to nibble at the proffered bait, notwithstanding the fact that her own detestation of Spain was (naturally enough) quite the equal of that felt by Ralegh.[17]

In the meanwhile, that stalwart soldier of Spain, Governor Berrio, was drawing to the close of his arduous and faithful, but by no means always fortunate, career. In July, 1595, he managed to escape from Vides, largely because that official dared not hold a fellow Governor and equal overlong, and, with only ten men, he visited the ruins of San José de Oruña on Trinidad. Thence he pushed onwards to the junction of the Caroni and the Orinoco where he founded a little fort called San Thomé.* Not long afterwards there arrived thirty more men, sent from New Granada overland by young Fernando de Berrio y Oruña, who added themselves to the original contingent, thus bringing the garrison up to the number of forty men.

This little band was holding San Thomé in March, 1596, when Ralegh's servant and emissary, Keymis, came up the Orinoco. It is not altogether clear what Keymis was looking for, but the indications are that he was in quest of gold, presumably that Ralegh might use it as material for making his Guiana venture more attractive to those at home. Keymis

* This is the form which the name usually has in literature; but it is likely that Santo Tomás would be more correct. Still, one does not wish to be pedantic, so the usual style will be used.

was told about, perhaps even shown, some kind of metallic deposit which immediately became the basis of a rather tall story about a gold mine said to exist not far from the confluence of the Caroni and the Orinoco. The presence there of San Thomé prevented Keymis from doing much of anything about the matter, and he and his men discreetly retired downstream and went home to England.[18]

During all this time Domingo de Vera had been fighting a picturesque and successful battle in Spain on behalf of Berrio. He had a marked tendency towards theatricality which led him to show himself about in public places arrayed in outlandish costumes which awakened the popular admiration. In addition to this, his stirring stories of shadowy, distant kingdoms and his clever diplomacy combined to bring about the raising of large sums of money, from the government and people of Seville and also from the King, who also granted six good ships. As a recruiting-officer Vera was no less successful than as a financial agent. His eloquence drew volunteers to his service so that in due course he had 400 married couples with their children and 600 bachelors, this needlessly large force taking ship for the Manoan realm early in 1596. On their arrival at Trinidad on April 19th, they easily recaptured the island in Berrio's behalf, and in the King's name, and thence they went onwards to the Orinoco and up it to San Thomé. The small walled town, with its little guns peeking pathetically over the battlements, with its houses and public buildings huddling along the inner side of the walls, and with its cistern in the middle of the central plaza, welcomed the horde of newcomers fresh from Spain as best it could. They came marching with flaunting banners and dressed in their gayest apparel, men, women and little children advancing to the sound of the churchbells and of military music.

It was a pathetic and a tragic show. Almost at once the fatal influence of a tropical environment upon a colony not yet accustomed to life in the wilds, and largely feminine at that, soon made itself felt. Sickness, discouragement, and nostalgia did their part; moreover, as always in such cases, when floods of gold were not immediately forthcoming, the morale of the men began to sink, nor could the clergymen of the expedition maintain it in sound condition. The faithful Alvaro Jorge died while leading an exploring expedition up the Caroni valley; Vera, grown proud, quarrelled with the chief whom he had served so devotedly, and withdrew to Trinidad. In a word, the whole thing went to pieces. It was the fate of many to end their lives in the jungles, swamps, and rivers of that land. Others perished at the hands of infuriated natives who resented the attacks made upon their homes, property, and persons. Amid a rising tide of disorders, desertions, sicknesses, and disasters none of which he could now successfully combat, Don Antonio de Berrio died, in 1597, shortly after the arrival of his son, Fernando, at San Thomé with further reinforcements brought from distant New Granada.[19]

6. The Significance of the El Dorado and Manoa Legend

Now that we have traced the main features of the El Dorado myth and of its development from the small but truthful beginning in the tarn of Guatabita to the overblown and tawdry vision of a reconstituted Inca-dom which drew Ralegh across the sea, we may well pause to examine the matter of El Dorado as a whole. Dispassionate appraisal shows that the myth—considered apart from the real Gilded Chief of Guatabita—had two major phases: The earlier and saner of these took the form of a belief that, somewhere east of the Andes, actual peoples dwelt in whose veins ran a proportion of highland blood, and in whose culture there were many elements derived from Incaic civilization. That there was a penetration eastward, not only of cultural elements and of ideas but also, to a less extent, of blood is a well-known fact of South American ethnology. Great ethnic groups, the Guarani-Carib for one, the Arawak for another, have milled about in South America and in the Caribbean for centuries, conflicting, merging, until the whole picture of the native population has become obscure under a tangle of cross-currents. For the moment it suffices to say that the earlier phases of the Golden Kingdom myth took its rise from the eastward ramifications of Incaic influence.

The later and eventually more fantastic phase of the myth came into being as a result of the journey of Ursúa and Aguirre and of the explorations made after their time. The Golden Kingdom came to rest, at last, in the hinterland of the Guianas, south of the Orinoco, and west of the Essequibo. There it was hunted for by Berrio and afterwards by Ralegh.

Not all explorations conducted from the Andean zone as a base had El Dorado for their objective. Journeys of quite different and more practical purpose were plentiful. By way of concluding the present chapter, we may notice a quaint truth: The real Inca Empire itself was once, as shown in Chapter II, something very like an El Dorado to men like Alejo García, Sebastian Cabot, Roger Barlow, and Francisco César. One of these, Roger Barlow, was an Englishman who thus, long before Ralegh, dreamed of adding the Golden Kingdom to the empire of England.[20]

NOTES TO CHAPTER VI

[1] This is made clear in a letter from Berrio to the King dated October 26th, 1591. See: Harlow-Ralegh, 1928, pp. lxx and 97. Also: Markham, 1912, p. 188.

[2] Berrio himself described his work, in his first journey, to the King in a letter dated May 24th, 1585, printed in Harlow-Ralegh, 1928, pp. 91–95. He had influential friends at Court who, throughout 1586, were working on his behalf, and with complete success. See: Harlow-Ralegh, 1928, pp. lxx–lxxiv.

[3] Harlow-Ralegh, 1928, pp. lxxv–lxxvii, and Berrio's Letter to the King, from Margarita, January 1st, 1593, at pp. 98–105 of that volume. Berrio's letter is, in effect, a rebuttal of the accusations made against him by the jealous Governor of Margarita, Juan Sarmiento de Villandrando, in a letter from Margarita on October 24th, 1591, printed by Harlow at pp. 105–106.

[4] Ralegh's reference to the matter ran thus: ". . . The relation of this *Martynes* (who was the first that discouered *Manoa*) his successe and end is to be seene in the Chauncery of *Saint Iuan de puerto rico,* whereof *Berreo* had a coppie, which appeared to be the greatest incouragement as well to *Berreo* as to others . . ." (P. 19.) From this we gather that Juan Martín even took to authorship and that his account of what he had seen—or rather of what he

said that he had seen—was known to Berrio and through him to Ralegh. There is also the hint that the original document may still be awaiting discovery in some repository at San Juan de Puerto Rico—a point which I commend to students of history in the Universidad de Puerto Rico, at Río Piedras. Ralegh, 1928, p. 20, repeats Martín's account of his long walk through Manoa's streets to the palace of the King of Manoa.

5 Harlow-Ralegh, 1928, p. lxxix. The official description of the city of San José de Oruña was: "Frontier and entry-port for the very rich provinces of Guiana, Dorado, and Manoa." (Quoted by Harlow from original sources, page cited, note 2.)

6 Harlow-Ralegh, 1928, pp. lxxix–lxxx, citing original sources.

7 Vera's report, or rather an extract from the copy of it, appears in Harlow-Ralegh, 1928, pp. 79–83, where Mr. Harlow indicates that the paper from which Ralegh was translating was an abbreviated version rather than a duplicate of the report made by Vera. The original report reached Spain safely, however, and was among the papers copied for the British Guiana boundary commission so that Mr. Harlow, by strange chance, is able to cite precisely both the original (in the Archivo General de Indias) and the transcript (in the British Museum), on p. lxxx, note 6.

The questions of *when* the Popham-stolen letters came to Ralegh's hands and of *how they affected him* are not easy to answer. Ralegh himself is by no means clear on the first point. He says: "Those letters out of which the abstractes following are taken, were surprised at sea as they were passing for Spayne in the yeare 1594 by Captaine *George Popham:* who the next yeare, and the same that Sir *Walter Ralegh* discouered *Guiana,* as he was in a voyage for the west Indies, learned also the reportes annexed. All which, at his returne, beeing two monthes after Sir *Walter,* as also long after the writing of the former discourse, hearing also of his discouerie: hee made knowne and deliuered to some of her Maiesties most honorable priuie Councell and others. The which seeing they confirme in some parte the substance, I meane, the riches of that Countrey: it hath beene thought fitte that they shoulde be thereunto adioyned." (P. 77 of Harlow-Ralegh, 1928.)

From this rigmarole one gathers that Popham took the papers in 1594 and that Ralegh did not see them until after his own "discovery" had been made and his account of it written, and that then, finding the papers to confirm what he had said, Ralegh printed abstracts of them with his book, published in 1596. If this is correct, the contents of the stolen papers cannot have had any part in determining Ralegh to fare forth in quest of Manoa the Golden.

On the other hand, Mr. Harlow, with reference to the report of Vera, which was represented by a short version of the original, said short version being among the papers taken at sea by Popham in 1594, remarks: "The fortunate capture of this document provided Ralegh with the key to Berrio's secrets." (Pp. lxxx–lxxxi.)

On the whole, in spite of Ralegh's statement, I am inclined to believe that the stolen papers reached him before he set out and that, moreover, they were the direct cause of his choosing the Guiana route for his proposed journey to the favor of his Queen which, as we shall see, he had lost. It is inherently more probable that a corsair captain like Popham would hasten to place such papers in hands likely to pay well for them than that he should roll around the seas with them during a year or two before making them known to others. An important argument against the theory that Ralegh was set upon the road to Guiana by the Popham papers is the fact that, in 1594, he sent Whiddon in that direction, as we shall see. Nevertheless, if the papers taken by Popham came to Ralegh's hands early in 1594, as they might have done, the sending forth of Whiddon may have been the first result of Ralegh's receipt of them.

8 Harlow-Ralegh, 1928, pp. lxxxiii–lxxxiv.

9 Harlow-Ralegh, 1928, pp. xxi and xcviii. Andrews, 1933, pp. 12–20; 1934, pp. 24–25. Fiske, 1897, I, Chs. i and ii. Historical Portraits, I, pp. 86–89. Chidsey, 1931. Konetzke, 1934.

10 Harlow-Ralegh, 1928, pp. lxxxiii–lxxxvi.

11 Harlow-Ralegh, 1928, pp. lxxxvi–lxxxvii, 13–14. See also: Williamson, 1923, p. 22, where he states that Berrio treated Whiddon and his men with civility.

12 Harlow-Ralegh, 1928, pp. lxxxiv–lxxxvi.

13 Harlow-Ralegh, 1928, pp. lxxxvii and 14.

14 Harlow-Ralegh, 1928, pp. lxxxvii–lxxxviii. Rionegro, 1914, p. 167.

15 Harlow-Ralegh, 1928, pp. lxxxviii, 16, 53–63. In 1613, Robert Harcourt, an infinitely better man and more able voyager than Ralegh, was still giving Ralegh the credit for "discovering" Guiana! (See Harcourt, 1928, p. 60.)

16 Harlow-Ralegh, 1928, pp. lxxxviii–lxxxix and 125–137, at which latter pages will be found contemporary Spanish accounts of the affairs here mentioned. They give the lie to Ralegh's own account of the same matters. One of the letters, that of Simón de Bolívar, from Margarita, July 8th, 1595, is particularly interesting as being by a close associate of Berrio's enemy, Osorio (see Rionegro, 1914, p. 165), and as being by a direct ancestor of the Libertador of northern South America. Governor Vides, it should be noted in passing, so far departed from his usual rascality as to make a very fine and successful campaign against Ralegh when the latter attacked Cumaná.

17 The precise nature of Ralegh's scheme becomes clear from a study of Appendix C in Harlow-Ralegh, 1928.

18 Harlow-Ralegh, 1928, pp. ciii–civ; 1932, pp. 64–67. Williamson, 1923, p. 74.

19 Harlow-Ralegh, 1928, pp. xci–xciii, and 108–113 (this being Vera's letter to the King, dated from Trinidad October 27th, 1597, and relating the affair from his standpoint). It is worth while to consult also: Simón, Part I, Noticia VII, Ch. xii; Fernández Duro, 1895–1903, III, pp. 101–106.

20 The variety of the El Dorado quest in general will be found tellingly set forth in Rodríguez, 1684, Bk. VI, Ch. iv, especially p. 385, where the true status of culture in Amazonia is described. See also, Gandía, 1929.

CHAPTER VII

THE RISE OF ENGLISH, FRENCH, AND DUTCH COLONIES IN THE SPANISH MAIN

1. *Non-Spanish Activities in the Spanish Main After 1598*

In Chapters III and IV we saw how English and French intruders in the Spanish Main did all that they could during the sixteenth century to hamper Spanish commerce there and to curtail Spanish power. Then, in Chapters V and VI we traced the El Dorado legend from its beginning to its culmination in the hands of a great Spanish soldier and of a celebrated English adventurer. Sir Walter Ralegh, the Englishman in question, represents not only the last phase of the quest for El Dorado (so far as we are concerned in the present volume) but also the beginning of a new tendency of the greatest importance for us, namely, colonization by Englishmen in tropical America. True, that tendency did not become a reality in the Spanish Main until after Ralegh's death; nevertheless, he should be credited with having prepared the way for it, and even, as we shall see, with having been connected with the first foundation of a tropical English colony in America in a manner almost direct, albeit unconscious.

Between 1598 and the founding of the English colony on St. Christopher in 1623 the English sea-rovers desirous of acquiring some of the American wealth which Spain was receiving were very active. This being the truth, we must ask ourselves what and how much was the annual wealth coming to Spain from America. Thanks to the magnificent research work of Dr. Earl Hamilton we are able very easily to obtain a bird's-eye view of this intricate matter. In addition to relatively modest amounts of what modern folk generally regard as "colonial produce" (such things as hides, tobacco, sugar, indigo, cochineal, copper), there were importations of silver and gold amounting, in general terms, to: 117,386,086 pesos for the Crown between 1503 and 1660; and for private persons 330,434,845 pesos for the same period.[1] Grouped by five-year periods the total yield of 447,820,932 pesos of *registered* treasure entering Spain from America between 1503 and 1660 rose from less than 2,000,000 pesos per quinquennium prior to 1536 to 11,207,535 in 1561–1565 and thence onward to the all-time peak of 35,184,862 in 1591–1595, after which there was a steady decline to 24,954,526 in 1626–1630, followed by an appalling drop to only 3,361,115 in 1656–1660. As Dr. Hamilton points out, the greatest yield came *after* the much-touted English victory over the Armada of 1588, and the ultimate decline in yield was certainly not chiefly due to the operations of foreign attackers working against Spanish power in America.[2]

These figures impress us still. To men of the sixteenth century Spain's empire in America was inconceivably rich and desirable, all the more so that they could not, from the shortness of the perspective, perceive the disadvantages of such an influx of gold and silver to the recipient nation itself.[3] Moreover, the religious contrast between Catholic Spain on the one hand and Protestant England on the other (with partly Catholic and partly Protestant France midway between them) was steadily growing sharper and more productive of ill-will on both sides.

The attitudes of Spain's three chief enemies—England, France, and the Netherlands—differed somewhat both in kind and in degree, having envy as a common denominator. Up to the end of Queen Elizabeth's reign the English attack on Spain's America had purposed chiefly to corrode the power of a formidable foe through the destruction of his source of wealth and of his imperial strength in general rather than it had purposed to create for England a rival realm in the New World. In this the Dutch tended to follow suit. In other words, the English, and later the Netherlanders, at first strove to ruin what Spain had built and only later did they endeavor to build overseas possessions for themselves. To them, in the earlier years, prior, roughly, to 1580 for England and to 1600 for Holland, raids on Spanish America were only a part of a long drawn-out campaign against Spanish power as a whole. France, in contrast with the two Protestant powers, had no special animosity against Spain, certainly none of a religious sort, and, although subjects of hers continued to prey upon Spanish colonial shipping for their own enrichment, the French government tended to take no part therein unless officially declared war was on. This, then, was the general situation between about 1580 and 1600.

After those dates a new trend developed—rival colonizing enterprise—which, being more constructive, was correspondingly more worthy of respect. One of the factors conducive to the formation of this new trend is curious and almost incredible, being the titanic stroll of one David Ingram, of Barking, from the Pánuco River on the east coast of Mexico north of Vera Cruz to a river not far from Cape Breton Island. It seems that Ingram, accompanied by Richard Browne and Richard Twide who, like himself, had served under Hawkins at San Juan de Ulúa and had been set ashore after the English defeat there in September, 1568, made his way on foot to the remote northern river mentioned. There Ingram fell in with Captain Champaigne, master of the fur-trading ship *Gargarine,* from Honfleur, by whose kindness the doughty pedestrian was returned to his native land, reaching there some time in 1569. Years later, in 1582, this humble, but certainly most remarkable, man came to the notice of several English magnates of his time: Sir Francis Walsingham, secretary to Queen Elizabeth; Sir Humphrey Gilbert, even then much interested in colonizing; Sir George Peckham, likewise interested in colonizing, but far more moved than the noble Gilbert by a wish to despoil Spain; and the younger Richard Hakluyt, leading propagandist on behalf of English expansion overseas. To these important persons David Ingram told his wondrous tale. It matters very little whether Ingram really took that mighty walk or whether the story which he told thirteen years afterwards was a majestic lie; the truth remains that the yarn spun by him fired the imaginations of his auditors and led two among them, Peckham and Hakluyt, to produce writings in which the English were strongly urged to emulate Spain by founding colonies of their own in America.[4]

Although it is easy enough to overemphasize the influence of Ingram's story one may safely say that it at least indirectly helped to form a policy of plantation-founding. It did so because it made known in high quarters in England the existence of vast regions in which English men and women could conceivably settle in order to carry on a kind of life—agricultural, pastoral, industrial—to which they were accustomed at home, without having to adjust themselves to violently novel and dubiously wholesome surroundings. In other words, country of the sort traversed by Ingram was clearly capable of becoming, as indeed it later did become, another England set up across the sea to serve the homeland in many ways, most of which were intended, in one way or another, to produce money. The plantations of England were motivated by other considerations also, of course, by the social escape motive, the self-betterment motive, the let-me-be-a-saint-on-earth-in-my-own-way motive, all of which are so well known as to require no special comment. But, in the last analysis, these motives had a common denominator in the fact that they were expected to produce benefit to individuals and to associations of individuals as well as to the nation as a whole or, specifically, to the sovereign.

The new and comparatively laudable policy of founding plantations in territories to which Spain had, at most, only an academic claim did not bring about an immediate cessation of piratical raids by Englishmen against the dominions of the King of Castile in America. Far from it! We mentioned, at the end of Chapter III, the exploits of George Clifford, Earl of Cumberland, in 1598, when he won a showy but not lucrative victory by capturing San Juan de Puerto Rico. He, in his ship called with rare aptness *Scourge of Malice*, was the prototype of the freebooting, smuggling, commerce-fostering sort of English nobleman whom we shall so often meet in later pages. Sufficient justification for his deeds was, in his own eyes and those of his contemporaries, Cumberland's possession of letters of marque bidding him to fare forth and do whatever damage he could. Even certain Spaniards, including Friar Francisco de Victoria and others of his exceptional broadmindedness (see pages 20-21), conceded a certain measure of rightness to letters of marque so long as they were not used to justify mere robbery and wanton spoliation of innocent people.[5]

Typical of this period was a raid by Captain William Parker who, on February 7th, 1601, with only 150 followers, attacked and captured Puerto Bello. It was a daring assault, but it produced only a small profit as all treasure except 9,000 gold pesos had lately been sent to Cartagena.[6]

Other and more serious-minded Englishmen, including both merchants and thoughtful politicians, desired peace with Spain and a restoration of that legitimate commerce with her and Portugal which their ancestors had enjoyed under the earlier Tudors. Through the death of Queen Elizabeth and the accession of James VI of Scotland as James I of England they were to have their wish, at least in part. That monarch, though a sufficiently unpleasant person in many respects, had never been an enemy of Spain any more than his Scots subjects had been. In the Treaty of London (August, 1604), although the English sought a legalized participation in trade with *all* dominions of the King of Spain, the latter was still insistent upon an exclusivistic policy. The chief consequence of the resultant deadlock was that piracy by English subjects was henceforth bereft of legality—at any rate in principle—which, however, did not cause that piracy to cease. The new situation, nevertheless, marked a real change, because it favored the new policy of founding colonies of England in parts of Spain's America not *effectively occupied*. To that bit of diplomatic cant we shall revert later.

In the meanwhile, France, now reunited under Henry IV, and a Catholic power once more, made peace with Spain by the Treaty of Vervins (May 2nd, 1598) in which, however, nothing was said about the Indies; so that, after the Treaty, the old principle of "No peace beyond the Line" once more became operative, in theory.

In this transitional interval, involving as it did the close of several long-lasting periods (Queen Elizabeth, Philip II, the wars of religion in France, and the struggle of the Netherlanders to attain independence) together with the commencement of new periods the Hollanders particularly distinguished themselves by working out and putting into practice new methods destined to be highly important in the colonial game among the nations. Their Dutch East India Company, founded in 1602, came to serve as a model for Willem Usselincx when, in 1606, he began the labors which, in 1621, culminated in the charter of the Dutch West Indies Company. The intervening fifteen years had been spent first in frightening Philip III into at least tacit acceptance of the "effective occupation" principle, and later, during the truce of 1609–1621, in internal preparations for future operations. As a result of these, at the conclusion of the truce period, the Dutch West Indies Company was ready to begin business under its new charter from Their High Mightinesses the Lords States General of the United Provinces in which document appears the illuminating statement that one of the Company's chief purposes was: ". . . to cooperate in extending national commerce, promoting colonization, crushing piracy, but above all in humbling the pride and might of Spain. . . ."[7]

In a word, although Spain still adhered in theory to her exclusive right in the New World, there was no possibility that she could now continue to maintain it as a reality, this situation being due in part to the growth in power of her three chief rivals and in part to her own interior maladies— of which Philip III's indefensible expulsion of the Moriscos in 1609 was only one—with the general result that Spain's enemies could now support their pretensions with strength against which her opposing strength was increasingly inadequate. Seventeenth century Spain presents the paradox of a country which led all Europe in the arts of civilized living while, at the same time, she was increasingly cankered with internal sickness, particularly in the economic field and in the political. This being so, England, France, and the Netherlands were able henceforward to flout Spain more and more by putting into practice the "effective occupation" principle against which Spain could no longer successfully contend.

As a result of the situation sketched above we have in the period now in question the beginning of colonization in tropical America by powers other than Spain and Portugal. Hitherto it had been chiefly through trade (regarded by Spain as illegal) that Spain's enemies had sought to reduce her strength; but now there began a new process, in which bits of territory which Spain still regarded as hers but which she had done little or nothing to settle, to fortify, and to hold, were nibbled off by her foes. The sickle-shaped line of the Lesser Antilles, neglected by Spain because of their goldlessness and because of the presence there of the intractable Caribs, were one area not "effectively occupied" by Spain; the Guiana coast was considered by the English to be another. In these two areas the new drama of colonial rivalry had its beginnings.

2. Sir Walter Ralegh's Last Voyage to the Orinoco, 1617–1618

Between the departure of Ralegh from the Orinoco in 1595 and his return thither in 1617 there were various English explorations both there and in the region to the south where the three Guianas now are. As they have only the slightest shadow of connection with the history of the Spanish Main we must pass them by in spite of their intrinsic interest.[8]

Sir Walter Ralegh, after the death of Queen Elizabeth and the accession of King James VI of Scotland to the throne of England as James I, found life decidedly difficult and unpleasant. Much of his time was spent in the Tower of London to which he was consigned on various charges into which we need not go as they have little to do with his career in Spanish America. Ralegh was still under a cloud and under sentence of death for treason when, despite the great hostile influence of the Spanish Ambassador, Count Gondomar, he was released from the Tower in 1616.

Ralegh at once set about preparing a new journey to the Orinoco. This time he was pursuing, not a phantom kingdom, but a phantom gold-mine. It was said to be somewhere near the junction of the Caroni and the Orinoco. As noted on page 135, Lawrence Keymis had heard rumors of a gold-mine, or of more than one, in that vicinity in 1596. Incidentally, the alleged gold-mine was not far from the Spanish post of San Thomé which Berrio had founded in 1595, and so was in effectively occupied Spanish territory. The object of the 1617 voyage was set forth by Ralegh himself in these words: "My one design was to go to a gold mine in Guiana, and tis not a feigned but real thing yt there is such a mine about three miles from S. Thomas. . . ."[9]

In short, the ostensible purpose of the trip was to obtain gold from mines on the Orinoco, the assumption being that, if he could bring home enough of the produce thereof, King James would pardon him of his death sentence. An impressive fleet was prepared at an expense of £30,000, of which Ralegh himself put up one-third. There was the *Destinye*, a great ship of 500 tons, and from 9 to 14 other vessels, the personnel numbering between 600 to 1,000.[10] Clearing from the Irish coast on August 19th, 1617, Ralegh arrived in Guiana on November 11th, having lost several of his ships through desertion and having much sickness among the men still with him. By the end of December he was at Trinidad.[11]

The Ambassador of King Philip III to the English court, Count of Gondomar, quite rightly claimed that Ralegh's excursion constituted an invasion of the King of Spain's realms. Astutely Gondomar observed that the real purpose of the journey was probably piracy and and that, moreover, if the gold-mine were the real objective, it was strange and needless to lead thither so impressive an expedition. In order to test the reality of the gold-mine objective, Gondomar offered the co-operation of his Royal master in the quest, which offer, being refused, revealed the fact that the gold-mine was a mere pretence.

Gondomar, who was nothing if not an active and efficient servant of his King, kept the Spanish government well posted on all that went on in England, thus enabling them to take adequate measures at home and in Guiana against Ralegh. Likewise, with the aid of Ralegh's enemies, he worked on James so cunningly that, by October, 1617, that monarch, with a weakling's duplicity, was actively plotting with the Ambassador for Ralegh's ultimate ruin.[12] The situation in which, unknowingly as yet, Ralegh was floundering because of his own king's treachery to him, is so tragic that, for once, it makes one sympathize with his intolerable lot.

In mid-January, 1618, some 400 English under the leadership of Lawrence Keymis attacked the humble little Spanish fortress-town of San Thomé. Because Ralegh, with characteristic caution (to avoid a harsher word), was safe at Trinidad he cannot be blamed for the atrocities committed by the English against the Governor Don Diego de Palomeque y Acuña and the Spanish defenders of the place.* Governor Palomeque died defending his post, and there were all manner of outrages perpetrated by the English upon the Spaniards, living and dead. It was one of the most disgraceful actions in English military history. Young Walter Ralegh's death in the fighting stands forth as a gallant sacrifice to an unworthy cause, and the suicide of Keymis, on board his ship, off Trinidad, in March, brought to an end a brutal career of piracy.[13]

On his homeward journey Sir Walter Ralegh well knew that his life was to be short, as is made very clear in his letter to Lady Ralegh from St. Christopher under date of March 22nd, 1618. His grand scheme for adding the imagined realm of the "Inga of Manoa" to the English possessions and for pro-

* Governor Palomeque had taken command at San Thomé in November, 1615, replacing Don Fernando de Berrio y Oruña. The latter, most unworthy successor of his great father, had been found guilty of illicit trade with interloping foreigners. (See: Harlow-Ralegh, 1932, pp. 360–361.)

ceeding thence utterly to ruin Spain's power in America had fallen to pieces; nor was he even bringing home a glittering bribe wherewith to purchase from his contemptible sovereign both pardon and honors.

In his proclamation of June 9th, 1618, King James, once more thoroughly subjugated to the far stronger will of Gondomar, came out frankly against Ralegh and against all attempts by Ralegh to invade the territory of the King of Spain. Gondomar was at last triumphant in his long struggle against Ralegh. On October 29th, 1618, Sir Walter died upon the scaffold.[14]

Several historical lines of importance lead forth from the second voyage of Ralegh. One is the chain of events connected with the beginnings of permanent English settlement in Guiana; another is the development of Spanish diplomacy in England during the last years of King James I. For us, however, the significant fact is that, by establishing his headquarters on Trinidad and by visiting the island of St. Christopher, Ralegh served, albeit unconsciously, as a link between the English activities on the Orinoco and the founding of English colonies in the Spanish Main. It is this line which we shall now follow.

3.   The First English Colonies in the Spanish Main

Down to about 1620 English attempts to colonize in tropical America had had for their chief purpose either the finding and exploitation of fabulous kingdoms—El Dorado or Manoa —or else the finding of gold in workable mines situated within effectively occupied Spanish territory. At about the date indicated, however, there came into play a new sort of motive for English colonization in tropical America, a motive altogether more sane and more solid and, incidentally, much more modern in character. This was a desire to build up trade in produce of kinds peculiar to the tropics: Sugar, cotton, dyes, fine woods, tobacco, gums, drugs, wax, spices, and so on. For things such as these manufactured goods from England were to be exchanged through the normal working of the new kind of proposed commerce. In short, the whole new development of colonies for the sake of general trade was profoundly wise and constructive; and in its formation England, France, and the Netherlands had each a great part, while Spain continued to lay far greater emphasis on cargoes of gold, silver, pearls, etc., than she did on trade in other varieties of merchandise.

Typical of the new trend in colonization for trade was the London Company for the Amazon Country.* Its prime mover was Captain Roger North, brother of Lord North. In April, 1619, Roger North formed a very powerful group of subscribers to the venture, including Robert Rich, Earl of Warwick, and various other noblemen, as well as merchants and other forward-looking persons. On September 5th, 1619, the patent of this Company passed under the Great Seal. Unfortunately for itself the London Amazon Company claimed as a field for operations not only Guiana, which was certainly not effectively occupied by Spain, but also considerable sections of Spanish Amazonia, already rather thickly speckled with Spanish settlements and mission-stations, and, still more unwise, a goodly part of Peru, the last being clearly a Spanish possession.[15]

In view of this somewhat ambitious attempt to expropriate a huge section of the Spanish empire in South America it is not surprising that that very diligent diplomat, the Count of Gondomar, should have gone into action. With great skill the Spanish Ambassador prevailed upon the English Privy Council to withhold permission to sail forth on the venture, so that North and his associates had to put up with seeing their ships remain in port with their crews devouring the backers' substance. Gondomar probably enjoyed the spectacle.

Finally, at the end of April, 1620, acting on a hint con-

---

* The official title of this enterprise was: "The Governor and Company of Noblemen and Gentlemen of the City of London Adventurers in and about the River of the Amazons."

veyed to him by the Duke of Richmond as to King James's *real* wish, North with three or four not very large boats skipped out of Plymouth without official permission and made for the Amazon. After being vigorously taken to task by Gondomar, James disowned the Company and North—it was rather a specialty of his to turn on his adventurous subjects after they had quitted his realm—and rescinded their charter, in addition to which he ordered the Lord High Admiral Duke of Buckingham to arrest North at sea and to bring him home to England.

North, however, reached the Amazon in May and, with a gentleman named Thomas Warner of whom we shall hear much later on, and with others of his following, he journeyed far up that stream. The region traversed seemed to the Englishmen a veritable Paradise rich in potentialities for commerce of the sort they had in mind. After some months there the expedition had to sail home for supplies and other considerations. Then, on January 6th, 1621, Governor North was sent to the Tower by order of King James and from that lugubrious if distinguished residence he was not finally released until July 18th, and then only on his solemn promise to trouble the Amazon no more.[16]

One of the chief outgrowths of the efforts to found English colonies in Guiana was an English interest in the Lesser Antilles. In view of the geographical conformation of that semilunar string of islands, with Puerto Rico at its northern extremity and Trinidad at its southern, it was inevitable that this should be so. Ships sailing from Guiana and the Orinoco for England naturally passed close to or stopped at one or more of the Lesser Antilles. Ralegh did so, as we have seen, on both his homeward trips, and so did some of North's party as well, doubtless, as others.

As we have said, Spain certainly did neglect and abandon the Lesser Antilles; some of them she never occupied at all. The reason for all this is simple enough: There was no gold to be found in islands which were mostly either volcanic or coral in geologic structure. In addition to this there was another factor almost equally unpropitious to Spanish settlement: The presence of Caribs discouraged cattle-raising and planting and, in general, made life precarious for Europeans.

These Caribs, truth to tell, were remarkable and respect-compelling people. Members, or at any rate relatives, of the great Guaraní stock which made itself dreaded in such widely separated areas, the Caribs nursed in their hearts a fierce love of independence and a passionate desire to continue their lives on the well-advanced archaic plane which they had reached. To this day a remnant of them survives in proud isolation on some of the least attractive islands. Neither Spaniard, Englishman, Frenchman nor Hollander has succeeded in breaking their fierce hearts; rather, they have been brought low in the world by the insidious forces of imported disease, by miscegenation and by economic oppression. Hail to their gallant and freedom-loving spirit!

One of the most lovely of the Carib Islands was Liamuiga, afterwards called San Cristóbal by Columbus and St. Christopher or St. Kitts by the English. With its neighbors, Nevis and Antigua, it lies near the northern end of the semi-lunar chain of Lesser Antilles, at about 17° north and 63° west. Although it was sometimes visited, from 1605 onwards, by English ships bound for or returning from the Guiana coast, it was left for the most part to the Caribs and, as were all the other gold-less islands along the eastern margin of the Caribbean, it certainly was not "effectively occupied" by Spain or by any other Christian state.[17] The establishment there of colonies by powers other than Spain was, consequently, justifiable.

The founder of the first lasting English colony in the Spanish Main was that same Captain Thomas Warner who had accompanied North to the Amazon in 1620. First hearing of St. Christopher from his colleague Captain Painton, Warner at once became interested in that island and, in 1623, while in England, he set about forming a company for the settlement of St. Christopher which island he and two other Englishmen had already visited a year earlier while on their way home.

This company seems to have been a sober and business-like undertaking in which Ralph Merrifield and other solid city-men invested their capital in the hope of substantial returns from tobacco-planting. In short, St. Christopher, from the very first, was planned as a commercial colony of the new sort already defined.

Having made all possible preparations Thomas Warner and fifteen or a few more prospective settlers sailed from England in the ship *Marmaduke,* reaching St. Christopher on January 28th, 1624. During his former sojourn on the island Warner had made friendship with the Carib chief who ruled there. But now, because the English built a fort and armed it with cannon, the island sovereign's suspicions were aroused and friction followed ending up with a war in which either side may have been the aggressor. The result of it was that St. Christopher was rid of its original inhabitants. Their chief being slain, they fled elsewhere. Thereafter the English set about all the necessary activities of building houses, planting tobacco, and in general of establishing themselves. On March 18th, 1625, came Captain John Jeaffreson with a contingent of new settlers and new supplies, from England, in the ship *Hopewell.*[18]

Shortly after that there arrived at St. Christopher a French ship commanded by a privateer of that nation, named Pierre Belain d'Esnambuc, who with his crew accepted Warner's invitation to exchange planting for marine adventure. Thus, in the summer of 1625, St. Christopher gained a European population partly English and partly French. It was lucky for the settlers that both parties were present; for, together, they were able to drive off a formidable Carib attack which neither could have withstood alone. As it was, the French received rough treatment before the English came to the rescue.[19]

All this time Merrifield in England and Warner on St. Christopher had been acting without any sort of official authority so that it was urgently necessary to obtain, if possible, a formal patent for the venture. Accordingly Thomas

Warner went to England to join with Merrifield in seeing what could be done.

The best thing for them would have been, of course, a proprietary grant with palatine privileges and all implied thereby. But Charles I was not in the habit of nicking bits out of the royal patrimony for the benefit of obscure and socially unimportant persons like Ralph Merrifield and Thomas Warner; to get him to do so one had to be a figure of note at Whitehall. In view of these circumstances, Merrifield and Warner did surprisingly well by themselves; for, in a patent passed under the Great Seal of the Privy Council on September 13th, 1625, Merrifield was recognized as the chief backer of the enterprise and Warner was appointed as the King's lieutenant with rule over St. Christopher, Nevis, Montserrat, and Barbados. This was the first document of the kind connected with lasting English colonies in the West Indies. The document was based upon a flat lie to the effect that the existent plantation had been made "with the consent and good liking of the Natives."[20]

Warner reached St. Christopher in August, 1626, bringing with him not only his new dignity but also some 60 slaves (probably caught in Africa on the way out) and upwards of 100 new settlers. He had three ships provided by rich and powerful backers who had added themselves to the original number, the new capitalists being Maurice Thompson of London and Thomas Combe of Southampton. Warner likewise had letters of marque, dated January 26th, 1626, by title of which, it is said, he endeavored, but vainly, to drive the Spaniards out of Trinidad.[21]

Subsequently, tobacco-planting became the chief interest of the English on St. Christopher. Often they put so much land under tobacco that their kitchen-gardens were dangerously reduced in size. At the same time a curious arrangement was arrived at with the French settlers whereby the English took a wide strip across the middle of the island and the French took the two ends, leaving certain salt-deposits at the southern point of the island common to both. This strange disposition of the land was first made by Warner and d'Esnambuc in May, 1627, and, although frequently confirmed afterwards, was a source of friction until the end of the eighteenth century. Harmony prevailed only when some common foe, Carib or Spaniard, was threatening an onslaught. It was agreed, however, that the two nationalities would not fight one another even if their respective monarchs went to war.[22]

In the meanwhile, the Court of Charles I contained numerous noblemen who were eager in quest of honor, power, and wealth. Some were interested only in the last. Once Merrifield, Warner, and their merchant associates had done the preliminary hard work of starting an English colony on St. Christopher, that island became far too fruity a morsel to be left in the hands of men so humble. On July 2nd, 1627, after some rather unedifying dickering, James Hay, Earl of Carlisle, received from Charles I a patent making him Lord Proprietor of the Caribbee Islands. Warner succeeded in making good his position with Carlisle and, after receiving a knighthood, Sir Thomas was appointed by Carlisle as his Governor for life over the English colony on St. Christopher. This was in late September, 1627.[23] After a struggle on the part of the colonists against the new dispensation, it was finally established. There was much unseemly bickering, however, not only on St. Christopher itself but also between Carlisle's officials there and those on Nevis. In short, matters proceeded with much disquiet, brawling and general unpleasantness.

It was not to be expected that even so weak a monarch as King Philip IV would long tolerate such a trespass upon his preserves, certainly not when he had so vigorous and acquisitive a minister as the Count-Duke of Olivares. Accordingly, in the autumn of 1629 a great Royal fleet of twenty-four men of war and fifteen frigates under Admiral Don Fadrique de Toledo suddenly swooped down on Nevis and reduced it to submission. In this the Spaniards were helped by the desertion to them of many indentured servants weary of being worse treated than so many slaves. The English planters on Nevis were obliged to surrender, some took service under the Crown of Spain while others, probably more numerous, were eventually shipped home by Admiral Toledo, who seems to have behaved with amazing clemency. The situation on St. Christopher was handled in like manner by the Admiral who, naturally enough, took nine hostages from the two islands to ensure the return of the ship in which he sent home the repatriated colonists. In all this the French on St. Christopher played a rather shabby part, retreating after slight resistance.

Both Sir Thomas Warner and Governor Hilton of Nevis were lucky enough to be in England at the time of Toledo's little visit. Therefore they were able soon afterwards to bring out new settlers who, joined with those of the first lot who had hidden among the mountains of the interior, started the enterprise anew with a persistence which compels admiration.[24]

When, in July, 1631, Sir Henry Colt reached Nevis in the ship *Alexander,* after a running fight with two Spanish men of war off Dominica (much to the disgust of Colt, a Catholic, but loyal to his country), affairs both on Nevis and on St. Christopher were in a bad way. The indentured servants were ill treated and full of resentment; there were no adequate houses; the tobacco-crop was not good. Nevertheless, from that time onwards things steadily improved so that, by 1639, the annual duties on the St. Christopher tobacco sent to England were £12,000. In that year the St. Kittsians tried to found a settlement on St. Lucia, some 300 miles to the south, but it was wiped out by the Caribs in 1641.[25]

No greater contrast can be imagined than that between the mountainous islets whose history we have been studying and the much larger and flatter island of Barbados. In those days it was well forested, was pleasantly free from native inhabitants and also from Spaniards, and lay some distance to windward of the usual route of Spanish ships. Here, if anywhere, one would think, the English had a right to settle and, having done so, a splendid chance to thrive.

Possibly, but by no means certainly, they might have prospered from their first coming to Barbados had it not been for the dire results of complicated and contentious conditions in Europe among English and Dutch business-men. The start of the settlement in Barbados was that the very solid Anglo-Dutch firm of Courteen Brothers, of London and Middleburg, long active in the smuggling trade to the Spanish and Portuguese colonies, became interested in founding a colony on Barbados. Sir William and Sir Peter Courteen were represented on the island by Captain Henry Powell who, in 1624 or 1625, had taken formal possession of it in the name of King James. Afterwards, in February, 1627, Henry Powell, acting for the Courteens, arrived at Barbados with the first contingent of English settlers. Two years later there were between 1,600 and 1,800 people on the island, including indentured servants.[26]

In short, the Courteens represented in Barbados by Captain Henry Powell and later also by his brother, John Powell, and the latter's son, John, Jr., made at considerable expense of money and of care a very creditable beginning of a sanely conceived English colony on Barbados, one that was based on agriculture and on animal husbandry which would produce a wide variety of articles in which profitable trade could be carried on. As we know, however, others than the Courteens were now avariciously watching the West Indies, and in particular the Earl of Carlisle. As early as 1626 Sir William Courteen became aware that he stood in danger of losing his venture to rivals. The best defense against such a misfortune was to obtain a proprietary grant from the English Crown which would convey quasi-regal powers (of the type called palatine) as well as absolute ownership held direct from the King. At the same time, Sir William, great merchant though he was, had not sufficient rank and social prestige to obtain such a patent in his own name. Accordingly he sought the co-operation of an influential courtier, Philip Herbert, Earl of Montgomery and, after April, 1630, Earl of Pembroke, by which title he is usually known. Acting on behalf of his friend, Sir William Courteen, this Earl obtained on February 25th, 1628, a palatine grant including: Barbados; Tobago; Trinidad, in reality held by the Spaniards; and Fonseca, a mythical island thought to lie some 300 miles east of the Antilles. As we know, Carlisle had received a palatine grant on July 2nd, 1627, which also included Barbados. From this situation there arose a grand squabble between the Carlisle party and the Pembroke-Courteen party, and, on April 7th, 1628, Carlisle won a second grant in which his title to Barbados was heavily emphasized.

The brutal and sordid strife on Barbados between the two parties need not detain us. Carlisle, although infinitely less worthy and less fit to control a colonial venture than were Pembroke, Courteen, the Powells, and that party in general, won out completely both in his intrigues at Whitehall and in the scuffle in Barbados.[27]

Eventually the Barbadians worked out a sound agricultural policy with tobacco, cotton, and, later, sugar as their chief exports to England. During the decade from 1631— when Sir Henry Colt found Barbados in a forlorn condition— to 1640 there was a great inflow of English. Some were persons of decent estate escaping from conditions which they liked not at home; many more were pitiable folk called "indentured servants" who had to pay for their passages out by servitude for a stated period during which their lot was often worse than slavery, its one redeeming feature being that it would end after a term of years—if they could but live through it.

We have now traced the chief circumstances under which English colonization in the Caribbean was begun. It is well, therefore, that we should now sum up the principal characteristics of English as contrasted with Spanish practice and theory in this connection.

From the beginning the English system laid predominating stress upon colonial produce and upon commerce dealing with it. The tobacco-crop was, in the earliest years, the most important, with sugar as a serious rival later on and other commodities also taking their part. All this marks a sharp contrast to the Spanish colonial trade wherein gold, silver, pearls, or other "precious" goods held a more important place than all other kinds of merchandise added together.

Furthermore, in the English system, it was the subject, not the King, who derived the greatest and most direct profit from colonial enterprise. This was equally true whether the administration of a given colony were given to a palatine proprietor having quasi-regal powers and privileges (as in the case of Carlisle) or whether it were confided to a company made up of private persons who subscribed their private money for the venture. In both cases the Crown of England delegated to subjects a very considerable proportion of its authority in governmental and in economic matters. In return the Crown received certain taxes. There was not, however, any degree of direct supervision and direction by the King of England in colonial affairs great and small, general and local, comparable to that exercised by the King of Spain in his dominions.

Finally, there was not, in the English colonies, anything like the official and all-pervading preoccupation with the problem of religious instruction for the Indians which was so characteristic of Spanish colonial rule. This was chiefly due to the fact that the earliest colonies of England were established on islands which either had Carib inhabitants who were soon expelled and afterwards excluded or else had no native inhabitants (as in Barbados). To all these points we shall revert later on.

4. The First French Colonies in the Spanish Main

Naturally enough we usually associate the name and the career of Samuel de Champlain with Canada. Nevertheless, from 1599 to 1601, Samuel Champlain made a long journey, at least partly in Spanish ships and service, during which he visited Santo Domingo, Cartagena, Mexico, Havana, and other places which he described with much care and portrayed with charming water-colors which are most informative. On his return to France he presented his illustrated *Brief Discours* to King Henry IV who rewarded him with a pension and an appointment as Royal Cosmographer, following this up in 1603 with a grant of minor nobility and of the title Sieur. There the matter stopped. Neither Champlain nor Henry IV was intending mischief against the Spaniards. In this the attitude of Champlain stands sharply contrasted to that of Ralegh, for example. It is to be observed that the report of Champlain on all the wonders which he had seen remained unpublished until 1859, never becoming the documentary basis of a proposed armed invasion as did Ralegh's so-called "Discovery" of Guiana.[28]

The French colonies in the Lesser Antilles: Guadeloupe (with its dependencies of Marie-Galante, Désirade, and Isles-des-Saints) and of Martinique were founded in the period which here concerns us. Both were younger than the French settlements on St. Christopher which had been formed under d'Esnambuc, as already told on pages 153–154. These islands, being either of volcanic or of limestone formation for the most part, were without gold and silver; still worse—from the Spanish point of view—they were peopled by the always intractable Caribs who offered no possibility of their becoming a disciplined laboring class. Unalluring to Spaniards as they were, the islands had unquestionably been abandoned by their theoretical owners so that here, if anywhere, the doctrine of "no title except by effective occupation" could be cited as convincing justification of settlement by others than Spaniards.

Hitherto the French government had taken no direct part in establishing, or in attempting to establish, permanent colonies in America. In October, 1626, however, d'Esnambuc formed under the protection of Cardinal Richelieu a Company of St. Christopher in order that the affairs of his little French colony might be properly administered. It was not, however, a very efficient organization. In June, 1629, a large French fleet under the Sieur de Cahuzac was supposed to defend St. Christopher from a great Spanish fleet which, as Cardinal

Richelieu well knew, was on its way to drive foreigners out of all the islands. But Cahuzac, who seems to have had the soul of a pirate rather than of a naval officer, went off on a freebooting tour in the Gulf of Mexico. A few days later, as we saw on pages 156–157, Admiral Don Fadrique de Toledo came with a very large fleet and dealt with the interlopers in a drastic manner.

With undeniable pluck both the English and the French came back very soon to St. Christopher and began their work anew. Then, in 1634, events arose which considerably enlarged the scope of interest in the Caribbees. A gentleman named l'Olive, who was well versed in the islands and in their possibilities as sites for colonies, chanced to be in Dieppe selling a shipload of merchandise which he had collected. Thus engaged he chanced to meet a certain Sieur Duplessis whom he succeeded in interesting in a pet scheme of his for the settlement of the island of Guadeloupe. The two Normans went to Paris and had an interview with the Seigneurs of the St. Christopher Company, the upshot of which was that the Cardinal Duke of Richelieu gave his active aid in the formation of a new and stronger enterprise, the Company of the Isles of America, whose contract was signed in Richelieu's house in the Rue Saint Honoré, Paris, on Monday, February 12th, 1635, in the afternoon.[29]

Armed with all such authority as the King of France could give them—the extent of which is open to debate—l'Olive and Duplessis formed, with the financial backing of the Company and of the merchants of Dieppe, a colony of 500 men who went out to Guadeloupe on the understanding that they would work for three years to pay for their passages. In two ships the expedition sailed from Dieppe on May 20th, 1635, under the joint and co-equal leadership of Governors l'Olive and Duplessis. With them went four worthy Dominicans whose duty it was to serve the spiritual needs both of the French and of the native folk of the island.[30]

As might be expected, the equality of the two Governors soon made trouble for the new colony. Wise old Father du

Tertre dryly observes: "If two Monarchs are incompatible in a Kingdom, two Governors are no less so on an island."[31] Indeed, even on the voyage out there was a certain amount of acrimony between the two leaders due to the greater vigorousness of l'Olive's character. Nevertheless, when they arrived at Guadeloupe on June 28th, 1635, the colony at once set to work to strengthen its position as much as possible. An altar and a Cross were erected the very next day and Mass was celebrated by the priests whilst the Caribs looked on and politely imitated the motions of the devout French as best they could in their uninstructed way. Matters did not, however, continue thus innocuously between natives and invaders; for, inevitably, there were many causes of dispute between them in the course of which the Caribs gradually arrived at a desire to be rid of their visitors. Duplessis, in all this, was for following a pacific and conciliatory policy in which the more pugnacious l'Olive was not a believer. Therefore when, in early December, 1635, Duplessis died, l'Olive (who at that moment was in St. Christopher endeavoring to obtain d'Esnambuc's support of his aggressive policy) was able very shortly to begin active warfare against the Caribs.

On January 20th, 1636, the war against the Caribs began in earnest. Pursuing their usual tactics the Indians fought in small groups, killing stray Frenchmen or parties of Frenchmen from ambush with poisoned arrows, tearing up plantations, setting fire to cabins, and in general working sad havoc among the unfortunate men fresh from peaceful Dieppe. We are told by the Abbé Raynal that the colonists were soon so reduced by hunger and by violence that those who did not perish were fain to dig up the dead bodies of their companions and to eat them, not to mention eating their own excrement also. In this we see a unique case of a "starving time" in a French colony, and this was due to the headstrong bad judgment of one man rather than to a general tendency of French colonists. Finally, in 1640, a new governor, named Aubert, succeeded in bringing the Caribs to a more reasonable frame of mind and so set the little colony on the path towards a greater prosperity.[32]

Martinique was founded in a manner quite distinct from that of Guadeloupe. Governor d'Esnambuc of French St. Christopher, in July, 1635, selected some one hundred tough and adventurous spirits from among his colony and with them took possession of Martinique. A fort was built and plantations were made. At first, apparently, the French seriously tried to establish friendly terms with the Caribs; but the latter resented their presence implacably and took to their usual guerilla warfare. Danger and disaster continued long in spite of reinforcements from St. Christopher until at last a French officer, M. du Pont, brought the Indians to terms. While carrying the good news to Governor d'Esnambuc this gallant du Pont was caught by a hurricane which drove his ship ashore on Hispaniola where the Spaniards captured him and put him into prison for three long years.[33]

French occupation of the islands of St. Christopher (in part), Guadeloupe, and Martinique was the result chiefly of accidental factors such as their being unoccupied by the Spaniards and such as the nature of the environment so attractive to Frenchmen bent on the peaceful pursuits of husbandry.

5. The Netherlanders in the Spanish Main

The enterprising Hollanders, so deeply imbued both with the instinct for business and with hatred for Spain, naturally took their part in the international sport of founding colonies at the expense of the King of Castile. Except for their settlements in Guiana, which lie beyond the scope of the present volume, the Hollanders had comparatively little importance as intruding colonists. Their activity tended rather to take the form of carrying on the trade between points in Europe or in Africa and points in America. It is as carriers and as naval fighters that they were chiefly renowned, rather than as colonizers.

Between 1621 and 1640 the Dutch West India Company of

William Usselincx's creation possessed itself of the islands of Curaçao, Aruba, and Buen Aire off the coast of Venezuela, and of St. Eustatius (or Statia), and Saba in the northern part of the Lesser Antilles. Of these tiny territories Curaçao was the most important and, incidentally, it was the only one wrested from Spaniards, in this case innocuous cattle-farmers who were transported to Venezuela by the Dutch. All the other islands, if not wholly deserted, were occupied by Caribs or by pirates. The manner in which the Netherlanders gave to the tropical island of Curaçao much of the outward aspect of their native country—especially in an architectural way— is an achievement that does them much credit.[34]

In spite of their modest rôle as colonists the Netherlanders were undoubtedly the deadliest and most efficient of all Spain's foes in America. From 1621, when the twelve-year truce between Spain and the Netherlands ended, to about 1633 the Dutch carried on furious and very largely successful naval attacks on Spain and her colonies. Their fleets harried the coasts of both the Atlantic and the Pacific sides of the continent. At the same time, contraband trade and carrying trade was very largely in the hands of Dutch smugglers. Naturally enough, the Spaniards regarded all this as abominable piracy.

Those twelve years of naval warfare constitute one of the glories of Netherland history. Backed by the then very prosperous Dutch West India Company, fleet after fleet, well equipped and well manned, fared forth to chop into pieces the commercial machinery so carefully set up by Spain. It was a multiplex attack on many fronts. Undoubtedly the high spot in the naval campaigns of the Dutch is the capture of the entire Plate Fleet, on September 8th, 1628, off Matanzas Bay in Cuba. The leaders on the Dutch side were Admiral Pieter Pieterszoon Hein and Pieter Adriaanszoon Ita. The commander of the fleet from New Spain was Don Juan de Benavides y Bazán, and the two ships from Honduras were commanded by D. Álvaro de la Cerda. The battle was of the running type, and the victory was overwhelmingly a Dutch one, largely because of vastly superior seamanship. The booty taken included huge amounts of gold, silver, pearls, spices, indigo, cochineal, logwood (for dying), hides, sugar, the whole ultimately liquidated for nearly 15,000,000 guilders to the Dutch West India Company which celebrated the event by declaring a 50 per cent dividend. Subsequently, Benavides, who certainly had been neither alert nor skilful, was executed in Spain for his part in the disaster, and even Cerda, who resisted bravely, was disciplined.[35]

Historians who chance not to admire and love Spain and her people tend to chortle a trifle too much about the undeniably gallant and brilliant action of Piet Hein and Piet Ita. They conveniently forget that this was a unique case and that it affected only one year's fleet. True, the loss was a grave one for Spain, and it hurt her credit in the international money-market; but it is absurd to say that it was a death blow to Spanish supremacy in America, or words to that effect. Moreover, as we have noted on pages 156–157, Admiral Toledo gave, the very next year, telling proof that Spain was anything but dead, and that she upheld her claims as vigorously as ever.

6. Conclusion

The period which we have been studying in this chapter was essentially one in which many tendencies destined to be important later had their inception. Chief among these tendencies was the process whereby Spain's enemies—England, the Netherlands, and France—began to supplement their traditional modes of attack, piracy (which *they* dubbed privateering) and contraband, with the far more constructive and therefore more laudable method of rivalry which consisted of founding rival colonies.

In this period, too, Spain might still assert her monopolistic claim in the Spanish Main and in tropical America generally with some hope of causing it to be acknowledged at least tacitly. Her kings, Philip III and Philip IV, were weak men, but the latter had a strong and pugnacious, if not deeply wise, minister in Olivares, as well as a truly great naval leader in Don Fadrique de Toledo. True, Spain at this time was in no condition to carry her claim to a logical conclusion by driving forth all foreigners in North America from Carolina northwards. Those territories lay beyond her natural zone of occupation, as her rulers must have understood, at least dimly. But she could, and did, maintain her supremacy in regions which she had long ago chosen for intensive occupation.

The truth of this is shown by the fact that Spain's only territorial losses thus far were extremely unimportant to her (except as a principle), and were mostly islands which, in any case, she had voluntarily abandoned. Not a single major island was captured and held by an enemy during this period, nor a square foot of Caribbean mainland.

Notes to Chapter VII

1 Hamilton, 1934, Table 1, p. 34. It is all but impossible to conjecture the dollar equivalent of the peso (of 450 Maravedís) used by Dr. Hamilton. Without any claim to accuracy, and hoping only to guide the reader's imagination, I suggest that the peso be taken as about $2.00, pre-war, with a purchasing power of about five times that sum. Kirkpatrick, 1934, pp. 351–352.

2 Hamilton, 1934, pp. 32–38. Other figures are given in Newton, 1933, pp. 31–32.

3 Hamilton, 1934, pp. 44–45. The "price revolution" so ably studied by Dr. Hamilton was but a part of the total mischief. See, for example, Nuix, 1780, and 1782, pp. 44–75, where he examines the various harms to Spain arising from the mines of Spanish America and from the resultant bullion commerce. A little-known, but very illuminating, study of this matter of good and evil arising from the Spanish colonies in America will be found in Juras Reales, 1828. Still other light is thrown upon the matter by Argüello, 1681, MS.

4 Brebner, 1933, pp. 142–147, where there are citations of Hakluyt's printings of Ingram's narrative and of modern editions of it, also of Sir George Peckham's writings, on which see also: Means, 1932, p. 231. Andrews, 1934, Ch. iii, is of the highest value for studying the English type of colonizing. Also: Wilkinson, 1933, Ch. iii.

5 Andrews, 1934, pp. 44–46, where he emphasizes Cumberland's influence on Robert Rich, Earl of Warwick, and on others, and where he traces the part played by illicit trade, often under letters of marque issued to Englishmen by minor continental sovereigns such as the Prince of Orange, the Prince of Courland, or the Duke of Savoy, especially after James I of England made peace with Spain in 1604.

For Friar Francisco de Victoria's astonishingly modern opinions with respect to letters of marque see: Scott-Victoria, pp. 232 and 284.

[6] For Parker's adventure at Puerto Bello see his own account of it printed in Gonzales Carranza, 1740, pp. 118–124. Also: Montesinos, 1906, Año 1601.

[7] W. L. Andrews, 1897, p. 19. C. M. Andrews, 1934, p. 78. Newton, 1933, pp. 123–130.

The Treaty of Vervins (1598) will be found in Dumont's *Corps universel diplomatique*, I, pp. 561–564. The "No Peace beyond the Line" principle reestablished thereby did not mean that the French government was free to wage war on Spain in America during the life of the treaty so much as it meant that Spain still refused to concede to France the trading and colonizing privileges which France wanted. As neither side would give in to the other's point of view, the Indies were not mentioned at all in the public part of the treaty.

[8] See: Williamson, 1923 and 1926.

[9] Quoted in Harlow-Ralegh, 1932, p. 67, from a statement made by Ralegh in 1618.

[10] Harlow-Ralegh, 1932, p. 24. Williamson, 1923, pp. 74–75.

[11] Harlow-Ralegh, 1932, Ch. iii. Williamson, 1923, p. 75.

[12] See: Harlow-Ralegh, 1932, pp. 153–155, where a letter from Gondomar to King Philip III under date of October 22nd, 1617, is given; and pp. 158–159, where a touching letter from Ralegh to that courageous lady, his wife, is given, the date being November 14th, 1617, from Cayenne, and its chief purport that he hopes that the Spanish King is not fortified to withstand him.

[13] See the letter from the Rev. Samuel Jones to the Privy Council. The writer, chaplain of one of Ralegh's ships, clearly displays the rascality of Keymis. (Harlow-Ralegh, 1932, pp. 232–237.) Mr. Harlow, with an impartiality which does him the greatest honor, gives us, on pp. 162–231 of his 1932 volume, Spanish documents pertinent to the Last Voyage of Ralegh, following them with English narratives, pp. 231–237. See also: Caulin, 1779, Bk. II, Chs. xi and xii, pp. 175–193.

[14] Ralegh's letter to Lady Ralegh from St. Christopher is in Harlow-Ralegh, 1932, pp. 243–245. The manner in which King James—certainly a far more despicable figure than his victim—did Ralegh to death as a result of his unsuccess is set forth on pp. 245–315. See also: Williamson, 1923, pp. 74–79.

[15] Williamson, 1923, pp. 80–83. Harlow, 1925, pp. lxxv–lxxvi. Andrews, 1934, pp. 47–48.

[16] Williamson, 1923, pp. 80–91. Harlow, 1925, pp. lxxv–lxxix.

[17] Williamson, 1926, pp. 13–20.

[18] Williamson, 1926, pp. 23–24. Harlow, 1925, pp. xv–xvii.

[19] Harlow, 1925, p. xviii. Williamson, 1926, pp. 23–24. Of the older sources for the French side of the matter one of the most important is: Tertre, 1667–1671, I, pp. 3–6.

[20] Williamson, 1926, pp. 27–28. Harlow, 1925, pp. xvi–xvii.

[21] There is some contradiction on minor points between our two chief authorities for all this part. Williamson, 1926, p. 31, gives the number of slaves as 60 and that of settlers as 100; but Harlow, 1925, p. xvii, gives the number of settlers as 400. The statement about the attack on Trinidad must not be taken too seriously as it comes from John Scott. Harlow, however, cites the place of the letters of marque precisely.

[22] Harlow, 1925, pp. xviii–xx. Williamson, 1926, pp. 20–23. Newton, 1914, pp. 27–28; 1933, pp. 142–143.

[23] Harlow, 1925, p. xxi. Williamson, 1926, pp. 40–41.

[24] Harlow, 1925, pp. xxi–xxiv. Williamson, 1926, pp. 25–32, 38–41, 70, 78–82. These two prime authorities do not always agree as to dates. I have followed Harlow as it seems to me that his are the more correct. See also: Fernández Duro, 1895–1903, IV, pp. 31–62, for data on Toledo's brilliant career. A very rare source for information on Toledo's achievements is: *Feliz/ Victoria qve/ ha tenido D. Fadriqve/ de Toledo. . . .* Valladolid (Iuan Lasso de las Peñas), 1630. (I know this work only through the reproduction of its title-page in Pedro Vindel's *Bibliografía Gráfica*, Madrid, 1910, No. 715. It appears not to be in The John Carter Brown Library.) See also: Newton, 1933, p. 160.

[25] Harlow, 1925, pp. xxiv–xxvi, and the charming narrative of Sir Henry Colt (1631), pp. 54–102. Williamson, 1926, pp. 152–153. Aspinall, 1931, pp. 214–231. Newton, 1933, Chs. x–xi.

[26] Williamson, 1926, pp. 36–37. Harlow, 1925, p. xxix; 1926, p. 4. Newton, 1933, p. 145. Andrews, 1934, p. 47, note.

[27] Williamson, 1926, pp. 38–47. Harlow, 1925, pp. xxxi–xxxii; 1926, pp. 7–10. Newton, 1933, pp. 156–158. Andrews, 1934, pp. 51–52, and note.

[28] The lovely original manuscript of Champlain's *Brief Discours* is, happily, in The John Carter Brown Library. It was first published in an English translation by Alice Wilmere under the editorship of Norton Shaw. (Hakluyt Society, 1859.) The first printing of it in French is that in Vol. I, pp. 1–48, of Abbé Laverdière's edition of Champlains *Oeuvres* (Quebec, 1870, six vols.). The definitive edition of Champlain's *Works* is that of H. P. Biggar, in both French and English, splendidly issued by The Champlain Society in six vols., one of them a solander case of illustrations, at Toronto, 1922–33. Curious bibliographic data may be gleaned from: Leclerc, 1878, p. 191; Winsor, IV, p. 133; John Carter Brown Library Catalogue, II, pp. 25–26. See also: Brebner, 1933, pp. 148–149; Parkman, *Pioneers of France*, Pt. II, Ch. ii; and Constantin-Weyer, 1931, pp. 25–31, for this part of Champlain's career. For this period in general see: Fernández Duro, 1895–1903, IV, Ch. viii.

[29] This unwonted precision as to time and place is due to: Tertre, 1667–1671, I, Ch. ii, pp. 46–50, where he tells us that the old Company of St. Christopher (October, 1626) was replaced by this larger affair which was to have weekly meetings at the house of Fouquet on the 1st Wednesday of each month at 2 P.M. The articles, pp. 51–55, were signed by the Cardinal, by Fouquet, and by other great men on February 13th, and the new company received its royal patent on March 18th, 1635, signed by the King of France at Senlis, as set forth on pp. 57–58. See also: Tertre, 1654, Pt. I, Ch. ii.

[30] For this task Father Superior Carré, at the behest of the Cardinal, appointed from the Paris house of the Dominicans Fathers Pelican, Griffon, Nicolas de Saint Dominique, and Raymond Breton. As the empowering of priests to work among the natives of America was, under the donation of Pope Alexander VI in 1493, the exclusive privilege of the Crowns of Spain and of Portugal, Pope Urban VIII, in appointing the French priests sent out by Father Carré, was obviously contravening his predecessor's arrangements.

The final Brief of Pope Urban VIII, March 17th, 1644, given by Tertre, relating to this question gets around the difficulty very neatly.

[31] Tertre, 1654, p. 34.

[32] Tertre, 1654, Pt. I, Ch. ii. Raynal, 1782, Bk. X, Ch. vii, Bk. XIII, Chs. xix–xx and xxvii–xxviii. It is curious to note the "philosophical" attitude of this eighteenth-century Frenchman who, speaking of the evil lot of the first French settlers on Guadeloupe, says: "C'est ainsi qu'ils expièrent le crime de leur invasion. . . . On est tenté de se réjouir de leurs désastres. . . ." Newton, 1933, pp. 158–161, 171–172, 176–178.

[33] Tertre, 1654, Pt. I, Ch. iii.

[34] Curaçao was taken in August, 1634, by Joannes van Walbeck. See: Fernández Duro, 1895–1903, IV, Chs. iii and vii. Newton, 1933, pp. 165–167. Aspinall, 1931, pp. 333–335.

[35] Newton, 1933, pp. 152–154. W. L. Andrews, 1897, pp. 19–27. Haring, 1910, pp. 48–50; 1918, pp. 237–242, where interesting sources are cited. Fernández Duro, 1895–1903, IV, pp. 98–106. Naber and Wright, 1928.

CHAPTER VIII

PURITANS IN TROPIC SEAS

1. *The Puritans in England*

Down to the first rupture between England and the Papacy, in the time of King Henry VIII, England had been, to all intents and purposes, a country of but one doctrine in things religious, namely, that of the Catholic Church whose head was the Pope. Except for a few sporadic exceptions, Englishmen had unquestioningly accepted the teachings of the Church and had regarded the mode of government, the dogma, and the ritual of the Church as not only right but also as necessary for their souls' good here and hereafter. Indeed, the large mass of Englishmen had thought little if any on religious matters; they had simply accepted what Authority bade them to accept. In all this they were precisely as were all other peoples of Western Europe in those times.

By the time when the final break with Rome took place, with the accession of Queen Elizabeth to the throne of England, the ancient uniformity of creed and method had vanished forever. This was the result of the great sweeping change which we call the Reformation, in which Luther represented a less sharp departure from tradition than did Calvin. In many countries of Northern Europe, particularly in Sweden, there was a complete severance of relations with the Papacy; but the outward forms of the Church continued in force under the new headship of the King and in consonance with the moderate Protestantism of Luther.[1]

In England, also, this development took place, but so likewise did more radical developments. A large part of the English nation who were willing enough to cease from subservience spiritual and political to Rome clung lovingly to the ancient ritual, or at least to a great portion of it, and still held that it was only right that the Sovereign should be the head of the Church of England and that rule in Church matters should remain in the hands of the archbishops, bishops, and duly appointed clergy. Thus came into being the Anglican Church or Church of England, of which our Protestant Episcopal Church of America is a daughter. Within the bournes of the Anglican Church were, however, wide variations of opinion and of practice, ranging from the very conservative High Church element on the one hand to a decidedly radical Low Church element on the other. All these variations had in common certain things, among which one of the chief was the adherence to the episcopal form of church government.

Beyond the limits of the Church of England, which, like the Church of Sweden and some others, was Lutheran in character, were still more radical new sects, influenced by the doctrines of John Calvin. The Puritans, disavowing Rome with special emphasis, and looking askance at episcopacy and all other surviving institutions inherited from an earlier and more authoritarian day, were the chief of the new and intensely Protestant communions in England. Moreover, as time wore on, they tended to become a distinct political and social category as well as one defined on religious lines.

Neither their best friends nor their worst enemies could truthfully say that the Puritans were jovial and light-hearted people. Intellectually they tended to lay great stress on the individual and to be desperately serious in connection with salvation as they understood it. They tended also to frown on all forms of frivolity, to regard pleasures as a snare for sinners, to question the righteousness of bright colors in dress, fair pictures or windows in places of worship, sonorous and cadenced music of ancient use in churches, and too-great luxury in any part of daily life. They were, in short, serious and solemn and austere. They were likewise apt to be impatient and often intolerant with all who thought not as they did. In this, although unconsciously, they bore a close resemblance to their special abomination, the ardent Catholic. Nevertheless, the Puritans had their virtues as well as their failings. One was an intense and awe-inspiring sincerity. This quality enabled them to go through all trials and temptations, to surmount all obstacles, for the sake of leading the sort of lives which they deemed to be godly.

Being, as they were, uncompromising and straight-laced, they were at home in a land which, like England or like our own New England, has a rough and rigorous climate with wide transitions of temperature from glacial coldness not unlike their own unemotional habit of mind to intense heat suggestive of the fires of hell to which sinners were condemned. A land whose skies are frequently gray and whose vegetation is chiefly of a sober green without a too exuberant or too colorful flora is one suitable to their sober outlook upon life. That is why both England and New England are countries eminently suitable to Puritans.

As already hinted, the Puritans were more than a religious sect. They were also a distinct element in matters political and social. As regards the first they had a strong tendency towards rule by the many and towards a strict limitation of royal power and of nobiliary privilege. They wished for the political predominance of Parliament rather than for control by the King. Socially, the Puritans were drawn from many classes, from the highest nobility of more modernistic mind as well as from petty landowners, yeomen, merchants, and the clerkly class. For the most part they were well educated and forward-looking. Moreover, in matters of business, they were realistic and practical. Money was good to them. It was something to be worked for, and to be worked for enthusiastically, all to the glory of God. They were, in fact, the establishers of our present attitude towards business affairs.

It is this trait in the Puritan character which, as much as their religious aspirations, explains why so many colonies in America were begun by Puritans. If a burning desire for freedom to worship as they saw fit in lands beyond the sea moved them to forsake their safe homes in England and to brave all manner of danger in the wilds, a wish to improve their economic and social condition was a motive scarcely less potent.

From these two causations, the religious and the social-eco-
nomic, arose the Puritan colonies in New England which, with
respect to natural environment, were set in a world enough
like that at home to enable the colonists to live in a manner
normal to them. From these same two causations arose also
the establishment of Puritans in various tropical places where
the maintenance of the Puritan mode of life and thought was
all but impossible.[2]

2.   *The Puritans on Providence Island*

We are here to trace the history of a Puritan colony on a
tropic island which lies at about 13° 30′ N. and 81° 30′ W.,
some 160 miles due east from what is now the Atlantic coast
of Nicaragua. Although not effectively occupied by Spain in
the second decade of the seventeenth century, the island had a
Spanish name, Santa Catalina. So also had a smaller island
sixty miles to the south, San Andrés. The first was renamed
Providence by the English and the second Henrietta. Today
both belong to Colombia and are called Providencia and San
Andrés, respectively.

Providence Island, as we shall call it, had long been an
occasional haunt for freebooters and their haven there had
now and then been raided by the Spanish authorities because,
owing to the fact that Puerto Bello and Nombre de Dios were
only some 300 miles away to the south, a pirate stronghold
on either Providence itself or on San Andrés would seriously
imperil Spanish commerce. Providence Island is about six miles
long by four miles wide, with its best harbor at the northwestern corner and, in the central parts, hills which rise to
nearly 1,200 feet. Fertile soil, good air, plentiful water, and a
happy lack of snakes and of venomous insects combine to make
it a place where, if anywhere, Puritans and other northern
folk should be able to thrive under tropical conditions.[3]

A third island must also be described in this connection. It
is the island of Tortuga, called Association Island by the English and Tortue by the French. Some twenty-five miles long

it lies parallel with and close to the north side of Hispaniola, in what is now Haiti, at 20° N., and nearby is the strait between the eastern end of Cuba and the western end of Hispaniola.[4] With these three tropic islands we shall deal in this study of a Puritan colony under tropical conditions.

It is not too much to say that the Rich family, and especially Robert Rich, second Earl of Warwick, already mentioned on pages 151–152, were the prime movers in the Providence venture. Robert Rich, third Lord Rich, had been a great owner of anti-Spanish privateering ships under commission from the Duke of Savoy; but, after King James I fell out with his brother-monarch of Spain in 1618, he was allowed to purchase for £10,000 the title of Earl of Warwick in spite of the fact that he had done much worse things against the Spaniards than had poor Ralegh, who, in that same year, had died on the scaffold for his actions against Spain. Lady Rich, wife of the first Earl of Warwick, had scandalized English society by becoming, quite openly, mistress of Charles Blount, last Earl of Devonshire in his line.[5]

The antecedents of Robert Rich, second Earl of Warwick, who here chiefly concerns us, and of his brother, Henry Rich, Earl of Holland, therefore, were picturesque, if not edifying. Lord Warwick, second of the title in the Rich family, and his kinsmen, were true to the family tradition of holding a high place in the world and of being both wealthy and important; consequently, we find Lord Warwick concerned in and often directing in all sorts of enterprises across the Atlantic, from helping the Pilgrim Fathers to establish themselves at Plymouth in New England to attempts upon Spanish fleets in southern waters which were eagerly traversed by privateersmen owned by him. In all this Lord Warwick was but acting the part of a powerful and active Puritan nobleman of multiplex interests. He, and Lord Holland, have lately been described as "not very good Puritans";[6] but this description requires qualification if it is to do them justice. As already said above, Puritanism had not merely a religious aspect; it had also its economic and social and its political aspects.

Therefore, if the religious aspect be considered, Warwick and Holland certainly were not "very good Puritans"; if, on the other hand, the economic-social and the political aspects be considered, they were very good Puritans indeed, being noblemen of extraordinary business ability (sometimes stained by questionable methods) and also they were keen politicians, particularly Warwick, an adept in the art of availing himself of opportunities as they arose. In short, Warwick, regarded as a Puritan, may be taken as representing the economic and political sides of Puritanism rather than the religious side.

Among the many colonial companies in which Warwick had a great part, both as to investment and as to interest generally, was the Somers Island Company which had charge of the English colony on the charming but by no means unduly warm island of Bermuda. Ever since it had been chartered in 1615, by King James I, the Somers Island Company resident in England and its colonists on Bermuda had tended strongly to quarrelsomeness and mismanagement, due to the already noted individualism and democracy which were an integral part of English colonial method. In 1629, when Governor Philip Bell, a protégé of Warwick, was having a difficult time on Bermuda, a certain Captain Daniel Elfrith, who had long travelled far and wide in tropic waters in the profession of a corsair or privateer, came into port and gave Governor Bell tidings of the islands called by the Spaniards Santa Catalina and San Andrés, and also he spoke of another island, named Fonseca or Fonseta, of which he had heard but which he had not seen for the simple reason that it never existed.

Knowing where his interest lay, Governor Bell at once wrote to his patron, Warwick, or rather to Nathaniel Rich (a kinsman), telling of the advantages of the islands as described by Captain Elfrith, and urging the Riches to found there a private colony of their own without reference to their colleagues in the Somers Island Company. He also stated that Elfrith's associate, Captain Cammock, or Chaddock (both spellings are found), was remaining on San Andrés with thirty men to hold it. This letter was received by the Riches at the end of April, 1629.[7] Thus, albeit a trifle left-handedly, the Providence Company was an offspring of the Somers Island or Bermuda Company.

While plans were being formed for putting into execution Bell's suggestion about Santa Catalina and San Andrés, a new factor came into play. It will be remembered from pages 156–157 that in 1629 Admiral Toledo wiped out the intruding colonies on St. Christopher and on its neighbor, Nevis. At that time Anthony Hilton was Governor of Nevis. After his colony there was wrecked he pitched on the island of Tortuga, off the north coast of Hispaniola, as a likely place for a new venture. Needing backers, Hilton went to England to find them and, opportunely, came into touch with the Riches who wove Hilton and his Tortuga Island, now renamed Association, into their new scheme, making Hilton their Governor on Association Island.[8]

On September 28th, 1629, letters of marque were issued to Captain Elfrith so that he might take Santa Catalina, now renamed Providence, and San Andrés, which Cammock and most of his men had deserted. Elfrith arrived at Providence about Christmas time 1629, and immediately set about building fortifications and founding a little town grandly named New Westminster on the strand of the best harbor. By the end of February, 1630, Elfrith was on his way home again from this preliminary voyage.[9]

During most of 1630 a plague in London prevented the formation of Warwick's new Company. On November 19th, 1630, however, it held its first meeting at Brooke House and, with all customary formality, "The Governor and Company of Adventurers of the City of Westminster for the Plantation of the Islands of Providence, Henrietta [San Andrés], and the adjacent islands lying on the coast of America" was established on December 4th.[10]

The make-up of the Company was strongly Puritan and, of course, equally anti-Spanish. Its members included Lords Warwick, Holland, Brooke, and Saye-and-Sele, together with various gentlemen, of whom John Pym was the most important, and a few merchants. This group, nineteen in number, subscribed £200 apiece, making a total of £3,800 all told.[11]

During January and February, 1631, a 200-ton ship, the *Seaflower,* was being prepared to take to Providence Island the first contingent of colonists. These were to be divided into three classes: Planters, tillers of the soil who were to share profits equally with the Company; Artificers, some of whom shared and others of whom were fed, housed, and paid £5 per annum by the Company; Apprentices, or Indentured Servants, upwards of fourteen years in age, who were to receive food, lodging, clothes, but money only in exceptional cases. The provisioning of the ship was entrusted to a merchant, John Dyke, member of the Company, who charged very high prices for the very modest quality of goods which he supplied from his own warehouses. Why John Pym, Secretary of the Company, did not at once learn of this we do not know. Only in 1632 was Dyke bought out of the Company.

The first contingent of colonists consisted of ninety men and boys, including a Welsh minister named Lewis Morgan, the group being under the command of Captain William Rudyerd, brother of Sir Benjamin Rudyerd, of the Company. Governor Philip Bell, of Bermuda, was made the first Governor of Providence; and Captain Daniel Elfrith became Admiral of the new colony. Both men were, to put it gently, beholden to Warwick, and the six members of the Council were closely bound by blood, marriage, or obligation to John Pym.[12]

As regards its organization both at home, in the Company resident in England, and on Providence where the colonists were ruled by Governor and Council, the new venture was a perfect example of English colonial method. Yet it had a special character in that here, although the members of the Company, as sound business-men, would have been glad to have a substantial return on their investment, their primary interest was religious. In a word, they were attempting a novel and exciting experiment, namely, the founding of a definitely Puritan colony on a definitely tropical island. As to the Spaniards, who might be expected to make an attack, the policy was to be defensive, not aggressive, to which end strong fortifications were prepared at New Westminster and at other strategic points. Another foe, hunger, in the past too often perilous in English colonies, was to be guarded against by planting food-crops in abundance and by taking care that tobacco and other profit-yielding crops should not crowd them. Admiral Elfrith was bidden to visit other islands in quest of new food-crops: sugar-cane, figs, oranges, and so on. (Owing to his piratical proclivities he neglected this duty badly.) Providence was planned to be a well-defended Puritan paradise, bounteously provided with all needful things, and set in a sea which reflected the deep blue of the tropic sky.

The *Seaflower* sailed with her passengers from the Thames in late February, 1631. The journey was made in reasonably good time but, because of the badness of the provisions supplied by Dyke and of the niggardliness with which his associate, the skipper, issued them, the passage was highly unpleasant. When the ship arrived at Providence in late May the colonists were in a weak and under-fed condition.[13] Dyke and Tanner (the skipper) seem to have been "not very good" Puritans in the sense that their religious fervor was not sufficiently strong to prevent an overdevelopment of their business instincts.

Governor Anthony Hilton, of Association (Tortuga) Island, was likewise a man who made money dishonestly at the expense of the Company and of its colonists. Dyewoods, potentially a source of considerable revenue for the Company, were plentiful on Association. Owing to the stringent laws against the importation of dyewoods into England (arising out of fraudulent and unskilful use that had been made of them), these commodities had, legally speaking, to be sold to Dutch or French purchasers. Such laws, however, were as easily evaded then as they have been in later times, and at least one cargo of dyewood from Association appears to have been sold in England with the connivance of the Earl of Ancram, holder of the patent for such goods.

Hilton, meanwhile, was not only allowing Dutch and French

ships to trade at Association in direct contravention of his contract with the Providence Company, but also he was complacent as regarded the congregating there of pirates and contrabandists who were a serious moral menace to the Puritan element. Still more important is the fact that John Pym, in England, and Secretary of the Company, agreed with Governor Hilton, on Association, that logwood cutting was work too heavy for Englishmen under tropical conditions and that, consequently, Negro slaves must be bought from Dutch ships carrying human cargo, this step being regarded by Pym and Hilton as necessary for the prosperity of Association's trade in dyewoods. When, in 1634, Hilton died, it came out that he had cheated the Company roundly and in many directions.[14]

Fraternal sweetness and light were not the universal rule on Providence. Trouble arose early between the pious Puritans fresh from England and the distinctly more earthy men from Bermuda who, to the number of eighty, joined them before long under Governor Bell. Friction sprang up and swiftly grew into a whirlwind of uncharitableness in which the Welsh minister, Lewis Morgan, took a part so unchristian that he had to be humbled from his sacred office and ignominiously shipped home. Moreover, life in this Puritan paradise was both toilsome and extremely dull so that, on the whole, it is not surprising that the relaxing warmth and the general exuberance inherent on any tropic isle induced some of the more jovial spirits there, including Captain William Rudyerd, to take to strong waters, to gaming, brawling, and to other still more ungodly amusements all of which the shocked Company at home sternly bade poor Governor Bell to suppress. In order to fortify the declining spiritual life of the colony three new ministers were sent out, of whom Hope Sherrard was a particularly fine example of Puritanism at its best, he being a staunch and truly righteous man.[15]

In short, on tropical Providence, Puritanism—at best an unnatural state of mind and replete with inhibitions—went rapidly rancid. Nor was the process confined to the colonists on the island. An important part in it was, paradoxically, the withdrawal from the Company of certain members, including Dyke, who were most intent upon making money through the enterprise. Their places were taken by new members disposed to let Pym direct matters as he deemed best. He was a man by no means averse to making money, albeit his religious convictions seem to have held firm to a creditable extent. Nevertheless, as we shall see immediately, Pym, no less than Warwick himself, desired that the Providence Company should make money.

The conditions of a voyage on the *Seaflower* and other Company ships having been noised abroad there arose a great difficulty in finding Puritans who were willing to go to Providence. In March, 1633, Pym learned at last that the island of Fonseca, which he had been holding in reserve as a possible source of revenue, did not exist. This, coupled with the disturbing diminution of emigration to Providence, necessitated new policies. One was an attempt, perhaps inspired by Drake's methods, to open up trade with the Indians on Darien who had never submitted to Spanish rule. This scheme, however, was spoiled by the fact that, before it could be put into execution, the Indians had been turned against *all* white invaders by a massacre perpetrated by some Dutchmen who, maddened by the sight of various golden trinkets adorning the persons of their hosts, had massacred many of them. Thereafter steps were taken by Pym whereby trade was to be established with the independent Moskito Indians of the Nicaraguan coast west of Providence, through the agency of Admiral Elfrith and other captains. Elfrith had been friendly with the Moskito folk for some time, one bond between them being their mutual hatred of Spaniards.[16]

These steps were successful—up to a certain point. That is, life on Providence was rendered pleasant and profitable by the development of commerce in two varieties of cotton, found wild on the island, in tobacco, in henequen (sisal hemp), madder, indigo, and dyewoods—all found on the Moskito coast. Also, what should have been a well-rounded and strength-giving diet was built up by the cultivation on Providence of potatoes, cassava, oranges, bananas, melons, hogs, poultry, fish, and turtles. By the end of 1635 there were some 540 English and other white folk in the colony, including 40 women and children. Surely a food-supply of the sort indicated ought to have enabled them to carry on their own work. But no, we find also a dangerous new element, namely, some 90 Negro slaves who apparently did all the hard work. This is a symptom fraught with serious implications. Nevertheless, had not Elfrith so far given way to his piratical tendencies that he quite needlessly outraged the Spaniards by capturing a ship of theirs in a Jamaican haven, all might have gone along well.[17]

At about the same time the Royal Audiencia of Santo Domingo became alarmed by the presence on Tortuga (Association), uncomfortably close at hand, of a large number of unsavory persons. They were the Puritans (now much relaxed in virtue) and the pirates and other rowdy folk whom Governor Hilton had allowed to settle there. In January, 1635, the authorities at Santo Domingo sent Don Ruy Fernández de Fuenmayor with 250 soldiers to clean out the interlopers. He did so, with considerable emphasis, finding some 600 English and French of all ages and sexes. The men he hanged, but he allowed the women and children to depart in a ship, after which he razed the settlement.[18]

Spanish ire was now aroused. Suspecting it, the Providence folk looked to their defenses, and to such good effect that they beat off, in July, 1635, an attack from Cartagena by a fleet of three or more ships bringing 300 soldiers.[19]

The successful Spanish attack on Association and the unsuccessful one on Providence combined to lead the Company into a period of anti-Spanish aggressiveness. Piracy, long secretly practised by Admiral Elfrith and other seamen associated with the Company, was now openly adopted as a policy by the Puritan controllers of the venture. Captain William Rous, a relative of John Pym, ventured to attack Santa Marta in October, 1636. He and his men were taken prisoner and sent to Spain. Mild and just Governor Philip Bell was rudely removed from office and replaced by a stern Puritan, Captain Robert Hunt, who served for two years from March, 1636.[20]

At the same time the meetings of the Company were becoming hot-beds of opposition to the King, particularly with regard to ship-money, which the King was raising in huge amounts by arbitrary means instead of, as the Puritans believed proper, through Parliament. In this we have a perfect example of the political aspect of Puritanism. Resistance to every attempt of the King to enlarge his power was a keynote of their political creed. When, on February 14th, 1637, ship-money was finally confirmed the Puritans of the Providence Company were so profoundly resentful that they wished to migrate in a body to their island. King Charles, by his silence regarding their petition for his license to depart, put a stop to that idea.[21]

It was also in this period that there arose, for the first time, a wish to "remove" New Englanders *en masse* from their northern homes to Providence and adjacent mainland areas. Providence had long traded with Boston and with Salem nearly as much as with England. Lord Saye-and-Sele, John Humfry and other backers of New England enterprise were displeased with conditions there, and the idea was alluringly presented in the north, much to the annoyance and alarm of authorities there. Fortunately, not much came of it.[22]

Altogether, there was a good deal of agitation in one way and another regarding Providence—in England, in New England, and in Providence itself. Things were not going really well. In England the political situation was serious; on the island of Providence there was a lack of complete harmony as well as a vague but pervasive feeling of apprehension.

The last was justified. In June, 1640, the Governor of Cartagena sent Don Antonio Maldonado y Tejada with a small fleet carrying 800 Spanish and 200 Negro troops to clear the English from Providence. But, as we know, the Puritans there were armed and prepared for defense; their forts, weapons, and munitions were in excellent condition, and discipline was tolerably good. Consequently, Maldonado, intent on plucking a poisonous weed from Spain's Caribbean garden, found that he had laid rude hands upon a stinging nettle. In fact, he was smartly defeated by the English in a short, sharp engagement during which his ships came to grief among the reefs while the batteries on Providence liberally sprayed them with shots. Maldonado had to withdraw after 100 of his men had been slain and many others had been captured while attempting to land. The glory of this victory of the Puritans was, however, much lessened by the fact that Deputy-Governor Andrew Carter, in spite of his solemn promise of clemency, put to death all the Spanish prisoners in his power. Against this tyrannical and shameful act Minister Hope Sherrard and three other honorable Englishmen stoutly protested. Their reward was that they were shipped home in chains by Carter.[23]

This affair had the twofold effect of increasing the vigilance of the Puritans on Providence and of really arousing the wrath of King Philip IV in Spain. When he heard of Maldonado's defeat he determined to take serious measures against the intruders on the island of Santa Catalina. Just then there arrived from Cartagena the Admiral Francisco Díaz Pimienta with a fleet of five galleons. This brilliant naval officer was in charge of the convoying of the fleet from America to Spain, but the King now bade him to return forthwith to Cartagena and from there to break up the English colony on Santa Catalina (as, of course, the Spaniards called Providence).

Accordingly, after careful preparations had been made, including a study of the island's defenses which was facilitated by certain Spaniards who had lately been there, Admiral Díaz Pimienta sailed from Cartagena on May 6th, 1641. He had 6 major ships ranging from 300 to 800 tons as well as 5 smaller vessels and his forces included 1,400 well-trained Spanish fighting-men. The island was sighted on May 17th, and navigation through the outer ring of reefs was carefully managed so that only on May 19th, despite a frantic defense by the island forts, a landing was made and battle was joined. It was a well-conducted and successful campaign that Díaz fought. On Saturday, May 25th, 1641, the flag of Spain once more floated in the island breeze and, the next morning, Mass was solemnly celebrated together with a *Te Deum Laudamus*. To his credit be it said, Admiral Díaz Pimienta did not follow the bad example set by Carter. He treated the frightened English women well and arranged for their transportation home by way of Cadiz (where their menfolk had to remain as prisoners). Thereafter a Spanish garrison was left on the Island of Santa Catalina, otherwise Providence, in order to occupy it "effectively." [24]

Díaz Pimienta found on Providence a situation which is full of significance for the student of that Puritan colony. There were 390 English of whom 60 were women, and there were 380 Negro slaves of all ages and sexes.[25] In other words, slavery, which constituted one of the major points of contrast between this Puritan colony and New England, had made great headway. In this we see an important and sinister manifestation of the effect of tropical environment upon Puritans. In New England, so much like England in point of climate and scenery, Englishmen could labor well with their own hands. In Providence they could not or, at any rate, did not. This, coupled with the already noted drift into piracy, explains a large part of what was, in truth, a decay of Puritan morale on this tropical island.

It was well for the Spaniards that they left a garrison behind them when they departed from Santa Catalina on June 6th, 1641. At that very moment John Humfry and a contingent of people from New England were sailing from Salem towards Providence. Humfry, at the time, was Governor-elect of Providence and this was a part of the projected "remove" from inclement (but wholesome) New England to the soft, warm air of Providence Island. When the ship from Salem arrived at the island it received a very warm welcome from the now Spanish batteries there. The Puritan pilot was killed, and the rest of the company on board were fain to turn back to the land whence they had come.[26]

John Pym, who all along had been the moving spirit of the Providence Company, as well as, in a sense, its evil spirit in that it was he who had introduced Negro slavery and open piracy, devoted the remainder of his life to anti-royalist politics in Parliament. He died in December, 1643, and was buried in Westminster Abbey whence, after the Restoration, his remains were removed by the hangman to a common pit. Warwick lived on and in 1643 became Governor-in-chief of all the English plantations in America.[27]

3. Interlude

So far as the activities of English Puritans in the Caribbean between 1641 and 1654 are concerned the chief link is the career of Captain William Jackson. He was in the service of the Earl of Warwick, taking wages from him in return for his activities as a privateer, his letters of marque being obtained through the Providence Company and through Warwick's influence.[28]

Although he was, in truth, a pirate, and although he was a man of unsavory character in many respects, William Jackson had the virtue of being an excellent sea-officer. After a preliminary series of despoiling voyages in 1638 to 1642, he began, in July of the latter year, an increased activity strongly reminiscent of that of Drake and other Englishmen. With three ships and some 900 men, mostly recruited from discontented and unemployed elements on Barbados, Jackson voyaged far and wide in the Spanish Main doing all the harm he could to the Spaniards. From Margarita Island he was sharply repulsed by Spaniards and Indians acting together; but elsewhere he was generally successful in his raids and did considerable damage to shipping and settlements. Maracaibo and various other minor ports of the Spanish Main were despoiled by him. His most important deed was the capture, from a defending force much smaller than his offensive force, of Santiago de la Vega, the Spanish capital of Jamaica. This took place in late March,

1643. It was also instrumental in drawing the attention of Englishmen to that island. Some of Jackson's followers found it so agreeable a place that they wished to settle there; but the time for that was not yet come.[29]

In the period between 1642 and 1654 events in England were rapidly changing the posture of the Puritans' affairs, lifting that party from obscurity to the height of power. The battles of Naseby (June, 1645), of Preston (August, 1648), and of Worcester (September, 1651), mark ascending steps in the military career of Oliver Cromwell from his original un-importance to a power even greater than that formerly held by Charles I—done to death in January, 1649.[30]

In all these years of tumultuous change at home the tropical colonies of England were the refuge of oppressed people, but with the difference that it was now the Royalists, not the Puritans, who were in flight from conditions at home. This was particularly true of Barbados, then held as a palatinate by Lord Willoughby of Parham by virtue of a twenty-one-year lease from Lord Carlisle.* By May, 1650, the King's party on that island was so strong that a proclamation of Charles II as King was solemnly made. This not only put Barbados ten years ahead of its day but also caused the Puritan government at home to forbid all trade between Barbados (and other recalcitrant colonies) and England or any other country. As the Barbadians were earnestly striving to arrange their affairs on a business-as-usual-during-repairs basis, they were forced now to trade with the Dutch and the French. Consequently, in February, 1652, a Parliamentary fleet under Sir George Ayscue came sailing in at Barbados and quickly reduced the colony to accept the new dispensation at home. Lord Willoughby and other Royalists fled south to Surinam, where, very courageously, they began their work anew.[31]

---

*The lease from the second Earl of Carlisle was dated February 17th, 1647, and was to run for twenty-one years, carrying with it full proprietary and palatine power. As it had both Charles's and Parliament's approval it could not well have been stronger.

4. The French in the Caribbean, 1639–1664

Our pre-occupation with the English in the Caribbean must not lead us to neglect the French activities there during the middle decades of the seventeenth century. This is all the more important that they were partly interwoven with English and Spanish colonial history in those parts.

After the Spanish victory at Tortuga in 1635 related on page 182, that island was for a time abandoned. Some four years later it was reoccupied, this time by a motley lot of English and French whose bickerings and general behavior was such that, in August, 1640, Governor-General de Poincy sought to regularize the situation by converting Tortuga into a Huguenot haven to which could be sent a portion of the population of the French Caribbees that had long been troublesome to him. For this task Poincy selected a Huguenot gentleman named Le Vasseur, who, with his Huguenot following, proceeded to drive the English settlers from the island. He then constructed an amazing fortress or citadel on the summit of a steep-sided crag which could be mounted only by a foot-way with steps cut in the living rock. Thereafter, this fortress frequently repulsed, with its great guns, Spanish attempts to retake Tortuga.

Likewise it seems to have filled Le Vasseur with some degree of mad pride; for, from 1643 to 1652, he passed through a crescendo of tyranny and folly, not only defying his original patron, Poincy, but even aspiring to be an independent Prince of Tortuga with a wild lot of outlaws for subjects. Thus Huguenot Tortuga, no less than Puritan Providence, went rancid under the tropic sun. In May–June, 1652, after Le Vasseur had been murdered by two rascals of his colony, Poincy sent a strong fleet to Tortuga under the Chevalier de Fontenay. He finally managed to re-establish the authority of the King of France in Tortuga.[32]

Fontenay continued for a time to rule Tortuga. His presence there, however, was an offense to the Spanish authorities at Santo Domingo, and particularly to the President of the

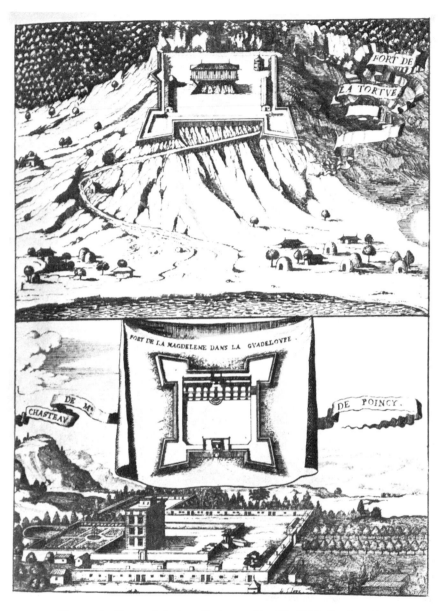

Upper: Le Vasseur's fort on Tortuga. (See Ch. VIII, Section 4.)
Lower: French constructions on Guadeloupe and on St. Christopher.
From a plate in Tertre. 1667–1671.

Royal Audiencia, Don Juan Francisco de Montemaior de Cuenca. This man, no less than Admiral Díaz Pimienta, victor at Providence, was of the best type of Spanish official in America. From August, 1653, onwards Montemaior busied himself with active preparations against the French. A well-disciplined and equipped force of 500 troops divided into two companies attacked Tortuga on January 10th, 1654 and, in less than ten days, fairly whipped the French under Fontenay in a good, clean fight. The vanquished were allowed to depart with their lives and personal belongings to the nearest French island, probably St. Christopher or Martinique.[33]

In 1654, when Spain was on the verge of the greatest loss of territory which she was ever to suffer at foreign hands in the Caribbean, the international situation there stood as follows:

England held: St. Christopher (in part), Barbados, Nevis, Montserrat, Antigua, and Bermuda out in the Atlantic. Also a few other small islands. She had lost fourteen years before her temporary possession, Providence. *Not one* of these places had ever been intensively occupied by Spain, and not one of them was won by England as the result of a military victory.

France held: St. Christopher (in part), Guadeloupe, Martinique, Désirade, Marie-Galante, Sainte Lucie, and Grenade, to all which the same remark applies.

The Dutch held: Curaçao (wrested from some Spanish cattle-breeders), Aruba, St. Eustatius (or Statia), Buen Aire, and Saba, all which were small places never intensively occupied by Spain.

All the rest of the Caribbean, islands and mainland, was *Spanish,* albeit certain parts, such as Darien and the Moskito Coast of Nicaragua, opposite Providence, were left in the hands of Indians as being regions unsuitable for intensive Spanish occupation.

So little had 125 years of unremitting effort by her enemies accomplished to the hurt of Spain.

5. *Cromwell's Design Westward*

Oliver Cromwell, having ensconced himself in the office of Lord Protector of the Commonwealth of England, held greater power than any ruler of England for a century past, including as it did both legislative and executive functions. As he had but lately, for commercial reasons arising out of his dread of their dominance in the carrying-trade, broken the power of the Netherlanders, Cromwell was left with but two serious rivals in Europe—and in America. These were France and Spain. Precisely as the dead Charles had long done, Cromwell for a time vacillated as to which of them should be his ally, for both, in the nature of things, could not be so. From the point of view of a Puritan ruler it was regrettable that, in either case, the ally would be a Catholic nation and therefore subject to the Pope or, as some Puritans so courteously phrased it, to the "whore of Babylon." France was, as it were, the less utterly Catholic of the two and therefore the less noxious to a Puritan potentate lately arrived in office and bent on deeds that would make his reign forever memorable. For one thing, France had no objectionably active Inquisition; for another, her ritual was perceptibly less "idolatrous" than that of Spain. These were among the considerations which led to Cromwell's finally allying himself with France.

With her aid, or at any rate without her opposition, England might, so Cromwell reasoned, deliver a terrible and a permanently disabling blow against the Spanish empire. It might even come about that Mexico, Peru, all South America except Brazil, and a large part of southwestern North America as well would become English instead of Spanish possessions. It was an enchanting vision which became known as Cromwell's Western Design.

The grandiose idea was not, truth to tell, original with Cromwell. Quite aside from the fact that Barlow, Drake, Ralegh, and other Englishmen had long ago had ideas closely similar, there was the fact that Admiral Coligny had laid an exactly similar scheme before the King of France a century earlier, as told on pages 65–66 and 77–78.

So far as Cromwell's part in the Western Design was concerned it was chiefly fostered by two very different men. One was a certain Colonel Thomas Modyford, a cousin of Monk,

the Puritan soldier who became Duke of Albemarle under
Charles II. Thomas Modyford, then in active political life
in Barbados, had gradually formed the opinion that a sharp
attack on Trinidad and the Orinoco would result in their capture and that, once they were won, they could be made to
serve as bases for still greater campaigns. These ideas Modyford was able to bring to the personal attention of Cromwell,
who, as it were, absorbed them and made them his own.[34]

The other and more important of the two chief fosterers
of Cromwell's scheme to take all Spanish America was a man
named Thomas Gage, of ancient Catholic gentry. As a young
man he became a Dominican and in that capacity went to the
Spanish Indies where he spent many years in priestly duties
at various places, especially in Mexico. His observations were
vivid if not invariably accurate. Their sum was that Spain's
America was enormously rich and was feebly held by an
effeminate people from whom it could easily be snatched. On
his return to England Gage turned Puritan and, in 1648, published the first edition of his celebrated book, *New Survey of
the West-India's.* . . . It was an inflammatory and provoca-
tive volume of the sort that Puritans and other English had
long loved to read. Later there was a second edition (1655)
sponsored by the reigning Puritan régime. Gage likewise
wrote letters to Cromwell that were even more inciting than
his book, and they aided in making Cromwell believe that
Spanish America could be easily conquered.[35]

Besides Modyford and Gage there were sundry minor con-
tributors to Cromwell's Western Design, some of them being
New Englanders still inclined to be discontented with the
climate and the land in their colony. For example, John Cotton, on July 28th, 1651, had written to Cromwell urging upon
him the desirability of ridding the New World of Catholic
Spaniards. Afterwards, Roger Williams, John Winthrop Jr.,
and others had expressed themselves in like sense. In this
piously imperialistic zeal we see, however, something more
than religious fervor on the part of New England's Puritan
theocrats; we see also a hope that Cromwell will conquer

from the Spanish some warm and cosy lands to which they could "remove" their ideas and their aspirations.[36] In short, they totally failed to comprehend what the fate of Providence should have taught them, namely, that Puritans cannot be their best selves in the tropics.

Cromwell combined these varied contributions into a coherent scheme of unprecedented proportions. In August, 1654, he made demands to Spain, through her ambassador, which he knew she would not grant. The desired breach followed automatically. Cromwell went ahead with his plans. Admiral William Penn was appointed to be in charge of the fleet and of the sailors, General Robert Venables was placed in command of the land-forces. The two were equals in authority and from this fact arose dissensions between them which spread to their men, disrupting the harmony which a unified command would have ensured.

Various instructions issued by Cromwell at this period make clear the spirit of the enterprise. From Whitehall, August 18th, 1654, he instructed Penn and Venables thus:

. . . And with the said Forces to Attaque the Spanyard both at sea and land in those parts; who hath unhumanly murdered diverse of Our people there, taken away their possessions, and doth exercise all Acts of hostility against them as open enemies . . .

Still more illuminating is a passage in the "Commission to the Commissioners of the West Indian Expedition," dated at Westminster December 9th, 1654, which runs thus:

. . . Having a respect likewise in this our undertaking to the Miserable Thraldome and Bondage both Spirituall and Civill, which the natives and others in the dominions of the said King [of Spain] in America are subjected to and lye under by meanes of the Popish and cruell Inquisition* and otherwise, from which if it shall please God to make us instrumentall in any measure to deliver them, and uppon this occasion to make way for the bringing in the light of the Gospell and power of true Religion and Godlines into those parts, Wee shall esteeme it the best and most Glorious

*From this it would appear that Cromwell was unaware that the Indians were never within the jurisdiction of the Inquisition.

part of any Successe or Acquisition it shall please God to blesse us with.

Finally, a more earthy and normal note is sounded in the instructions to Venables (December, 1654) in which he is bidden to capture the Silver Fleet from Puerto Bello with the treasure from Peru on board.[37]

Cromwell had plenty of fine ships of war. He likewise had a well-manned army which had had splendid training during the Civil War. Nevertheless, the army which he now assembled for use in America was terribly bad, being made up of the dregs of the London regiments whose commanders were delighted to be thus rid of their most undesirable troops. This force left England on December 25th, 1654, in a fleet of thirty-eight sail carrying some 2,500 soldiers of the quality indicated. They arrived at Barbados in January, 1655.

On that island there were many unfortunate men who had been thrown out of work by the rapid growth of great sugar-estates worked with slave labor. Some 3,000 of these now joined up with Venables. To them were added about 1,200 much better volunteers from St. Christopher, Nevis, and Montserrat. At last there were 6,873 men in the expedition, of whom 916 were officers. The quondam Dominican, Gage, went along as a Puritan chaplain in Venables's own regiment.[38]

The first step in the great Puritan campaign to conquer the entire Spanish empire in America was an attack on the city of Santo Domingo. The Spanish Governor there was Don Bernardino de Meneses Bracamonte, Count of Peñalva, lately arrived from Spain. Although Santo Domingo had fallen away from its original greatness as a center of Spanish power, it still had great prestige in foreign eyes. Hence the English desire to conquer it. Between April 17th and 25th, 1655, the entire English force did its best to capture the city. But, with only a few hundred fighting-men, Governor Count of Peñalva routed them utterly. English historians agree that this was nothing less than a national disgrace.[39]

After the Santo Domingo fiasco Penn and Venables were

bitterly at odds, and their respective commands were likewise. Still, something must be done. The island of Jamaica
came to mind. At this period there were only some 1,500
Spaniards there, of whom about 500 were men capable of
fighting. Under the benign rule of Governor Juan Ramirez
they had been engaged in such unmilitary pursuits as cattle-
raising and agriculture. Between May 10th and 17th, 1655,
Penn and Venables and their more than 6,000 followers managed to make Jamaica an English possession.[40]

Jamaica, certainly a modest recompense, was the sole fruit
gathered in by Cromwell's celebrated Western Design. Penn
and Venables went home not very long afterwards, and were
imprisoned in the Tower because they had returned without
permission from Cromwell. Their men were left in the Indies
in a sad state of semi-starvation and of illness from dysentery
and other tropical diseases. In that condition they were found
by a very distinguished New Englander, Major-General of
Massachusetts Robert Sedgwick, whom Cromwell had placed
in command of an auxiliary force of ships and men for the
purpose of co-operating with the army and navy from England. General Sedgwick did all that lay in his power to
ameliorate the miserable condition of the troops, but he could
make no real headway against either the physical evils of
their lot or against the insubordination and general worthless-
ness of the men themselves. He died of a broken heart at
Jamaica, May 24th, 1656. General Sedgwick it was who made
a remark illustrative of the attitude of many reflective Englishmen in that day anent the Western Design. He said:

This kind of marooning cruising West India trade of plundering
and burning towns, though it hath long been practised in these
parts, yet is not honorable for a princely navy, neither was it, I
think, the work designed, though perhaps it may be tolerated at
present.

What men of uprightness and vision, such as Sedgwick,
wanted was that England, in the course of honorable warfare
properly conducted, should take Cartagena or some other first-

rank Spanish port in the Caribbean as a permanent English base for further war against the Spaniards in America.⁴¹

This, however, is precisely what neither the Western Design nor any later English expedition accomplished. In fact, the Western Design was intrinsically impossible in any case and the manner in which it was carried into execution made it a dismal and ludicrous failure. Cromwell, in a "Declaration" made on Friday, October 26th, 1655, endeavored to justify the affair on the ground that the Spaniards had "attacked" the English at Providence Island and elsewhere; but in so doing he ignores the fact that the English were the aggressors in the Spanish Main far oftener than were the Spaniards and also the further fact that, in the case of Providence, the Spaniards were but repossessing themselves of an island which had been taken from them by Englishmen to the great hurt of their commerce.⁴²

Having acquired Jamaica in the manner indicated, Cromwell seems to have been somewhat at a loss what to do with it. The deed had been done without a shadow of sanction from Parliament and in the face of opposition from many sober-minded and far-seeing English merchants who would far rather have seen a restoration of the ancient trade between their country and Spain. This worthy class of Englishmen took no satisfaction in the rape of Jamaica. That island, however, was now English and something must be done to give it an English population. Consequently, various steps were taken both in England and in New England. From the former were sent out various unsavory elements from the gutters of London, and to them were added numbers of unfortunate people from Barbados and other English islands where slave-grown sugar was causing white unemployment to become a tragic problem. In New England, at the behest of the home government, Daniel Gookin tried to induce a large number of better-class men and women to "remove" to warm, sunny Jamaica; but only a few of them did so.⁴³

Unquestionably the reason why England was able to retain Jamaica in spite of repeated and varied Spanish attempts to regain it was that Admiral Robert Blake, one of the truly great naval men of his nation, paralyzed the naval power of Spain in waters close to Europe. By cruising off Cadiz, and by harrying Spanish ships as they approached their destinations, and, most brilliant action of all, by destroying a great Spanish fleet under the very guns of Santa Cruz de Tenerife, in the Canary Islands, in April, 1657, Admiral Blake, in honorable warfare of the sort visualized by Sedgwick and others, gave his compatriots time in which to consolidate their hold upon Jamaica.[44]

Presently Jamaica became the centre of English power in the Caribbean, it being the largest and finest island they ever conquered in those parts. Although lovely to behold from a ship out at sea, and in its higher districts sufficiently salubrious for northern folk, it was by no means ideal in its coastal areas. In time there grew up a small class of English landowners interested in agriculture and kindred matters who depended for labor upon a very large Negro slave-class whose blood afterwards sometimes spread surprisingly high in the social scale. On later pages more will be said of the history of this Greater Antille taken from Spain and made English.[45]

6. Conclusion

Puritan England's effort against Spain's empire in the Caribbean had three main parts: The Providence venture, in which a deserted island was taken and occupied for ten years until its occupants were ejected by a Spanish expedition; the career of William Jackson, a freebooter who wrought much mischief against Spanish ships and settlements, but who did naught of lasting importance; the Western Design, which, probably intending to take the whole of Spanish America, and certainly most of the Caribbean, took only one largish island where less than 1,500 Spaniards were living. If this be a glorious tale of gallant warfare, let him who will make the most of it.

In the French Caribbean colonies there was an interlude between 1648, when the *Compagnie des Isles d'Amérique* which had been in charge of them went out of existence, and 1664, when Louis XIV's great minister Colbert took matters in charge. The interval was marked by a transitory use of the proprietary system in a form somewhat similar to the English. The most important development of this period was the fact that, from possessing Tortuga only, the French came to hold the entire western end of Hispaniola, which is now the French-speaking Negro republic of Haiti. It is a curious product of the colonial genius of the French people that, although there were not more than 12,000 of them in all the Caribbean colonies, they succeeded without apparent conscious effort in impressing the Negro masses with a collective character distinctively French. It was not merely that the Negroes spoke French—or a jargon based upon it—but also that in their ways of life and in their surroundings there was an unmistakable French cast which marked them as apart from all other Negro populations. This arose, in great measure, from the singularly sympathetic and conciliatory spirit which Frenchmen have always displayed towards races distinct from their own with whom they have come into contact as rulers. One sees the same thing today in French North Africa and in the French colonies of the Far East. For themselves the French in the Caribbean succeeded in reproducing much of the elegance and amenity to which they were accustomed at home. For example, General de Poincy built for himself on the French part of St. Christopher a château in the purest style of France at that period, surrounding it with formal gardens, promenades, stables, and offices which would be perfectly suitable in any part of France itself and which, strangely enough, succeeded in looking perfectly suitable also in St. Christopher. This was a work of genius. It points the special adaptiveness which is so large a part of the French character. The same results can be seen in the old engravings of plantations, sugar-mills, and other industrial establishments set up by the French in their possessions. They were, in short, great colonizers who ruled other races better than did either the Spaniards or the English.[46]

Notes for Chapter VIII

[1] See: Andrew A. Stomberg, *A History of Sweden*, New York, 1931, Chs. ix and x.

[2] For the Puritans in England see: Abbott, 1924, I, pp. 344–345, 416–419, 497–505; Adams, 1921, Ch. iv; Andrews, 1934, Chs. xviii and xxi; Morison, 1930, pp. 339–346; 1935, pp. 43–46; Wilkinson, 1933, Chs. iii and iv.

[3] Alcedo, 1812–1815, article on Providence Island. Newton, 1914, p. 12, and map there; 1933, Ch. xii.

[4] Alcedo, 1812–1815, article on Tortugas Island. Newton, 1914, p. 12.

[5] This is no mere low gossip. It is set forth by two reliable English historians on sound documentary bases. See: Newton, 1914, pp. 16, 21, and note, 34; Wilkinson, 1933, p. 96. Also: S. R. Gardiner, *History of England, 1603–1642*, London, III, p. 215, where sources are cited.

[6] Andrews, 1934, p. 497, note. Morison, 1935, p. 43, speaks of ". . . puritans like the great Earl of Warwick who were swearers of great oaths and notorious loose livers."

[7] Newton, 1914, pp. 31–34, for Bell's letter; 1933, pp. 171–172. Wilkinson, 1933, pp. 240–244. Andrews, 1934, pp. 136–137, note, where, on the basis of source materials, he shows that Elfrith was a servant of Warwick and captain of a ship chiefly owned by him which may have been engaged in carrying slaves, at that time a perfectly respectable thing to do.

[8] Newton, 1914, pp. 101–105.

[9] Newton, 1914, pp. 52–56.

[10] Newton, 1914, pp. 56–58.

[11] Newton, 1914, pp. 58–59, for a list of the members of the Company and details of their subscriptions and of other and later financial arrangements. See also: Wilkinson, 1933, pp. 244–245; and, C. E. Wade, *John Pym*, London, 1912, pp. 150–153.

[12] Newton, 1914, pp. 85–95.

[13] Newton, 1914, pp. 95–100; 1933, pp. 173–174. Wilkinson, 1933, pp. 248–249, where he tells us that the *Seaflower* stopped at Bermuda and took on some sturdy additional settlers for Providence, adding that in the summer of 1631 eighty more Bermudians, this time of poor quality, were sent to Providence. At pp. 252–253, Mr. Wilkinson describes the first voyage out of the *Seaflower*, with specific mention of Tanner who had held back supplies from the passengers in order to sell them later.

[14] Newton, 1914, pp. 107–111.

[15] Newton, 1914, pp. 110–122.

[16] Newton, 1914, pp. 122–145.

[17] Newton, 1914, pp. 145–150, 153–155. Beer, 1908, p. 20.

[18] Newton, 1914, pp. 187–193, citing a report of the raid on Tortuga by the Audiencia of Santo Domingo under date of June 12th, 1635. See also: Tertre, 1667–1671, I, pp. 169–172.

[19] Newton, 1914, pp. 193–197.

[20] Newton, 1914, Chs. viii and ix. It was in this period, in 1637, that King

Charles refused to allow the Company to sell Providence Island to the Dutch West India Company for £70,000. (Newton, 1914, pp. 238–239, 249–250.) May it not have been that His Majesty hoped that the Company would be ruined by having to retain the Island?

21 Newton, 1914, Ch. x.

22 Strong, 1899a, pp. 81–85. Newton, 1914, Chs. xi and xiii; 1933, pp. 179–181. Andrews, 1934, pp. 496–498. Morison, 1930, pp. 98–100. For the New England side of the matter see: Winthrop, 1908, I, pp. 332–335; Bradford, 1908, pp. 305–310, 320.

23 Newton, 1914, pp. 297–298. Díaz Pimienta, 1642 and 1642a.

24 Newton, 1914, pp. 298–303; 1933, pp. 190–192. Harlow, 1923, pp. ix–xii. Fernández Duro, 1895–1903, IV, pp. 333–340. Díaz Pimienta, 1642 and 1642a. Fernández de Navarrete, 1851, I, p. 453. Toynbee, 1935, II, p. 35, and note. Rowland, 1935, gives an important account of the later history of Santa Catalina Island.

25 Díaz Pimienta, 1642.

26 Johnson, 1910, pp. 205–209. Winthrop, 1908, I, p. 333, II, pp. 11–12, 33–35. Newton, 1914, pp. 304–305.

27 Newton, 1914, pp. 314–318. See also articles on Pym and on Warwick in DNB. Also: Historical Portraits, II, pp. 112–114, for Warwick, and 115–118, for Pym.

28 Harlow, 1923, pp. vi–viii. Newton, 1914, pp. 265–271. Andrews, 1934, p. 145.

29 Harlow, 1923, pp. viii–xx. Wilkinson, 1933, pp. 268–269. Newton, 1914, pp. 314–317. Haring, 1918, pp. 234–235.

30 Abbott, 1924, I, pp. 502–505, II, pp. 7–15.

31 Harlow, 1925, pp. xxviii–lv. Lord Willoughby, an attractive and brave figure in history, died in a storm at sea, in the Lesser Antilles, in October, 1666. (Harlow, 1925, pp. 196–198.)

32 Charlevoix, 1730–1731, II, pp. 12–21. Labat, 1931, II, pp. 207–210.

33 Montemaior, 1658, pp. 1–5. Charlevoix, 1730–1731, II, pp. 21–24.

34 Strong, 1899, pp. 228–232. Harlow, 1926, pp. 104–105. Newton, 1933, pp. 211–213. Buchan, 1934, pp. 411–413.

35 Gage, 1648, 1655. Gage, 1929, which has a valuable Introduction by A. P. Newton. Harlow, 1926, pp. 104–105. Thurloe, III, pp. 59–61 (letter from Gage to Cromwell) and I, p. 537, III, pp. 62–63 (papers by Modyford). Strong, 1899, pp. 233–238. See also Watts, 1924, Ch. viii.

36 Strong, 1899, pp. 237–241. Beer, 1908, pp. 377–378.

37 These materials will be found in: Venables, 1900, Appendix A, pp. 107–115. See also: Newton, 1933, pp. 213–216; Strong, 1899, pp. 242–243; Bridges, 1827–1828, I, pp. 195–197; Watts, 1924, Chs. viii and ix.

38 Venables, 1900, Appendix B, pp. 116–122 (for statistics of troops), and Appendix C, pp. 122–126 (for commissioned officers).

39 For the Spanish side of this affair see: Montemaior, 1658, pp. 22–23, verso. A fine copy of this very rare work is in the John Carter Brown Library. See also, Fecundo, 1655, of which there is a copy in The John Carter Brown Library; Wright, 1926, where many Spanish documents are given; and Watts, 1924, Ch. xi.

[40] Cundall and Pietersz, 1919, Ch. iii. Wright, 1923. Strong, 1899, pp. 242–244. J. K. Laughton's article on Penn, in DNB, and C. H. Firth's on Venables, in DNB. Firth's Introduction to Venables, 1900. Harlow, 1926, pp. 105–113. Buchan, 1934, pp. 413–414. Watts, 1924, Ch. xii.

[41] See, for Sedgwick's views on these matters: Thurloe, IV, p. 604; R. L. Jones's article on Sedgwick in DNB. Mrs. Venables, who accompanied her husband on the expedition, made sharp remarks about the poor quality of the troops (in Venables, 1900, p. xli). Watts, 1924, Chs. xii–xiv.

[42] See: Cromwell, 1655; "N.N.," 1655, which was published in London on July 6th, 1655, possibly prior to the arrival in England of full knowledge concerning the capture of Jamaica. The author's name is unknown, but the book was registered at Stationers' Hall, on the date given, by Thomas Peake. The book, in a disguised and roundabout way, strives to stir up English envy against the Spaniards and to egg on the English to snatch a part at least of Spain's American empire whose riches are described in glowing language calculated to incite. (I am indebted to Mr. Lawrence Wroth, Librarian of The John Carter Brown Library, for my knowledge of this exceedingly rare work.) See also: Pelleprat, 1655, Part II, from p. 121 onwards, where there is printed a French letter from St. Christopher under date of June 14th, 1655, describing a courtesy visit of the English fleet, said to be of 70 sail, to Poincy, Governor-General of the French Caribbee Islands. (This rare work, also, is in that supreme collection, The John Carter Brown Library.)

[43] Strong, 1899a, pp. 89–94. Andrews, 1934, p. 499. Beer, 1908, pp. 382–383. Thurloe, IV, pp. 130 and 634, V, pp. 6–7, 510. Bridges, 1827–1828, I, Ch. vii.

[44] See article on Blake in DNB. Newton, 1933, pp. 220–223.

[45] Further citations on Jamaica are: Charlevoix, 1730–1731, II, pp. 26–27; Drouin-de-Bercy, 1818, entire: Cundall, 1900, pp. 12–22; Fernández Duro, 1895–1903, V, pp. 19–44; Long, 1774, *passim*; still others, with brief comments, are: "I.S." (under S, in Bibliography), 1655, which is an attempt to make Cromwell's Jamaican effort seem a glorious thing; Messrs. Maggs Brothers, however, in their *Bibliotheca Americana*, Part IX, p. 99 (London, 1930), have the fine gallantry to point out the truth of the matter. (I know this rare item only through their description of it.)

Sloane, 1707, Introduction. This great work, which I have studied in The John Carter Brown Library, describes the Natural History and environment, trade, etc., of Jamaica, showing the advantages and disadvantages from the point of view of English occupation.

Trapham, 1679, described by Messrs. Maggs in work cited, p. 110, thus: "A scarce medical work. The author especially treats of the Flux, Fevers, Dropsy, Worms, Venereal Disease, Dry Belly Ache, etc." These maladies probably had a great part in the condition of the English troops found by Sedgwick. Needless to say modern science has greatly mitigated their ravages.

West Indies, 1657; this book contains a description of "an attempt on the Island of Jamaica, and taking the Town of St. Jago de la Viga [*sic*], beating the Enemy from their Forts and Ordance [*sic*], being a body of 3,000 men, and so took possession of the Island, May 10, 1655 . . ." (quoted from Maggs, IX, p. 120). If the figure, 3,000, refers to the defending force it is a gross exaggeration, the true number of fighting defenders being 500; if it refers to the English force it is an understatement, the true number being well over 6,000. (A copy of this book is in The John Carter Brown Library.)

[46] Tertre, 1667–1671, III, pp. 9–35, for French Caribbean history in general. Labat, 1930, for important descriptions of life in the French colonies. Mims, 1912, entire, for a splendid study of French colonial policy and technique, particularly in the time of Colbert. Also: Fernández Duro, 1895–1903, IV, Ch. xviii; Newton, 1933, pp. 199–200; Rochefort, 1665, for pictures of the French colonies which can be consulted profitably in conjunction with those in Tertre, Labat, etc.

CHAPTER IX

MORGAN AT PANAMA, THE SCOTS AT DARIEN, AND THE TWILIGHT OF PIRACY, 1660–1700

1. *New Alignments and Policies in Europe*

IN Spain the last forty years of the seventeenth century marked the deepest degradation both of the Spanish Hapsburg dynasty and of the Spanish people. From having been in, let us say, 1585, beyond all doubt the greatest and most powerful state in Europe, Spain under Philip III (1598–1621), Philip IV (1621–1665), and Charles II (1665–1700), had rapidly declined from her lofty place in the world. For a time the Spanish people maintained their traditional conviction that they were the mightiest folk on earth; the fact that they hailed Philip IV, that monarch of a mouldering monarchy, as "Don Philip the Great, of all Kings the Greatest" is symptomatic of the manner in which the illusion of grandeur was still preserved. No less significant is the fact that his son was frankly styled "Charles the Bewitched," a title betokening a national consciousness that things were not as they had been. In fact, under that cretin royal, Spain, once so virile and so proudly expansive, was a discouraged nation which clung feebly but stubbornly to the mere shadow of a once substantial greatness.

Spain's colonies overseas remained, however, the widespread and wealth-containing realms they had long been. True, their monetary yield had declined alarmingly,[1] but their potentialities for commercial development of the sort found in the English, French, and Dutch colonies had not been realized. The fundamental weakness of the Spanish system was its habit of over-emphasizing gold and silver at the expense of other kinds of merchandise. This arose largely from the fact that the anciently flourishing industries of Spain had been ruined by

202

taxation and by other factors, and also from the fact that gold and silver were needed to pay for imported goods of kinds which Spain had once manufactured but which she no longer produced. In a word, Spain was far inferior to all her rivals in commercial sagacity and consequently in commercial strength.[2]

Contrasted with the steadily declining commercial life of Spain and of Spanish America was the condition prevailing in the colonies of the three chief rival powers. In none of them were the precious metals an important item. On the other hand, those powers worked on the whole intelligently to produce wealth by developing the products of the colonial soil and by making the colonies important markets for the manufacturers of the home-countries. Even after England had taken Jamaica and after France had taken, from the island of Tortuga as a point of departure, the western end of Hispaniola (the modern Haiti), the territories held by the rivals of Spain were insignificant in comparison with the still Spanish territories on the mainland of America and on the other islands of the Caribbean. Seeing the Spaniards make so little of what they had, and believing that they themselves could make many times more and better use of those so imperfectly developed realms, England and France, during the last forty years of the seventeenth century, naturally desired more and more to possess themselves of Spain's American territories.

In those same forty years the United Provinces of the Netherlands ceased to be an important factor in the Caribbean. It came about in this way. As noted on pages 186–187, certain of the English colonies in the Caribbean, notably Barbados, had not accepted the Commonwealth and had stood by the King until beaten into submission by the Parliamentary fleet under Sir George Ayscue in 1651.[3] Previous to that time the English colonists had been wont to trade with Holland as much as with England. It was perceived in England that a very high percentage of the shipping-business and of the slave-trade was in the hands of the Dutch. To end this situation the Commonwealth, in October, 1651, passed the Navigation Act which limited the carrying of English trade to English ships, either of the home country or of the English colonies, and those ships were to be manned predominantly by English subjects. Thus did the Puritan Commonwealth pay its arch-enemy, Spain, the ultimate compliment of imitation. Thereafter the English commercial monopoly was fully as rigid and as exclusivistic as that of Spain.

Naturally, the Netherlanders fought against the new policy of England which meant nothing short of the ruin of their trade with America. The first Anglo-Dutch war, 1652–1653, largely grew out of the Netherlanders' determination to resist the change. That war was a crushing defeat for them. Nor did the Restoration in England alter the matter. Charles II detested the Dutch and was a firm friend of Portugal, chief rival of the Dutch in the slave-trade. Out of this situation arose the second Anglo-Dutch war, 1665–1667, which resulted in a further reduction of the maritime importance of Holland. Finally, in 1672–1678, England and France together crushed the Dutch still more, leaving them in a very weak state until, in 1688, the greatest of all Hollanders, Prince William of Orange, mounted the English throne as King William III, doing so by virtue of his marriage to Mary, daughter of King James II of England, now driven into exile in France. After that Holland was hardly more than an appanage of England, so that Spain's chief enemies were France and England.[4]

They were, however, enemies of Spain in a new sense and each of them in a different way. This was a period in which constructive activity in the form of commerce was constantly growing both in the public esteem and in importance while at the same time merely destructive activity, whether by pirates or by privateers, was losing ground. It is in this period, for the last time, that the traditional employment of individual despoilers was countenanced by the authorities in England and France, or in their colonies, as a means of damaging Spanish power. The use of proper navies for the defense of com-

mercial interests and for the furthering of colonial ambitions
succeeded to the older method of attack by means of individuals of the sorts denominated corsairs by the Spaniards.

Behind this change, which was naturally slow, there were
the fundamental attitudes of England and of France towards
Spain. These we must now examine.

Charles II of England was eager to make peace with Spain
in the hope that he would thereby gain some part in the commerce of the Spanish colonies. For this purpose the entering
wedge would be an *asiento* (contract of license permitting the
importation of slaves into Spanish America) such as that
which Spain had given to her own subjects and, between 1580
and 1640, to Portuguese subjects over whom the King of
Spain then ruled. For a time the Dutch had had, as already
indicated, a near-monopoly of both the general carrying trade
and the slave-trade, their important part therein being largely
due to Spain's resentment against the lately liberated Portuguese. But Charles II of England, no less than his predecessor
in power, Cromwell, was determined to crush the maritime
power of Holland and so to aid his friends, the Portuguese.
One of Charles's instruments for this was the Royal African
Company, founded in 1662 directly under the personal patronage of the King. One of its functions was to be opposition
to Dutch commerce wherever possible, both in America and in
Asia as well as in Africa. The King likewise hoped to win
for the Royal African Company the *asiento* or slave-trading
privilege, and also a right to share in the general commerce of
the Spanish Indies. To gain these ends Charles II in 1664
sent an able diplomat, Sir Richard Fanshawe, to Madrid to
conduct negotiations for him. While Philip IV remained
alive little headway was made; but, after his death in 1665,
the regency for Charles II of Spain was found to be somewhat
more tractable. The chief obstacles to success on the part of
English diplomacy in Spain were the refusal of England to
give Jamaica back to Spain and the English continuation of
the use of buccaneers as an arm of offense, largely from
Jamaica as a base.[5]

Thus the English contemplated and desired a share in Spanish-American trade; the French, however, wanted infinitely more than this. Very early in the reign of King Charles II of Spain it became apparent to every one that he would have no heir and that, consequently, he would have to bequeath his throne either to a French Bourbon or to an Austrian Hapsburg, these being his nearest kin. There followed many years of court intrigue, tortuous diplomacy, and all sorts of efforts to sway the will of the ailing and unhappy man who was ostensible ruler of Spain and of all her dominions. The two parties, the French and the Austrians, were evenly balanced. In turn they achieved matrimonial victories by marrying the King first to a French princess and later to an Austrian one. Not until the King died, however, was the issue finally decided by his will in which he nominated as his successor Philip, of Bourbon, Duke of Anjou, grandson of King Louis XIV of France.

During the long diplomatic struggle which turned upon the question of Charles's successor Louis and his government tended to ward off all who would injure Spain and her colonies which, it was hoped, would soon belong to the House of Bourbon. This did not at all mean, however, that France invariably refrained from attacking Spain herself if it seemed wise to endeavor to terrorize the Spanish government into playing a part favorable to France. We shall now see, indeed, how both England and France comported themselves towards Spain in the period now under consideration.

2. Sir Thomas Modyford and Sir Henry Morgan

As noted a little way back, the English continued to use the traditional methods of piracy even after the home government had begun earnest endeavors to arrive at a satisfactory arrangement with Spain by the more civilized methods of diplomacy. In so doing the English officials who backed the pirates were, to be sure, largely acting on their own initiative and without approval from the home government.

Jamaica, which had become the principal colony of England in the Caribbean, was one of the chief bases for operations of this kind. Its governor, Sir Thomas Modyford, whom we have already met as one of the prime movers of Cromwell's "Western Design," was naturally inclined to continue his life-long offensive against Spanish power. As he had no regular naval forces belonging to the King of England at his disposal he necessarily used whatever forces he could find at hand. In those days the community of sea-rovers, calling themselves the "Brethren of the Coast," were plentifully supplied with good ships and with large numbers of men. The trouble was, however, that they often disobeyed the orders given them by their official patrons.

An example of this piratical independence is found in the various raids carried on during 1665–1666 by Captain Edward Mansvelt (called Mansfield by the English), one of the Brethren of the Coast. Although commissioned by Governor Modyford to attack the Dutch—with whom England was at war— at Curaçao, Mansfield went raiding up the San Juan River and so into the rich pastoral country around the Lake of Nicaragua. The Spaniards there had never been invaded before and, being for the most part peaceful herders of cattle and tillers of the soil, they had little experience in warfare. All the same, they made whatever resistance they could and received decidedly rough treatment for their pains. The plunderers, true to type, pillaged churches and houses, exacted a price for their departure, and finally made off with considerable plunder.[6]

On the way back Mansfield, in the latter half of 1666, captured Providence Island from the Spanish garrison stationed there. But after all these exploits against the Spaniards, in direct disobedience to his commission from Modyford, Mansfield did not care to face his possibly angry official friend. Instead, he sent a young lieutenant of his, Henry Morgan, a Welshman, to Port Royal in Jamaica with the announcement that Providence was once more an English possession. Thus first came to Modyford's attention the man who, during the years to come, was to win widest notoriety as a formidable and skilful despoiler of Spanish America.[7]

In order fully to understand the significance of Henry Morgan's career as a pirate acting in close co-operation with Governor Modyford of Jamaica we must remember that King Charles II of England had sent Sir Richard Fanshawe to Madrid to negotiate a treaty which would ensure England a share both in the slave-trade and in the general commerce of the Spanish Indies. Diplomatic events followed in rapid succession. Philip IV, who would do nothing for England while she held Jamaica and favored corsairs, died on September 17th, 1665. Exactly two months later Fanshawe and the Duke of Medina de las Torres, who was acting for the Queen Regent of Spain, mother of Charles II of that country, signed at Madrid the first of a series of agreements which were destined to regularize both Anglo-Spanish relations and the status of English colonies in America. Likewise the anger of Spain towards Portugal was abated at this period, largely through Fanshawe's influence. In June, 1666, Sir Richard died of an ague, shortly after the arrival of the Earl of Sandwich as a special envoy to help in the work begun by Sir Richard Fanshawe. In May, 1667, Sandwich made a new agreement with Spain which further improved the relations between Spain and England, but which made no mention of the Indies. Therefore pirates such as Morgan and governors such as Modyford could still continue in their usual courses without risk of breaking solemn treaties between nations.[8]

In the autumn of 1669, however, the situation was profoundly changed by the arrival in Madrid of an exceptionally able diplomat, Sir William Godolphin, who, with rare skill, brought about the signature, on July 18th, 1670, of the momentous Treaty of Madrid. In that treaty Spain for the first time recognized the right of England to possess and to rule the many American territories which she already held and which subjects of the English crown already occupied. In other words, after claiming for a century and three-quarters that she alone had title to those parts of America that lay west of the Papal Line of Demarcation, Spain now conceded that England, also, had established a right to colonize in the Western Hemisphere.

Nor was this all. The Treaty of Madrid, although it gave neither of the signatory Powers trading rights in the other's territories, did contain various provisions for reciprocal abstention from all hostile acts *in all parts of the world*. This was immensely important in various ways. In meant not only that the ancient sophistry anent "No Peace beyond the Line" was dead as far as England and Spain were concerned but also that official connivance at buccaneering was doomed. Hereafter, if England permitted her subjects to conduct raids on Spanish places during the life of any treaty of peace such raids would rightly be regarded as acts of war. In these circumstances it was incumbent upon England to do everything possible to suppress buccaneering or, in other words, to put it beyond the pale of law.[9]

The Treaty of Madrid was not designed, however, to go into immediate effect. It contained provisos for a four-month period during which ratification was to be obtained and for a further eight-month period to allow for its publication in the colonies of each power, so that only in May, 1671, did Governor Modyford receive formal notification of the treaty and instructions to carry out its provisions. In the ten months between July, 1670, and May, 1671, significant events took place in paradoxical contrast to both the letter and the spirit of the Treaty of Madrid.

Early in 1668 rumors reached Modyford that the Spaniards were about to attack Jamaica in order to recapture it. He sought to protect his island by using Morgan as a weapon, and accordingly he appointed his young friend as "Admiral" of the buccaneer fleet. An attack upon Cuba was planned. Morgan's boldness was seasoned with caution so that, instead of assaulting the strongly fortified city of Havana from the sea with his fleet, or of investing it from the landside with his small army of 500 men, he contented himself with a naval demonstration outside the harbor and then, with a great deal of cruelty, swooped down upon a poor little town near the eastern end of Cuba. The inhabitants did what they could to defend themselves, and the mayor of the town was slain in the combat. Morgan, however, triumphed. Persons who might pay ransom were taken prisoner and tortured until they disgorged their gold. Humbler folk were merely murdered. Women and children were crammed into the church where they were subjected to every sort of indignity and terrorism. All this befell in Holy Week, late March, 1668.

Puerto Bello, in June-July, 1668, was Morgan's next victim. By a cunningly executed nocturnal attack from the rear occasioned by the knowledge that the city was well defended on its seaward side, Morgan, with only some 400 men, quickly possessed himself first of the landward defenses and then of the city itself. The Governor, Castellón, and all that were left of the garrison after a terrible massacre, retreated into the one remaining castle and resolved to die there with honor rather than to surrender shamefully. It was at this point that Morgan hit upon a scheme which shows the diabolical ingenuity of which he was capable. Various hapless monks and nuns had been captured in the town and these were now forced to march at the head of the English invaders carrying great scaling-ladders to be set up against the walls of Santa Gloria castle. True to his resolve not to submit, Governor Castellón ordered that they be mowed down by Spanish fire so that the ladders could not be used. It was in vain, however, and in the end the Governor and his surviving soldiers were slaughtered by Morgan and his men. Thus, after many hours of desperate but far from heroic fighting, Morgan captured one of the greatest nerve-centres of the Spanish Empire.

Esquemeling, who saw it, describes what followed. He speaks of "very honest women, . . . who being threatened with the sword were constrained to submit their bodies to the violence of these lewd and wicked men." A night of hideous lust ensued, and on the morrow the grand hunt for treasure began. The rack, burning of feet, and still worse tortures were used liberally to extract information as to hidden wealth. In the end, a ransom of 100,000 pesos and a mass of jewels and of merchandise (including slaves) amounting to 200,000 pesos more were wrung from the wretched survivors of the carnage. When, in August, 1668, Morgan returned to his patron, His Excellency Governor Sir Thomas Modyford, he bore with him this considerable booty as the result of the foray.[10]

Thereafter Modyford and Morgan continued in their wonted course for two years. The Governor commissioned his seafaring partner as "Commander-in-Chief" of the Jamaican ships. Neither one gave much heed to the diplomatic events proceeding in distant Madrid or, if perchance they thought of them, they looked upon them as a danger to be dodged as long as possible. Therefore, between August, 1668, and August, 1670, a series of minor but lucrative depredations was carried on by Morgan, always under the ægis of Governor Sir Thomas Modyford, and at the same time preparations were being made for a culminating achievement in piracy.

This was to be nothing less than an invasion of the city of Panama, which, besides being a point of the highest importance in the commercial and political system of Spanish America, was a rich, populous, and strongly fortified place on the Pacific side of the Isthmus. Morgan was wise, therefore, to go warily and to take more than usual care in shaping his plans for this supreme blow against the hated Spaniards. Gradually a fleet of 28 sail English and 8 sail French, with 180 guns English and 59 guns French, manned by 1,326 Englishmen and by 520 Frenchmen, was prepared. They were all, of course, corsairs, "Brethren of the Coast," without a shadow of authority from their respective home governments. Meanwhile, the Treaty of Madrid had been signed, and Modyford had to go through with a considerable and intricate mummery in order to preserve an appearance of ignorance concerning at least its general tenor.

He managed it of course. Such men always find a way. In August, 1670, Morgan began to assemble his followers, his ships, and his supplies at the Isle des Vaches, a tiny speck of land near the southwest corner of Hispaniola. He departed thence on December 16th, 1670, and, pausing at Providence Island, which he took with ease on account of the smallness of the garrison and of the pusillanimity of the Spanish commandant, he proceeded to the Isthmus and, on January 9th, 1671, was already master of Chagres, both the river and the port of that name.

Truth to tell, Morgan's march across the Isthmus was a remarkable accomplishment; he was a devil and a wretch, but he was also a great leader of men. The obstacles to advance were enormous and complicated. For the pirate host life was anything but sweetly easy. Weevilly bread and maggotty meat are not the most succulent viands; lice, jiggers, and mosquitoes are not the most alluring of bed-mates; alligators playfully snapping at hands and feet are not the most pleasing of pets; and the hot, damp atmosphere of that region, never quite free from the stench of decaying organisms, is not exactly bracing. Into all these conditions they were plunged. As they pushed onwards through the matted jungles, fighting malaria, yellow-fever, and dysentery, their clothes alternately soaked with the slime of bogs and caked with stinking mud, they grew hungrier and hungrier. Indeed, only a chance-found treasure of maize in a forgotten granary saved them from starvation, and the good of that was nearly made void by a rashly copious quaffing of wine into almost empty bellies.

On January 17th or 18th they drew nigh to Panama city, where the President Don Juan Pérez de Guzmán had made ready to resist at all costs, albeit in this he was not invariably well supported by his inferior officers. Pérez himself was of the superstitious type of Spanish Catholic—very common in the days of the King Charles the Bewitched—so that, instead of relying upon proper military measures, backed up by a reasonable amount of prayer, he wasted precious time and strength in useless religious processions and in services galore. Meanwhile the freebooter army was coming onwards, nor could volleys of arrows from Indian allies stop invaders who promptly took to fighting native-fashion, doing it as well as the Indians themselves.

Undoubtedly Henry Morgan had certain of the qualities of a great general. On January 19th, 1671, upon the plain of Matasnillo outside the old city of Panama, he whipped the Spaniards in a fair fight, out-manœuvring them at every point. The defenders, in despair, resorted to a weird stratagem, causing a herd of frenzied cattle to charge the English rear. But, when the English turned and fired into the on-rushing bovine faces, the great beasts wheeled about and charged back upon the Spaniards. After that all morale and discipline seems to have deserted the defenders. Pausing in his retreat from the doomed city, President Pérez gave a last agonized order: The powder-magazines in different places were to be touched off. In the thunderous roar of their explosions the proud city sang its last pæan of defiance, and it died in a flood of flame.

Then, while the embers were all too slowly cooling, the usual sordid treasure-hunt began with its customary concomitants of raging lust and implacable torture. The booty assembled was found to be worth between 400,000 and 750,000 pesos. Morgan took for himself a sum deemed by many rather large. It is likely, however, that Morgan, aided by Governor Modyford, cheated not his followers but his King and that King's brother. Those gentlemen were to have received considerable monetary proceeds from this last adventure in *quasi*-official piracy. It was not that they were personally implicated in the matter; rather, their ostensible shares seem to have been treated by Modyford as a pool into which he could dip his hands without undue risk to himself.[11]

Morgan's return to Jamaica in mid-March, 1671, was a veritable triumph for him. On the last day of May he was accorded the formal thanks of the Governor and Council of Jamaica for his noble deeds in defense of English freedom.[12]

The destruction of Panama had astonishingly little harmful effect on the Spaniards. Beyond the undoubtedly great shock to their nervous-systems and the loss of valuable buildings, chattels, etc., they received more benefit than injury because the city was moved to its present site which is infinitely better for commercial and hygienic reasons than the old location.

In later life Morgan became respectable. Nagged incessantly by the Spanish ambassador, Count of Molina, King Charles II of England went through the motions of disciplining Modyford and Morgan for the gratification of King Charles II of Spain. Later, the two worthies were both kicked upstairs, the Governor becoming Chief Justice of Jamaica, and the pirate being dubbed a knight by the King in person. Afterwards he was on three separate occasions Governor of Jamaica, in which office he was enthusiastically severe at times against the piratical profession of which he had once been so conspicuous a member. Finally, after a riotous and varied life in the course of which he begat various half-negro children whose descendants fill the Yallahs Valley in Jamaica with ebon portraits of Sir Henry, the famous corsair died in August, 1688, and his funeral received a salute of twenty-one guns.[13]

3. The French in the Caribbean, 1660–1700

The life in the French colonies is described in an inimitable manner by the Dominican missionary, Father Jean-Baptiste Labat, one of the shrewdest observers of men and of things ever to travel in America.[14]

Born in Paris in 1663, of a family which came from the *Landes* near Bordeaux, Labat became in 1682 a novice in the great Dominican monastery called *les Jacobins* which stood in the rue Saint Honoré about midway between what is now the Place Vendôme and the church of Saint Roch; and there, on April 11th, 1685, he made his profession in religion. In a word, he could not well have been more thoroughly a Frenchman and an ecclesiastic. He had not, however, the contemplative type of mind. He was a monk, certainly, and on many occasions served admirably as a priest and as a consoler of the unfortunate; but beyond all that he was also a man of enormous vitality, eager for action and not at all averse, when needful, to pugnacity. His portrait shows him with a twinkling glance, a mocking twist of the eyebrows, a very massive and businesslike nose, and a firm chin, altogether the face of a red-blooded kindly man capable of great energy in many directions.

In 1693, responding to a letter from the Dominican missions in the French Antilles asking for new workers, Father Labat abandoned the pensive tranquillity of the Jacobins and crossed the rolling seas to seek an appropriate outlet for his varied gifts. He remained in the French islands until 1705. Spiritual labors were only a part, albeit a considerable one, of his work in his new sphere of activity. He was a great builder of houses for his Order, of canals, of batteries, and of sugar-mills. He was a buyer of slaves and their master, but not a cruel one as things then went except when black magic drove him to fury; he was a friend, and sometimes even a colleague, of filibusters; he took part in fighting with English invaders, and he had at least two exciting adventures with serpents. He travelled frequently and widely in the Islands, always noting even the minutest details of the scene with those bright satirical eyes of his; and when there was naught else to do he ate, drank, and enjoyed such society as came his way, loquacious and merry always, and at times decidedly naughty in his talk but never vulgar because never stupid, but always refusing to gamble at cards. Father Labat found the jiggers with which his legs were often infested a strangely fascinating subject for study, and his accounts of their domestic habits, of his adventures with them, and of their painful persistence, are lively and absorbing. For the rest, every aspect of the daily life of all classes in the French islands and of the customs there is vividly portrayed by this most brilliantly witty Frenchman. To him should turn all who wish to get at the very soul of the subject.[15]

In general it may be said that the history of the French colonies in the Caribbean and in all parts of America was marked by a gradual strengthening of the authority of the King of France. On pages 162 and 188 we have seen how, after royal French authority was established on Tortuga it was gradually spread to the whole western end of Hispaniola, which became the French colony of Saint Domingue, and which is today the Franco-Negro republic of Haiti. This constituted a sizeable seizure of territory by France from Spain, being, in fact, a French parallel to the Jamaica affair between the English and the Spaniards. In Saint Domingue, as in Santo Domingo (the Spanish eastern end of the island), life was based on sugar-growing, on indigo, and on similar industries which produced raw materials for European industries. The French part of Hispaniola was, however, far more prosperous and better administered than was the Spanish, the latter having declined greatly in all respects.[16]

As said on page 197, there was a brief period in which the French Caribbean colonies were administered on a proprietary basis somewhat like that once in vogue in the English colonies. Such an arrangement did not accord, however, with the growing tendency to concentrate all power in the hands of the King of France. In November-December, 1663, the Sieur Prouville de Tracy was appointed to be Lieutenant-General for the King of France over all French possessions in America. This was followed in April-July, 1664, by the formation, under the auspices of King Louis XIV and of his great minister, Jean-Baptiste Colbert, of the *Compagnie des Indes Occidentales* (Company of the West Indies) which, after it had bought out the proprietors of colonies, was placed by the King in charge of all French holdings in the West Indies. The final step came in 1674 when King Louis XIV definitely added the Isles of America to the domain of his crown, thereby achieving a position with respect thereto identical with that which the Spanish crown had held from the beginning.[17]

Certain treaties made in Europe during this period must now be mentioned. In July, 1667, England, France, and the Netherlands made the Treaty of Breda regularizing their respective holdings in America (and elsewhere) so far as the signatory powers were concerned. Among the territories which changed hands were New York, which became English instead of Dutch, and the English part of St. Christopher, lately taken by the French, was returned to England in ex-

change for Acadia (New Brunswick). The Treaty of Nym-
wegen, August-September, 1678, ended the third Anglo-Dutch
war, but made no mention of American affairs. In May, 1680,
at Windsor, Spain and England made a treaty in which they
agreed that if either was molested in any of its possessions by
any other power, the offended party was to receive the aid of
the other signatory, and this principle was to hold in all parts
of the world. In the nature of things it would be France who
would make depredations against either English or Spanish
possessions. Finally, in August, 1684, the twenty-year Truce
of Ratisbon was signed by all the leading countries of Europe.
Its main feature was that it established peace in all parts of
the world, this being a general recognition of the fundamental
unity of interest between affairs in Europe and affairs in
America. The Truce of Ratisbon was the final blow to official
piracy and to the use of it by civilized governments as a
weapon of attack. Thereafter piracy was utterly outlawed
and the authorities of all nations did their utmost to suppress
it during times of peace, albeit in times of war corsairs
might be taken into favor if they would give up their criminal
ways and become regular fighters in the service of their respective countries.[18]

This new status of piracy is well illustrated by the procedure of France towards the end of the war which Louis XIV
began in 1689 against William III of England and in behalf
of the exiled James II. In that war England, the Netherlands,
and Spain were allies against the King of France who, mind-
ful of his designs upon the throne of Spain, determined, in
1697, to attack the very centre of Spanish power in America.
To that end he sent forth Admiral Baron de Pointis as leader
of an impressive expedition. Leaving Brest in January, 1697,
with a royal French fleet of over 13 sail and 4,015 regular
troops of the French army, Pointis was joined in American
waters in March by the Governor of Saint Domingue, Jean-
Baptiste du Casse, with nearly 1,000 additional men and 7
frigates. Although the colonial contingent led by Casse is
frequently said to have consisted of "buccaneers" so to refer

to it obscures its real character. In reality, Casse's force had for its nucleus the regular garrison of Saint Domingue, consisting of about 170 men. To them were added over 700 more who, ordinarily, were by profession buccaneers. On joining up under Casse, however, all these men became automatically, at any rate for the time being, soldiers of the King of France, then at formally declared war with the King of Spain. Because of all this, the colonial forces led by Admiral and Governor du Casse against Cartagena, in conjunction with the much larger regular force from France under Admiral de Pointis, was as different as possible from, for example, the rabble of corsairs led by Morgan against Panama. Morgan had had no better commission than that of Modyford, and Modyford's master, the King of England, had not been at war with the King of Spain. In short, the French expedition was good clean warfare; the English one had been merest piracy.

The military aspect of the French attack on Cartagena has often been studied. It was brilliantly executed, and with noteworthy martial gallantry on both sides. The map opposite shows clearly the manner of it. Coming along the shore from the north the combined French squadrons passed by the city and made for the Boca Chica, the only entrance to the harbor, where was the Fort of San Felipe, commanded by our old acquaintance, Don José Sánchez Jiménez de Orozco, reconqueror of Providence Island. He and his small garrison conducted themselves with such splendid courage that their French vanquishers were moved to show them chivalrous courtesy. Thereafter, from April 15th to May 3rd, 1697, the siege of Cartagena proceeded. On the latter date the great Spanish city surrendered.[19]

Everything was done in an honorable military manner, even to the collection of heavy money-payments from the defeated citizenry. The French held Cartagena until the end of May under the military governorship of Casse who did all that he could to maintain discipline and to check looting and other outrages. In view of the circumstances he succeeded remark-

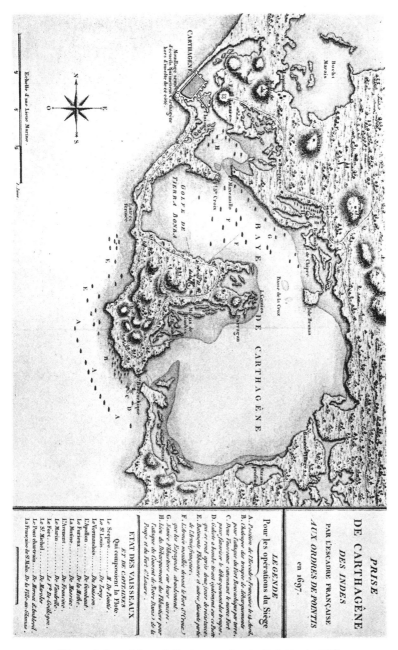

Map of the taking of Cartagena, by de Pointis, in 1697.

Reproduced by courtesy of Francis Russell Hart, from "Admirals of the Caribbean."

ably well. The worst disaster of the siege was suffered by the invaders rather than by the invaded. A terrible plague, either malaria or yellow-fever, carried off hundreds of Frenchmen. There was also much wrangling among the victors about the distribution of booty, Pointis behaving in a manner far from generous to Casse and his followers. (Later King Louis XIV strove to do justice to the injured parties.) All that, however, has naught to do with the honorable conduct of the French towards the Spaniards in which we have proof that the former were no mere brigands, but a proper army. In due course Cartagena was evacuated by its invaders, and at the end of August 1697, Admiral de Pointis was again in France, and three weeks later the Peace of Ryswick brought the war to a close. This was the last war fought between Spain and France until the Napoleonic period. A few years later, in 1700, a Bourbon sat upon the throne of Spain and it may reasonably be assumed that a large factor in his being there was the French victory of 1697 which finally convinced poor failing Charles II that his heir should be a Bourbon rather than a Hapsburg.[20]

4. Contraband and Other Commerce Gain in Importance

Piracy supported by governments as an instrument of war had been traditional in the Spanish Main for 150 years on the basic assumption that there was "No peace beyond the Line" and that consequently no peace-treaty binding in Europe was binding in America, so that depredations might continue there regardless of the treaties in force in Europe. All this was terminated in 1670–71 so far as England was concerned and in 1684 so far as France was concerned; for, as we have seen, the Treaty of Madrid and the Truce of Ratisbon cut the ground out from under piracy-in-peacetime in America by ending the hitherto theoretical non-existence of such peacetime. Piracy, therefore, declined into a mere brigandage and ceased to have political importance except as a symptom of imperfect social control precisely similar to crime among ourselves. In times of war, to be sure, pirates could join up as volunteers in this or that army or navy. But piracy as such was no longer of importance.

What *was* important was contraband trade. Originally, as we saw in Chapter III, corsairing and smuggling were practically conterminous and both were indulged in by the same individuals in many instances. But in the period which now concerns us—and after it—they diverged more and more. It was realized at last that piracy was inimical to the growth of both public and private wealth and that commerce, whether legal or illegal, was the chief source of wealth. Since the Hapsburg government of Spain, even in the darkest years of Charles II's reign, would not tolerate the slightest infraction of its monopoly of trade, the rival nations were obliged to do what they could for themselves through contraband trade.

In all this the slave-trade under *asientos* (slaving privileges) was a great aid to non-Spaniards wishing to carry on business in Spanish America. Having no African colonies of her own whence slaves could be obtained Spain, necessarily, gave *asientos* to foreigners who could tap the sources of supply. With slaving as an opening wedge, evasion of Spain's laws of trade became a fixed system with its special etiquette and technique, the whole being hallowed and made respectable by widespread public complacency in this regard. In short, at the end of the seventeeth century, as also throughout the sixteenth century when men like Hawkins and Drake did a thriving business with the help of Spain's colonials, it was the subjects of Spain who made possible this most deadly foe of the official monopolistic commerce between Spain and her American possessions.

It is Father Labat who gives us the clearest view of the methods of illicit traders. He tells us of the solemnity with which local Spanish officials in minor ports would pretend to believe that some visiting foreign ship was in dire distress requiring immediate repairs under plea of which the ship would be admitted into the harbor. Her cargo would then be removed before careening and would be officially sealed in a warehouse as the law required. But he goes on to tell us how, by night, and through some unsealed side door, a vast array of indigo, cochineal, vanilla, ginger, tobacco, sugar, and other colonial produce would be passed into the warehouse in exchange for all manner of European goods taken out.[21] This was but one of many methods employed, the general result of the contraband trade being that it came to outrank the legitimate commerce by more than ten to one.[22] It was clandestine commerce far more than the fortunes of war that caused the conspicuous shrinkage in the revenues flowing from America to Spain during the last decades of the Hapsburg period.

5. The Scots at Darien

A perfect example of the magnitude to which contraband commerce arose is the career in Darien of the Company of Scotland which is illustrative also of other matters, as we shall see.

The venture in question was the Company of Scotland Trading to Africa and the Indies. It was in large measure the product of the genius of William Paterson, native of Dumfriesshire, who, after founding the Bank of England in 1694, returned to his native land in the next year and there guided the formation of the aforesaid Company of Scotland to its formal inauguration on June 26th, 1695.[23]

Very emphatically King William III of England, who was also King of Scotland, did not give his blessing to the new enterprise of his Scots subjects. His attitude, in this matter, was a faithful reproduction of that of his English subjects of the merchant class on whose good will his power and place largely depended and who saw their own interests seriously threatened by this new rivalry of the merchants and other leaders in the northern kingdom. As, however, Scotland was a separate and sovereign state neither the hostility of the English merchants nor the unfriendliness of the King could prevent the carrying out of the Scots plans.[24]

According to the terms of the Act of June 26th, 1695, the

Company of Scotland was to enjoy for thirty-one years a monopoly of trade between that country and any part of the world *not possessed by any European sovereign*. Very ample civil and military powers were conveyed along with the commercial powers. After many preliminary difficulties with the English House of Lords and English capitalists it was decided that the capital subscribed for the venture should be wholly Scots. Over 1,400 Scots of all classes subscribed £400,-000 (of which £219,094 was paid in cash) prior to August 1st, 1696.[25] In short, the Company of Scotland was the outcome of a national endeavor to join in the great game of transoceanic trade.

That it was not originally intended to undertake contraband trade is made sufficiently clear by the presence in the incorporating Act of a significant phrase about trading only with lands *not held by any European sovereign*. It was chiefly through the influence of Paterson that that phrase was early forgotten by the Company. Paterson himself had for many years been keenly interested in the idea of founding a Scots colony in Darien whence active trade could be carried on across the Isthmus and so to the Far East. He had even made suggestions in this sense to King James VII of Scotland (II of England) who, however, was soon after driven from his thrones by William III so that nothing came of it.[26]

Notwithstanding the aforementioned restriction, Paterson's long-cherished plan for a colony at Darien was accepted by the Company on July 23rd, 1696. This was a serious mistake. The Company was now committed to participation in contraband trade of a kind expressly prohibited to them. To this mistake was added another fully as fatal, namely, an extraordinarily ill-chosen array of merchandise to be dealt in at Darien. As the prospective customers were unsubjugated Indians of rather low native culture, with perhaps also a few Spaniards if they could be induced to trade, the freight was wildly unsuitable: Cloth, shoes, slippers, stockings, hats, wigs, and, by way of climax, 1,500 Bibles in English of the King James version.[27]

When finally ready to sail from Leith, on the east side of Scotland, in mid-July, 1698, the Company's fleet consisted of five vessels with a total tonnage of about 1,300, and 175 guns. These last were to be used solely for defensive purposes. There were 1,200 colonists, including 300 young men from the gentry of Scotland and sixty army officers, the rest being respectable artisans and tradesmen. There were also documents providing instructions and outlining the colonial government by a self-renewing Council of seven, but without, unfortunately, clear regulations concerning the choice of a president.[28]

These were the chief antecedent conditions under which the first Company of Scotland Expedition to Darien set forth in mid-July, 1698. At the end of August the fleet was at Madeira where, instead of buying needed victuals, twenty-seven pipes of fine Madeira wine were bought. Here we have a first hint of the marked bibulosity which was a recurrent feature of the enterprise. Sailing from Madeira on September 2nd, the fleet came to Crab Island, now called Vieques, off the eastern end of Puerto Rico, on October 3rd. It was intended that Crab Island should be a way-station on the route to Darien. As it was not occupied, the fleet had no difficulty in taking Crab Island. There the Scots were joined by an experienced sea-rover, Captain Allison, who became a useful guide and adviser to them. Obeying orders, the fleet went on to Golden Island near the northern end of the Gulf of Darien. There, on November 3rd, 1698, the colony of Caledonia was formally established.[29]

The Scots having thus reached their destination, what were the conditions under which they remained there from November 3rd, 1698, to June 20th, 1699?

They were seated on an oval bay some seven miles long and three and one-half miles wide, running from northwest to southeast and having its wide mouth at the southeastern end. Golden Island lies on the eastern side and is one of a string of islands enclosing the bay from the ocean; opposite, some two miles to the west, is the peninsula where New Edinburgh was established.

Although the Scots tried to view their surroundings opti-
mistically, sending home glowing accounts of the charms and
advantages of the country, in solemn truth no scene could
possibly be more unsuitable for occupation than was this,
their colony of Caledonia. Humid heat, swarms of insects,
torrents of steel-gray rain utterly different from the opalescent
mists of Scotland, blistering sunshine, a deep mould covering
the earth and bearing a coarse and largely useless tropical
vegetation but not at all favoring intensive agriculture of the
kind known to the Scots, all these factors combined to make
Caledonia nothing less than a death-trap for the hardy north-
erners who sought to occupy it.

Moreover, the place was "possessed by a European sovereign," or at any rate Charles II of Spain and his government could with a great degree of plausibility claim to possess
it. Within a radius of 300 miles were such important Spanish
centres, effectively and intensively occupied, as Cartagena,
Santa Marta, Puerto Bello, and Panama. Caledonia lay, indeed, within the jurisdiction of the President of Panama, and
it was from Acla (almost on the site of Caledonia) that Nuñez
de Balboa had discovered the Pacific in 1513.[30]

Finally, there was the question of the prospective customers. It was obvious from the first that trade would have
to depend upon the circumambient Indian population. It was
made up of tribes governed by chiefs whom the Scots styled
"Captains." They were all friendly enough with the Scots
whom they perceived to be very different from the Spaniards
whom they hated and to whom they had never bowed their
heads in homage. But they were distressingly poor prospects
from the point of view of sales. They were, indeed, well adjusted culturally to their environment; but they were perfectly hopelessly as purchasers of stockings, wigs, hats, and
Bibles in English.

Altogether the outlook for setting up a contraband trade
was decidedly bleak. To make matters worse it early became
evident from the visit of an English man of war out of Jamaica, in mid-November, 1698, that the hostile southrons were

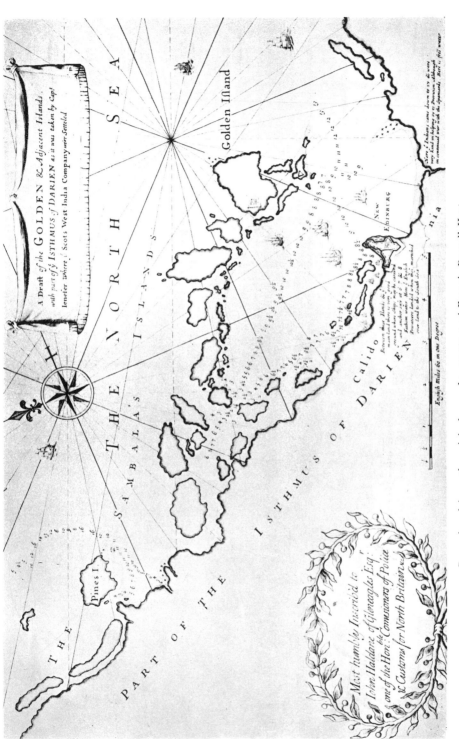

Reproduced from the original map, by courtesy of Francis Russell Hart.

bestirring themselves. There were, too, constant rumors of impending Spanish attacks. Then, on December 24th, a friendly French ship, the *Saint Antoine,* which was to have carried home dispatches to the Company, went to pieces on the rocks as a result of a tremendous jamboree held to celebrate her departure. Here again we have the Demon Rum.[31] Nevertheless work proceeded actively on the fortifications of New Edinburgh and elsewhere in Caledonia. The eyes of Spanish authorities both in Spain and in America had been on the Scots enterprise ever since it left Madeira, but there was only one small skirmish with Spanish soldiers, on February 6th, 1699. It showed, however, that the Dons were beginning to stir. In April Governor Beeston of Jamaica, a one-time associate of Modyford in his dealings with Morgan, made a rancorous proclamation against the Scots forbidding that any aid or comfort be given them. To all this were added continuous wrangles among the Councillors and among the rest of the colonists, much bad health, recurrent shortage of food, and a steady deterioration of the fleet of ships because of the harm done by parasites abounding in the tropical water. In short, there was a general decline in all respects under the irresistible adverseness of the surroundings. And no business was done.

In the end it was the grave illness of William Paterson which determined the withdrawal of the first expedition from Caledonia. Mrs. Paterson had died of a fever some time before. The departure was made on June 16th–19th, 1699, and, after a horrible voyage marked by shipwreck and other calamities, only one ship succeeded in reaching Scotland, November 20th, 1699, with less than a quarter of the original number of those who had set forth so bravely.[32]

While the first expedition was still at Darien the wrath of both Spain and France had been aroused against King William because of the presence of his subjects at Darien in the rôle of intruders probably intent upon all kinds of mischief. Neither of those powers could then believe that the King of England might be bitterly opposed to what the subjects of the

King of Scotland were doing. A king ruling two separate and by no means mutually affectionate kingdoms was to them anomalous and incomprehensible. The reason why the French were thus siding with the Spaniards was that, by now, Louis XIV was tolerably sure that a French Bourbon would soon mount the throne of Spain so that it behooved him, Louis, to do all that was possible to help the Spaniards in the protection of their commercial routes, already sufficiently endangered by the English at Jamaica. In March, 1699, the English ambassador at Madrid managed to make the Spanish government understand King William's position and attitude, but all that he got for his trouble was a cool suggestion that, if the King of England objected to the Scots colony at Darien it was for him to crush it.[33]

While King William was thus being spurred on to action against the Scots, than which he would have liked nothing better, the Spaniards themselves were becoming active. In their cumbersome, tardy way the officials of Spain in Mexico, Panama, and Cartagena, as well as at home, were preparing a punitive expedition in order finally to eject the interlopers.[34]

The sad fate of the first expedition was not yet known in Scotland when the first section of a second expedition set forth for Caledonia in mid-May, 1699. It consisted of two ships carrying 300 new colonists and plentiful supplies. Arriving at Darien in mid-August, 1699, this advance section of the second expedition of course found Caledonia deserted. A few days later, on account of carelessness in the drawing of brandy from a hogshead, one of the ships burned at her moorings with all her supplies but without loss of life. Posting a few volunteers as a garrison to hold the place if possible, the remaining ship took all the rest of the colonists to Jamaica.[35]

The main body of the second expedition, consisting of four fine ships with 1,250 colonists, set forth from Scotland in late September, 1699, in spite of the recent receipt, via London, of dolorous tidings about the state of affairs at Darien. Caledonia was reached on November 30th. As in the case of the first expedition there was unwisely chosen freight, and also a

strong tendency towards all manner of bickerings and dis-
sension among the colonists, probably because of their decline in morale in that deadly climate. On this occasion, however, there was one sizeable military engagement. It took
place at Topocante, somewhere in the vicinity of Caledonia,
in the hills of the Isthmus behind the settlement. In mid-
February, 1700, Colonel and Councillor Alexander Campbell
of Fonab and Lieutenant Turnbull, being freshly arrived from
Scotland, inflicted an indecisive defeat upon the Governor of
Darien, Don Miguel Cordones. There were only a few hundred fighters on either side. The Spaniards had the advantage
of a palisadoed fort in a good position and they knew that
sooner of later they would be reinforced. The Scots, in spite
of the hideous difficulty of the country, managed to work
them considerable damage.[36]

Soon afterwards, on February 23rd, 1700, Don Juan Pimienta, Governor of Cartagena, blockaded Caledonia harbor
with a fleet of eleven tall and gun-bristling Spanish warships.
The might of outraged Spain was to the fore at last. A period
of stout but vain resistance followed. Then came long-drawn-
out negotiations between Spaniards and Scots, using French
and Latin as vehicles of expression. The stalwart pride of the
Scots touched the no less proud Pimienta so that, in the end,
they were allowed to depart in their ships "with colours
flying, and drums beating." The departure, honorable to both
sides, was made on April 11th, 1700. While making for Scotland the entire squadron was lost in one way and another so
that only a few of the 1,250 colonists ever saw gorse again,
or ever breathed the glorious air of Scotland.[37]

What Mr. Hart has so aptly named "The Disaster of
Darien" was the product of many factors. By laying itself
open to Spanish hostility through its seizure of land "possessed by a European sovereign," the Company of Scotland
created one enemy which it could not possibly vanquish; by
daring to enter the field of contraband commerce which England hoped to make peculiarly her own the Company of Scotland set its own king against its enterprise; by selecting un-

saleable goods wherein to attempt to trade, the Company of
Scotland undermined its economic position at the outset;
finally, by choosing one of the worst parts of all America
wherein to settle, a region so insalubrious that not even Spaniards hardened to life in America could withstand it, the
Company of Scotland subjected itself and its colonists to the
implacable hostility of Nature.

In spite of these errors pre-inducing failure the Darien
venture of the Company of Scotland was a daring and an admirable experiment. It had none of the piratical features
which had marked previous attempts to invade Spanish territory, and all its armament was destined solely to defensive
purposes. As planned by William Paterson the Darien colony
was intended to be a new and grandiose kind of contraband
trade in the very heart of the Spanish empire, and it was
designed ultimately to be a station on a trans-Isthmian route
leading to Scots factories on the Pacific side and thence to new
commercial fields in the Far East. Had all this been seriously
attempted in accordance with Paterson's original vision and
plan the Spaniards would probably have wrecked it precisely
as they wrecked what was actually begun at Caledonia. From
their point of view they would have *had* to wreck it. But, as
it turned out, the environment at Darien sapped all vigor
from the Scots and even laid the indomitable Paterson low
with grievous illness so that their original impetus was brought
to nothing.

NOTES TO CHAPTER IX

[1] Compare, for example, the imports of treasure into Spain from the Indies
in the five years from 1591–1595, being 35,184,000 pesos, with those for 1656–
1660, being 3,361,000 pesos. On this see: Hamilton, 1934, pp. 34–35.

[2] Haring, 1918, Ch. vi. Altamira, III, sections 723–742, where this great
Spanish historian shows the myriad burdens and evils which general commerce
in both Spain and the colonies had to support, as a result of which the general commerce of both was but a fraction of what it might have been. Argüello, 1681, MS., describes the decay of Spanish industry.

[3] Harlow, 1926, pp. 68–70.

[4] Abbott, 1924, II, pp. 14–17, 55–57, 61–63. Newton, 1933, Chs. xiii–xiv,
xvi–xx. Scelle, 1906, I, pp. 473–549, 703–752, II, pp. 16–34. Wright, 1924.

[5] Abbott, 1924, II, pp. 85–87. Newton, 1933, pp. 240–242, 282–284.

[6] Esquemeling, Pt. I, Ch. vii. Hart, 1922, pp. 48–50. Fernández Duro, 1895–1903, V, pp. 161–178. Newton, 1933, pp. 259–261.

[7] Governor Modyford, naturally enough, hailed the capture of Providence with satisfaction, and, on November 10th, 1666, his brother, Sir James Modyford, was appointed Lieutenant Governor of Providence Island. The matter did not end there, however, because the President of the Audiencia of Panama, Don Juan Pérez de Guzmán, immediately took active steps to win back the Island for Spain. He sent Don José Sánchez Jiménez de Orozco in command of forces drawn from Puerto Bello and from Cartagena to regain the lost island, which was done in so emphatic a fashion that Sir James Modyford was never able to take possession of his hoped-for jurisdiction. See: Esquemeling, Pt. II, Ch. iv. This author had a wide experience as a pirate in the Caribbean and, although not always accurate, he is usually informative and exciting. Mr. Philip Gosse has lately shown that Esquemeling, whose nationality has hitherto been in doubt, was a native of Honfleur, in Normandy, and that he later lived in Amsterdam where the first of the innumerable editions of his book was printed in 1678. (See: Gosse, 1932, pp. 145–147, for documentation on this point.) For the adventures of Mansfield and of Morgan in his early period see: Hart, 1922, Ch. iii; Roberts, 1933, pp. 62–69; Newton, 1933, pp. 258–261; Fernández Duro, 1895–1903, V, Chs. iii and xi. Very important is: Rowland, 1935, pp. 304–308.

[8] See, for details on Fanshawe's diplomatic career in Spain: Fanshawe, 1907, especially pages 176–197 and 234–251. See also: Newton, 1933, pp. 240–242, 261–262.

[9] Newton, 1933, pp. 269–271. Haring, 1918, pp. 250–251. Roberts, 1933, p. 143. Altamira, III, section 664.

[10] Esquemeling, Pt. II, Ch. vi. Gosse, 1932, pp. 156–157. Roberts, 1933, Ch. v. J. K. Laughton's article on Morgan, in DNB, XXXIX, pp. 17–21, 1894. Newton, 1933, pp. 263–266.

[11] Roberts, 1933, pp. 180–183, where he cites a special monograph on Morgan by a Welsh author, namely: W. Llewellyn Williams, *Sir Henry Morgan, the Buccaneer,* published by the Honourable Society of the Cymmrodorion in their Transactions for 1903–1904, London, 1905. I have not succeeded in seeing it.

[12] Esquemeling, Pt. II, Ch. vii; Pt. III, Chs. i–vi. Gosse, 1932, pp. 158–159. Newton, 1933, pp. 266–277. By far the most satisfactory book on Morgan known to me is the oft-cited Roberts, 1933, especially Chs. v–ix, and Appendix A, pp. 281–290, where a letter written to the Queen Regent of Spain by President Pérez, on February 19th, 1671, from near Panama, describes the Morgan raid from its victims' standpoint. See also: Hart, 1922, pp. 54–91; Fernández Duro, 1895–1903, V, Ch. xi.

[13] Roberts, 1933, Chs. x–xv. Newton, 1933, pp. 275–276, 289–290, 332. Fernández Duro, 1895–1903, V, Chs. xi–xii. Haring, 1918, pp. 249–254. See also: Sosa, 1919; Villestreux, 1930; Sternbeck, 1931.

[14] So far as I know Father Labat and his work are utterly unknown to modern American writers with the exception of Prof. C. H. Haring, who cites him but who mistakenly calls him a Jesuit. He wrote several books,

but the only one which concerns us here is his *Nouveau Voyage aux Isles de l'Amerique,* published in a legitimate first edition at Paris in 1722, by Guillaume Cavalier, in six volumes, and in the same year in a pirated edition of the same dimensions at The Hague, *chez Husson.* The edition used by me is the admirable one prepared and introduced by Monsieur A. t'Serstevens, Paris, 1931, 2 vols. (Éditions Duchartre.)

[15] Father Labat returned to Europe in 1705 and travelled widely there, on religious errands not exempt from mundane incidentals. His last twenty years were spent in the great monastery in the rue Saint Honoré, where he died on January 6th, 1738. His personality was so vivid and so sharply drawn that it made him a figure of legend in his own time and down to the present in the Isles of America where once he dwelt. Lafcadio Hearn often speaks of him in *Two Years in the French West Indies,* New York, 1890, and Monsieur t'Serstevens tells us that *Pé Labatt* is still a living person to the Negroes of Martinique.

[16] Hazard, 1873, Chs. v–vi.

[17] Tertre, 1667–1671, III, pp. 14–23, 36–76. Charlevoix, 1730–1731, II, p. 35 to end of Bk. VII. Mims, 1912, entire, for Colbert's colonial policy.

[18] Newton, 1933, Chs. xix–xxiii. Abbott, 1924, II, pp. 57, 63, 73.

[19] Altamira, III, section 664. Alcedo, 1812–1815, article on Cartagena.

[20] Labat, 1931, Pt. IV, Ch. iii. Baron de Pointis, *Relation de ce qui c'est fait la Prise de Carthagène,* Brussels, 1698, translated into English and published in London, 1740. Baron Robert du Casse, *L'Amiral du Casse,* Paris, 1876. Charlevoix, 1730–1731. Hart, 1922, Ch. iv. Niles, 1924, pp. 148–154, where she gives a picturesque reconstruction of the surrender of Fort San Felipe. Fernández Duro, 1895–1903, V, Ch. xviii. Mr. Hart's admiral account of the taking of Cartagena is particularly to be recommended. His bibliographical notes, 1922, pp. 193–194, are most useful.

[21] Labat, Pt. VI, Ch. vii, 1931, II, pp. 253–255.

[22] Haring, 1918, pp. 115–122. Chapman, 1933, pp. 164–167.

[23] In his youth Paterson had travelled widely in the West Indies and had there met various corsairs, perhaps including William Dampier and Lionel Wafer, from whom he gained much information. On this see: Wafer, 1934, pp. l–lxvii; Insh, 1932, pp. 98–100; Hart, 1929, pp. 149–151.

On the establishment of the company see: Hart, 1929, pp. 21–22; Insh, 1932, pp. 19–21; Barbour, 1907, p. 8; Anderson, 1911, p. 474. Although the actual founders of the company were two Scottish merchants, Robert Blackwood and James Balfour, there can be no question concerning Paterson's powerful influence and guidance.

[24] Hart, 1929, pp. 12–13.

[25] Hart, 1929, pp. 36–40. Insh, 1932, Bk. I, Ch. ii. A list of the subscribers will be found in Barbour, 1907, pp. 255–284.

[26] Hart, 1929, pp. 45–48. Anderson, 1911, p. 474.

[27] Hart, 1929, pp. 48–49, where he quotes in full the list of goods given by: Walter Herries, *A Defense of the Scots Abdicating Darien,* Edinburgh, 1700, p. 22. See also: Insh, 1932, pp. 85 and 235. It is thought that the unwise choice of freight was due to influence brought to bear by certain Scots merchants holding stock in the Company.

28 Hart, 1929, pp. 51–56. Insh, 1932, pp. 109–120. Barbour, 1907, pp. 81–89, gives a list of the first expedition's members.

29 Hart, 1929, Ch. iv, and the *Journal* of Mr. Rose in Appendix II of that work. Insh, 1932, pp. 118–128. Dampier, 1927, p. 25, states that Golden Island had been a favorite haunt of pirates for many years, and Wafer, 1934, pp. 34–35, 149–150, also gives us information about the place.

30 A Spanish town was founded at Acla in 1514, by Gabriel de Rojas, but it had been abandoned *because of its unwholesome climate* in 1532. (See Alcedo, 1812–1815, article on Acla.) If Spaniards could not thrive there, how could the Scots?

31 Hart, 1929, pp. 66–77. Insh, 1932, pp. 133–139.

32 Hart, 1929, Ch. vi. Insh, 1932, pp. 160–168.

33 Hart, 1929, pp. 86–88 and Appendix XVIII. Insh, 1932, pp. 146–153. To the Spaniards, of course, the Scots at Darien were simply "pirates" in spite of the fact that their true character was that of contrabandists on a would-be large scale.

34 Hart, 1929, Ch. vii. Documents listed in Hart, 1931.

35 Anderson, 1911, p. 490. Hart, 1929, pp. 121–123.

36 Hart, 1929, pp. 136–137. Insh, 1932, pp. 184, 188–192.

37 Hart, 1929, pp. 138–145. Insh, 1932, pp. 196–198.

CHAPTER X

TWO CENTURIES OF TITANIC STRUGGLE:
A RETROSPECT

1. The Conquest of the Itzas, 1697

THE same decade which saw the defeat of the Spaniards by the French at Cartagena and the triumph of the Spaniards against the Scots at Darien saw also the last great victory won by Spanish power against a native American civilization. This last was the culmination of a long and intricate endeavor which, as it has received only the slightest attention from modern historians, deserves to be referred to briefly here.

Soon after Don Fernando Cortés had reduced the great empire of Mexico to obedience to the King of the Spains, in 1519–1524, two other conquests befell. The one was that of northern Yucatan, where the civilization of the Mayas still existed, albeit in somewhat humbled and disunited circumstances. Francisco de Montejo and his son of the same name, originally sent to Yucatan by Governor Diego Velásquez of Cuba, made the northern part of the peninsula of Yucatan into an orderly Spanish-Indian province between the years 1526 and 1545. The other conquest was that of Guatemala by Pedro de Alvarado in 1523–1524.

As a result of the labors of Cortés, of the Montejos, and of Alvarado Mexico, northern Yucatan, and central Guatemala were definitely parts of the Spanish empire by 1545. Between them, however, there remained a vast area where dwelt refugee remnants of the once great Maya folk. Of these remnants the most important was the miniature kingdom of the Itzas of Tayasal, on Lake Peten and in the country round about, where the reigning house of Canek maintained a simulacrum of the ancient pyramid-studded and stone-built cities which had flourished of old in Yucatan and in Guatemala. The Itzas, safe in their forested wilds, long withstood the encroachments of Spanish power. Both from the north and from the south efforts were made to bring them under the sway of Spain. Neither soldiers nor priests, nor yet both together, could manage to deprive them of their prideful and often insolent independence so that, in 1695, the Itzas were still ruled only by their pagan king, Canek, from his strongly fortified island of Tayasal rising from the water of Lake Peten.

One factor in the non-success of the Spaniards in their attempts to break up the Itza kingdom was the King of Spain's prohibition against the use of war for their undoing. It was the policy of Spain that spiritual methods only be employed to bring these pagan Indians into the fold of the Church and under the civil authority. And so, in the end, it was done, with the powerful aid of an economic motive backed up by military force, as we shall see.

The religious leader in the final conquest of the Itzas was the Franciscan friar, Father Andrés de Avendaño y Lóyola. Accompanied by various religious men of his own and of other Orders Father Avendaño made two attempts to reach the domain of King Canek, Lord of the Itzas of Tayasal, with the idea of bringing him and his people to the Faith. From the beginning Father Avendaño was backed up by the civil authority in Yucatan from which he received for his aid and defense a force of 115 Spanish soldiers under the command of Captain Alonso García de Paredes.

The civil leader of the enterprise was Don Martín de Ursúa y Arizmendi, Count of Lizárraga Vengoa, governor of Yucatan. This gallant Basque gentleman had written a letter to the King of Spain (Charles II), from Mexico, on June 30th, 1692, offering to open up a royal road from Yucatan to Guatemala and to bring the Itzas and other independent tribes to obedience to the King and to the Faith, all this to be done at Ursúa's own expense. The King, or rather his government in the person of the Count of Adanero, then

President of the Royal Council of the Indies, promptly accepted the generous offer of Ursúa and issued orders to all authorities in Yucatan and Guatemala and other parts to cooperate with him to the fullest possible extent. Ursúa, in turn, gave Father Avendaño and the other friars all the authority he could.

The first journey of Avendaño and his colleagues was intended by Ursúa to be in the nature of an embassy to Canek, King of the Itzas, calling upon him to become a Christian and a vassal of the King of Spain. The expedition departed from Merida on June 2nd, 1695, and passed southwards through wild and difficult country covered with forests and only scantily supplied with water. García de Paredes and his soldiers, who should have aided and protected the friars, constantly made trouble for them by raiding the Indians along the route and stealing their possessions. All efforts to change the behavior of the soldiers were vain even though Father Avendaño frequently reminded them of the King's laws and of the wishes of Governor Ursúa. When, in July, the town of Tzucthok, far in the south of Yucatan was reached the violent actions of García de Paredes and his men made Father Avendaño and the other priests give up all hope of being able to bring the Itzas to the Faith by peaceful means. After a conference they decided to return to Merida without the troublesome soldiers and with the idea of finally reaching the Itzas by some other route, and without troublesome military companions. The return journey was terrible, dangerous, and slow, so that they reached Merida only on September 16th, 1695.

Finding themselves deserted by the friars, García de Paredes and his men hastened to send back to Merida abusive letters containing all sorts of charges against them. Neither Governor Ursúa nor the religious authorities took these accusations seriously, and both increased their efforts on behalf of the friars.

Accordingly, on December 13th, 1695, Father Avendaño and his companion friars departed again from Merida. They followed the same route as before and found García de Paredes at an Indian town called Batcab, where some work on the projected road was being done. The friars pushed onwards in an easterly direction to another town known as Chuntucí where, on January 6th, 1696, Mass was celebrated by them. A week or so later Avendaño and his party arrived at Tayasal where they had satisfactory dealings with Canek, but where some of that king's subjects seemed very decidedly to hate the newcomers. It seems clear that there were two opinions among the Itzas at this time concerning what policy should be pursued. King Canek and his party were all for accepting the inevitability of Spanish rule with the best grace possible; but the opposite party was strongly determined to resist it to the end.

Both the Christian priest, Avendaño, and the pagan king, Canek, were men of tact and patience; moreover, both were gentlemen of honor. Consequently they could understand one another. The priest and his colleagues, all well versed in the Maya tongue, expounded the Christian doctrines to the Indians as clearly as circumstances permitted. For a long time, however, they could not persuade any of their hearers to accept baptism. Whenever the Fathers suggested it, the Indians always replied, "We will answer soon." At length King Canek offered one of his own children as a subject for the still incomprehensible ceremony. As soon as they saw that, far from being the horrid and gruesome sort of rite that they had imagined, it was merely a pouring of water upon the head and a giving of a new name, the Indians hastened to bring hundreds of their children to be baptized. All this befell on the steps of a pagan temple upon the island of Tayasal, towards the end of January, 1696.

Father Avendaño was not content with merely baptizing a few hundred little Indians. His aim was to bring Canek and all his nation of some 80,000 people to the Faith. For this he prepared the way by interpreting certain ancient Indian prophecies to the people in such a way as to make it seem that the time was at hand when great changes would come to pass among them. Still the hostile party resisted, so much so that a plot was formed to kill and eat the friars as they were departing from the Itza country. But King Canek himself saved them by bidding them to depart by the end of the lake opposite to that by which they had entered, where their ill-wishers were lurking.

The advice was good, but it led Father Avendaño and the other friars into terribly difficult country to the east and north of Lake Peten. There they floundered onwards as best they could for many days through bogs and through thorny thickets. Their course lay first towards the north and then turned westward. After some time had thus been spent, Father Avendaño sent two of his younger and stronger colleagues ahead in quest of aid. With some faithful Indian servants brought from Merida the heroic Avendaño, now in a fearfully fatigued condition, with wounds from thorns all over his sadly under-nourished body, pushed on until he could advance no more. He then sent the Indians from him, bidding them to save themselves if they could, and to leave him to the will of God. Reluctantly they departed from him, leaving him under a tree. Solacing himself by reading his Breviary, and preparing to meet his death in a holy mood, he was according to his own narrative, miraculously nourished by a fruit brought to him by a squirrel, there being no fruit near at hand.

As so often happens to men lost in the woods, Father Avendaño was in reality close to aid. His Indians had not been gone from him more than an hour and a half when they suddenly came to the town of Chuntucí. There they found other Indians who returned with them in quest of Father Avendaño. With a little difficulty they found him and rescued him early the next day. With tears streaming down their faces they greeted their well-loved pastor and, wrapping his chilled frame in warm blankets, they placed him in a hammock which they had brought and carefully bore him to Chuntucí, where he arrived safely on Septuagesima Sunday, February 19th, 1696, at about three o'clock in the afternoon. After a period of recuperation he returned to Merida by the road which he had already traversed.

On arriving at Merida Father Avendaño was astonished to learn that, during his absence, Governor Ursúa had received an embassy from King Canek headed by a nephew of that woodland chieftain. The ambassador, Can by name, was accompanied by his brother and by several other Indians of high rank as well as by a large retinue. In the name of their Lord, King Canek of the Itzas of Tayasal, they proffered to Governor Ursúa a richly wrought diadem of exquisite feather-work as a symbol of Canek's submission to the Catholic King of Spain. The feather-work diadem was accepted by Governor Ursúa with appropriate ceremony, and afterwards he and all the most distinguished Spaniards in Merida, both clergy and laymen, entertained the Indian envoys with all possible splendor in recognition of the importance of the event.

Of this embassy and submission Father Avendaño had heard no hint or rumor while he was staying with King Canek on the island of Tayasal. Consequently, on learning of it after his return to Merida, he was filled with suspicion as to the sincerity of the gesture. In this he did less than justice to his Indian friend who, in all likelihood, had refrained from mentioning what he had done for the reason that he greatly feared the strong anti-Spanish party among his subjects.

Governor Ursúa, after entertaining Ambassador Can and the other envoys right royally, and after they had all been solemnly baptized, sent them homewards with suitable messages to Canek concerning his submission to the King of Spain and concerning the Christian religion. Ursúa followed this up by sending orders to Captain García de Paredes to hasten the building of the road as much as possible. At the same time, the governor determined that he would take the leadership of the matter into his own hands.

This decision was strengthened by the receipt of encouraging letters from King Charles II and from the Count of Adanero, dated from the Palace of Buen Retiro in Madrid on May 29th, 1696. They reached Ursúa at Merida towards the end of the year, and were accompanied by ample authorization for the continuance of the work begun with respect to the building of the road from Merida to Lake Peten and thence to Guatemala, and with respect to the conquest of the Itzas. All officials in New Spain and elsewhere were bidden to do everything in their power to help Ursúa in his labors.

Accordingly, Governor Ursúa took personal charge of operations. From Campeche on the west coast of Yucatan he entered the country as far as Tzucthok. Work on the road was pushed ahead rapidly by means of labor drawn from many villages of Yucatan so that, when Ursúa reached the Lake of Peten in March, 1697, it was already completed to that point, its northern end being in Yucatan. A galley and some smaller boats had been built upon the lake in order to protect the Spaniards, numbering only about 180, but well armed, and to give them prestige among the Indians.

It was now March 10th, 1697. Governor Ursúa and his officers, soldiers, and accompanying priests made their camp beside the lake. It was quite clear that there was much excitement among the Indians, but King Canek himself was not to be seen. The truth of the matter was that the anti-Spanish party among the Itzas had temporarily got the upper hand and, while holding Canek a prisoner in his own palace, they sought to force the Spaniards into a fight. From all quarters they came in their canoes and arrayed in war-paint, brandishing their weapons and shouting insults. The Spaniards, on their side, were eager to join battle, and only the iron discipline of Ursúa prevented their doing so. In spite of the warlike advice which all his officers and men gave him Governor Ursúa was determined not to fire upon the subjects of Canek, now a vassal of his own King, Charles, until absolutely obliged to do so.

At last, on March 13th, 1697, Governor Ursúa and his followers boarded their vessels with the intention of sailing over to the island of Tayasal. It was urgently necessary that they get into touch with King Canek so that the situation might be put in good order. Thousands of menacing Indians in great numbers of canoes thronged about the Spanish boats. Soon the Indians began to shoot their arrows and to hurl their javelins with fatal aim. Presently the Spanish musketry spat forth its deadly fire, turning all the boldness of the Indians into panic. Sharp, fierce, and short was the strife. Within an hour or two of its commencement the Spanish standard was unfurled over the palace where King Canek had ruled. Tayasal and all its realm was a possession of Charles II of Spain.

The next day solemn Mass was celebrated in the newly purified temple of ancient idols whose cult was driven forth into still more remote places. Before long King Canek, having got away from captivity among the irreconcilables who had taken him over to the mainland, came with the High Priest of Idolatry and other chief men of the Itzas to make their homage to Ursúa in the name of King Charles and to be baptized into the Christian Faith. In doing so Canek made it clear that, when he sent his feather-work crown to Merida by his kinsman, Can, he had been sincere, but that afterwards his opponents had overpowered him for a time.

Before long the road was completed to Guatemala. In this manner Spain consummated her control over what had been the last of the unconquered native civilizations of America. Thereafter, the former realm of Canek became a peaceful and productive Spanish-American province living under a new rule and under a higher Faith than any known there before.[1]

For us the significance of the conquest of the Itzas is this: It shows that Spain, even in the dark period when the Hapsburg dynasty was drawing towards an inglorious end, still stood by the ancient theory that the spiritual conquest of Indian populations was fully as important as military conquest. It also shows that, at need, two hundred or so Spaniards could still vanquish an Indian nation numbering many tens of thousands. This, indeed, was done within a few months of the time when a French expedition captured Cartagena. It was followed in a few years by the Spanish victory over the Scots at Darien. In short, although the Hapsburg system was rotting at its very centre, the colonial subjects of Spain were still capable of being honorably beaten in

a fair fight and also of winning against other adversaries. The
spirit of the Spanish people still lived, and was often strongest
in the places where strength could least be expected. In the
case of the Itza conquest a generous and far-seeing soldier,
working in conjunction with particularly self-sacrificing
priests, sought to serve his king by building a much needed
artery of commerce and by putting an end to a survival of
idolatry which was an insult to all subjects of Spain.

2.   Certain Fundamental Aspects of Spain's Colonial Career

In the conquest of the Itzas, as we have seen, religious and
civil authority worked hand in hand from the beginning to
the end of the enterprise. In a word, Spain in the 1690s was
as true to her special tradition in matters colonial as she had
been at any time during the previous 200 years. It is well
that we refresh our memories as to the nature of that special
tradition.

As told in Chapter I, Columbus's venture into the unknown west followed immediately upon the close of a long-
sustained conflict in Spain against the infidel Moors. That
conflict, involving both inimical civilizations and mutually
repugnant religions, was for the Spaniards in the nature of a
crusade, and as such it filled the entire Spanish people with a
fierceness and a pride which they have not yet wholly lost
and which supplied them with a powerful motive throughout their colonial career in the New World.

On arriving in the Caribbean the Spaniards found themselves amid peoples and scenes which, though utterly strange
to them, were yet familiar in the sense that they constituted
a world which obviously required something of the same
crusading treatment that had been meted out to the Moors
during so many centuries. The low-cultured folk of the Caribbean islands first visited were from the outset a serious problem for the Spaniards. There the Indians were, in great numbers, with their fantastic and sometime repellent customs and

their unheard-of surroundings, and, above all, with their glittering golden baubles which to them were pretty toys and nothing more. What should be done with such people? How should they be ruled? How should they be put to work in spite of their indolent habits? Had they souls? If so, how were they to be saved?

From the very first the Catholic Church and the Catholic Sovereigns together on the one hand and the bulk of the Spaniards in America on the other answered these questions in their several ways. Church and sovereign held that the Indians certainly had souls and that they could be saved only by instruction in and acceptance of the Christian Faith. Church and sovereigns also held that the Indians must work, but not under unduly severe conditions, for the glory of God and for the support of the king. In order to combine the necessity for regulating the labor of the Indians with the no less pressing necessity for instructing them in the Faith, the *encomienda* was developed. Through this institution, peculiar to Spanish America, persons whom the king wished to favor received the right to take the tribute of certain allotments of Indians who worked under their own chiefs, and in return for this privilege the holder of an *encomienda* was obliged to provide for the spiritual and temporal welfare of his Indians. There were many provisions connected with grants of this kind intended to preserve the Indians from ill-treatment and to ensure their being well taught in matters of the Faith. In the spirit and form in which it was planned, the *encomienda* was a generous and high-minded institution altogether more benign than slavery, its only alternative short of systematic extermination of the natives.[2]

Such, in brief, were the theoretical attitude and policy of Church and State with regard to the native population of Spain's America. The reality was the work of the men of many characters and qualities who went to America, either as officials and representatives of the Crown or of the Church, or else as settlers. Although there were numerous individuals of intelligence and worth among them, it is tragically true that the great majority of Spaniards in America were persons who, having gone thither in quest of riches, scrupled not to pervert the *encomienda* and other institutions benevolently conceived in order to serve their own rapacity at the expense of the Indians. The dolorous contrast between the benign intentions of Church and State and the malign practice of all too many Spanish settlers in America sounds a tragic note throughout colonial history in the New World. Yet, again and again, it is offset and at times drowned by a glorious and faithful fiulfill-ment of the laws of Both Majesties—Divine and Kingly—so that often we see unrolling before us scenes of heroic explora-tion and audacious conquest conducted with all the fire and devotion which had marked the centuries-long wars of Reconquest against the Moors in Spain. True, in many of the wars which Spanish conquerors waged against Indian nations in order that a Christian and Spanish empire might be built up, there were countless cruelties committed, sometimes on one side, sometimes on the other. But as often as not these were the result of military necessity rather than of innate ruthlessness. Inevitably, when a people of advanced civiliza-tion sets out to found a colony in the land of a people less advanced, that colony is raised upon blood, grief, and shat-tered freedom. Any other European people placed in the situa-tion of the conquering Spaniards would have behaved both as well and as ill as did they. There is a world of truth in the couplet:

> Estas maldades fueron la saña
> de todo un tiempo y no de España.
>
> (These wickednesses were the fury
> Of a whole age, not of Spain only.)[3]

With all its shortcomings Spain's rule in those parts of America which she occupied most intensively, and held against all foes for three hundred years, resulted in a more perfect preservation of the ancient native race of America than in the parts ruled by any other European nation. It so happened that none of the regions where the Spanish-Indian colonial culture grew to greatest strength is suited by nature to wholly White Race occupation. One tries in vain to imagine a Mexico or a Peru inhabited only by folk of European blood. The very quality of the sunlight there makes it difficult if not impossible for men of pure white blood to perform for long periods the more arduous kinds of toil. In the Caribbean islands the native race was early exterminated because the Spaniards had not yet mastered the technique of building a bi-racial society having a culture in part derived from native sources and in part from Spanish. To the extermination of the Caribbean Indians their own unrobust physique and the tenuous character of their culture greatly contributed so that their fate was very different from that of the more civilized populations of Mexico and Peru. In the islands Negroes soon replaced the vanished Indians, and all the Europeans there, the English at Providence and Jamaica, the French in Saint Domingue and the islands held by them, as well as the Spaniards in all the lower-lying regions around the Caribbean, yielded to the inevitable in relying upon Negroes for manual labor.

In Mexico and throughout the Andean region the native element in the population remained a large proportion of the whole and, under Spanish rule, the Indians not only survived but increased and formed an integral part of colonial society under conditions which permitted the most capable of them to hold respectable positions.[4] In this respect Spanish America differed from and was superior to those parts of America held by other European nations. One can only guess what the results would have been if France or England had taken the regions held by Spain, but all things considered it is likely that the English would have pushed the Indians into the eastern jungles and replaced them with Negro slaves, and that the French would have built up an even better bi-racial civilization than did the Spaniards, doing so with far less hardship to the native element.

3. Contrasting Governments in Europe: Spain, England, France

So far in this Chapter we have considered the internal character of Spain's colonial system, particularly with regard to the Indians. We must now give some thought to the nature of the Spanish government at home and we must compare it with its chief rivals.

Without plunging ourselves into the intricate history of monarchy in Spain prior to the final overthrow of the Moors, at Granada in 1492, we may remind ourselves that, in the time of Ferdinand and Isabella, the formerly numerous and disunited kingdoms of Christian Spain were drawn together under central authority in the persons of those Catholic sovereigns. Their power represented not only a triumph of kingship over the forces of disunion latent in the ancient feudal nobility of the Spanish realms but also a partial victory of royalty over other local authorities such as municipalities and parliaments.

In Charles I (grandson of Ferdinand and Isabella), who reigned from 1516 to 1556, Castile and all the other Spanish kingdoms had both their first Hapsburg monarch and their first really absolute sovereign. From his day onwards to the Napoleonic period, the king was undoubtedly the paramount and guiding force in Spain and in Spanish possessions everywhere. Under Philip II (1556–1598) Spanish kingship reached its apogee of splendor and might. The once well nigh indepent nobles were rendered politically impotent and looked to the king for leave to seek glory by serving him. At the same time, the once influential municipalities and parliaments spoke humbly when they spoke at all. The later Hapsburg kings of Spain, Philip III (1598–1621), Philip IV (1621–1665), and Charles II (1665–1700), were a series of progressively worthless men whose vast prerogative was largely suffered to lapse into the hands of favorites and ministers, usually with disastrous consequences. Nevertheless, the august supremacy of the Crown remained unshaken and unquestioned.[5]

In England the course of governmental development was exactly the opposite to what it was in Spain. Henry VIII was the last English king whose power verged upon the absolute, and even he had to consider Parliament sometimes. His daughter, Elizabeth, sometimes achieved a *quasi*-absolutism, but it was due to her own amazing skill in dominating parliamentary and other opposition rather than to her constitutional position. Indeed, the crux of the contrast between the Spanish Hapsburg monarchy and the English monarchy was the fact that in Spain the people had no constitutional rights (having lost those which formerly, and in a regional, limited way, they had possessed), whereas in England there had been a Constitution ever since the Great Charter of 1215. From the parchment penned at Runnymede grew the liberties of England, rising age by age until, by the time of James I, the power of the king and that of his subjects was so nicely balanced that the king could rule as he listed only when he could prevent Parliament from meeting. The reign of Charles (1625–1649) was fundamentally a prolonged strife between King and Parliament, with the King's death and the triumph of Parliament at the end of it.

An important point in this connection is the fact that, in England, there has not been for many centuries a wide and impassable chasm between nobles and commoners such as many other countries have known. At Runnymede the barons were fending for the common man as much as for themselves, and, when oppression by the sovereign was in question, English nobles and English commoners fought it, almost always, shoulder to shoulder. Moreover, in England, the sons and daughters of even the highest peers have always been commoners in strict legality, using titles by courtesy only. Finally, in no country has it been so easy as in England for a man of talent to rise from humble to lofty position in society and in political life. In all this we have proof of the fundamental democracy of the English people, which is throughout history their most salient characteristic.

Midway between Spain and England, not only geographically but also in many other respects, is France. In that country, down to the first quarter of the seventeenth century, the king was hardly more than the greatest of noblemen, his authority being unquestioned only within his own domain, all the rest of the realm being held in vast feudal fiefs whose lords grudgingly accorded allegiance to the monarch. Not until the rule of Cardinal Richelieu (1624–1642) was the strength of the feudal nobility broken forever and the King of France made absolute. At no previous period had the nobility been defenders of the people as the English nobles were. Therefore, when they were bereft of all political functions, the people were merely left with one all-powerful master instead of many lesser masters. The nobles, in turn, were confronted by the choice of becoming courtiers in attendance on their king or of retiring to their estates to lead a monotonous and inelegant life as *hobereaux* (rusticated nobles, squireens). Naturally enough, all those who could do so flocked to the Court in droves, and with the king as their unquestioned lord, dispenser of all favors and privileges, they led frivolous, amorous, gaming, polished, and utterly useless lives based on the bowed shoulders of the populace.[6]

Thus France became, a full century after Spain, a monarchy no less absolute than her southern neighbor. There was, however, an enormous difference between them, typified by the contrast between the sombre, monkish majesty of the Escorial and the jovial, elegant worldliness of Versailles.

The Escorial, 745 feet by 580 feet, and containing sixteen courtyards, was built by Philip II in 1563–1584 when at the peak of his prestige. Its centre is a vast church, sedate but austere, and a great proportion of it is occupied by a monastery and by a college managed by the monks. The pantheon of the Kings of Spain is also there, a place of sad splendor with but one of its niches still unfilled. On one side of this stupendous monastery-palace is the royal residence, containing the far from luxurious chamber where, with his eyes upon the altar of the adjacent church, Philip II led his mournful and inscrutable life and conscientiously strove to rule the affairs, no matter how minute, of all his vast dominions. To stand in that bleak apartment and to visualize what the life of its inmate must have been, with its constant subjection to religious dread and its immense amount of administrative labor, is to understand, at least a little, why the Spanish empire was as it was. The keynote there is, not the glorification of kingship, but the dedication of the king to the service of God. That service, however imperfectly performed, was the central motive of the Spanish Hapsburg theory of government.

The palace of Versailles is even more vast than the Escorial. Built by Louis XIV in 1668–1689, precisely a century after its Spanish analogue, it symbolized the French type of absolutism as perfectly as the Escorial reflected the Spanish. At Versailles the atmosphere was almost deliriously mundane and madly pagan in its riot of allegorical ornamentation drawn from classic inspiration, the whole being a bright-hued and gilded setting for a monarch who thought far more of earthly splendor than of life beyond death. The chapel, far from being the centre of *this* palace, was tucked awkwardly enough into a courtyard. It was, moreover, an afterthought, built in 1699–1710, and is much more like a theatre or a salon than like a shrine where a human soul might humbly seek to know God.

There were, in short, three kinds of government behind the history of colonial America: The absolute monarchy of Spain in which the king controlled all earthly matters in the name of his master, the Almighty; the constitutional monarchy of England, resting on an increasingly broad base of popular sanctions as expressed by Parliament; and, between them, the absolute monarchy of France, not at all preoccupied with mystical religion, but practical, and chiefly interested in gaining the things of this world.

4. *The Colonial Systems of Spain, England, and France*

Politically and economically considered the fundamental contrast between the English (and by implication the Dutch) mode of colonial administration and the Spanish mode was, to use modern terms, the contrast between individualism and totalitarianism.

English and Dutch colonization were so similar that they may fairly be considered together. The major fact concerning both, as has been said, was that, although the authority of the State was in each case the theoretical source of all activity, it was in reality the initiative of private individuals or of companies which accomplished the task and which reaped the profits, the State receiving its share in the form of taxes. As Professor Andrews has made very clear, the company, in several forms which he describes, was the instrument whereby English and Dutch expansion into the Western Hemisphere was carried into effect. The companies were business enterprises designed to make money for their members through the formation of settlements overseas whence profit could be derived through trade. The companies set up colonial governments and created commercial machinery. The authority of the State was, at the beginning of the process, so slight that it could not have done what the companies did; moreover, in neither England nor in the Netherlands, did the State possess experience in rule beyond its own bournes. At the same time, the whole tendency of the age was one of expansion, both as regards the scope and volume of the mercantile activities of the peoples concerned and as regards the territories in which they carried on those activities. It was inevitable, therefore, that the Spanish claim to exclusive possession of the entire Western Hemisphere should be attacked and that, as Spain weakened, those attacks should be delivered and the territories which they won should be successfully held, not only in the regions beyond Spain's natural zone of occupation as defined on pages 19–21, but also, in the seventeenth century, in the very heart of Spain's natural zone. In the world-as-it-is might, after all, does make right, or at any rate, it makes realities paramount over theories. *Vae victis.*

Essentially, the companies, both in England and in the Netherlands, were a manifestation of a nascent trend towards democracy. True, as already said, they derived their privileges from the State; but they were not the State; rather, they were States within the State. They were machines whereby wealth arising from colonial enterprises was distributed among a large number of private persons. Sometimes they were for business only; sometimes they had a powerful religious motive working in conjunction with the business motive; but the business element was always present and very strong. As the companies grew, a process began whereby piracy, alias privateering, which had formerly been invested with high respectability and even with quasi-official standing, began very slowly to sink into disrepute with thoughtful Englishmen and Netherlanders, albeit hot-headed blades in plenty clung to it fondly still, regarding it as a glorious weapon against detested Spain. At the same time a process began whereby contraband trade began to be a chief function of the companies and to receive approbation from the State which authorized those companies.[7]

A few words must also be said of the proprietary type of English colonization. Companies were, in a sense, often proprietors, but here one has in mind the proprietary and palatine grant to an individual. In the area with which we are concerned this sort of grant was far less important and widespread than it was on the mainland of North America; there were, in fact, but two such grants in the Caribbean area, those of Carlisle and of Pembroke. In both cases the King of England arbitrarily divested himself of a portion of his royal prerogative and gave it to a subject along with a deed to the territories so conceded, thus making that subject a king in his own lands and answerable only theoretically to his sovereign. Thus we have, side by side, the trend towards democracy represented, as yet in embryonic form only, by the companies and an extraordinary assertion of kingly authority represented by the proprietary palatine grants to Carlisle and to Pembroke, which grants were probably not as altruistic as they looked on the surface.

To a Spanish king, sacred and absolute sovereign of all his

people, sole owner of all lands and wealth held by his subjects in America, ultimate fount of authority on all questions whether great or small concerning those lands and their inhabitants, neither colonization by companies nor colonization by proprietors would have been conceivable. Every benefit which Spaniards derived from their activities in America came to them as a personal "grace" from the king; title to all their possessions was derived direct from him and sooner or later reverted to him; every enterprise undertaken by them was a royal enterprise in which the men engaged in it were acting as emissaries and servants of the king; and the king was not only the ruler of the nation, but also the head of the Church in his dominions by virtue of concession from the Pope.

In this last point we see one more startling contrast between the Spanish and the English (and the Dutch) philosophies of colonization. In the America of Spain the Church was all-pervasive, omnipresent. A high proportion of all that was done in America by Spaniards was done for the Church and by churchmen. Because, from the Spanish point of view, it was imperatively necessary to bring the native populations within the fold of the Church as speedily as possible, tremendous journeys were made and enormous perils were confronted. The purpose was that of carrying the Faith of Christ and the rule of the king as far afield as might be. In this we have the explanation of the fact that in Spanish America there never was a frontier or a pioneer fringe in the sense that those terms are used in English America. Not only in theory but also very largely in fact when the Spaniards possessed themselves of a country both the Faith and the royal authority were established therein almost immediately, reaching even into remote districts where as yet there were few Christian settlers. The manner in which the Inca-ship and other native political structures became appanages of the Crown of Castile is illustrative of this truth; so also is the creation of bishoprics extending over vast areas even before any missionary work had been performed within them. The point is that the existence of those bishoprics, at first a theory rather than a fact, in itself constituted an acknowledgment of the obligations inherent in the royal office towards the native Americans, and, equally, it constituted a promise to fulfill that obligation as rapidly and as thoroughly as circumstances permitted. Consequently, there was no such thing as a frontier line beyond which the royal power and the royal responsibility did not pretend to extend.

Nor should we neglect the position of France with respect to colonization in tropical America at this period. France, no less than Spain, was a Catholic nation, and one in which, thanks to Richelieu, the royal authority was rapidly becoming supreme and all-powerful. Therefore we need not be surprised to find that the strong commercial sense of the French was rendered operative by a form of company rule, varied for a time by a version of proprietary rule. It was done, however, with two major differences from the English mode. In the first place, the Crown, through its ministers, formed the companies and afterwards controlled their every act with a rigidity unknown in the English companies; in the second place, the attitude of the French government and of the Church in France towards the Indians was one of sympathy and love which made it no less imperative in French eyes than in Spanish that the natives encountered should be brought to the Faith. Indeed, because of the special graciousness, flexibility, and resourcefulness which characterize the French intellect, coupled with an innate distaste for violence, harshness, cruelty, or any other extremity, the French made, by gentle means, far more headway among the native peoples whom they encountered than did the more vehement and unbending Spaniards. From the standpoint of relations with the Indians, as well as from that of colonial administration the French stood midway between the Spanish and the English positions, and their rule was better than that of either Spain or England.

5. A Backward Glance at Two Centuries of Colonial Rivalry

The several colonial systems being so different among themselves, and the rivalries of the respective nations being so keen, it inevitably followed that strife between them arose and remained active throughout the colonial period.

In the course of this book it has been shown how Spain, in the very beginning of her colonial expansion, tolerated if she did not encourage, participation by foreigners in her enterprises. It soon became apparent, however, that if Spain were to remain paramount in her chosen part of America, foreigners and foreign influence, including foreign trade, must be rigidly excluded. Therefore, soon after 1525, the Spanish monopolistic system came into being. Against it the rival nations fought incessantly, by piracy, by contraband trade, by diplomacy, and by openly declared warfare. In all this, as we have seen, there was a noteworthy trend from the destructive methods of the corsairs, backed by their home governments, to the saner methods of creating colonies and of fostering trade which, as time went by, was protected more and more by the regular fighting forces of the nations concerned. Each advantage won was followed up by diplomatic adjustments so that, in time, Spain was forced to acknowledge the right of other nations to form colonies of their own in places which she had not effectively occupied.

In one respect the Spanish concept of colonial administration was vindicated. Her monopolistic and exclusive policy, against which her rivals contended so long, was in the end imitated by them to some extent. The French government had its Royal Company for the exploitation of colonies; the English and the Dutch had their Navigation Laws designed to protect their respective shipping interests from foreign intrusion. It became, in short, a fixed and general principle that colonies should trade only with their mother countries.

The territorial losses of Spain in America were, after all, insignificant. In the Caribbean, so long the focus of her rivals' envy, she lost only unoccupied islands at first, and later only Jamaica, but weakly held, to the English, and western Hispaniola to the French. On the mainland she lost nothing during the period prior to 1700. To all intents and purposes the chief islands of the Caribbean—Cuba, eastern Hispaniola (Santo Domingo), and Puerto Rico—and practically all the continental regions around that sea are today predominantly Hispanic or Indo-Hispanic in language, customs, and general civilization. Her struggle was long, stubborn, and, despite many grave reverses and disasters, very largely successful.

*   *   *   *   *

On the night of October 31st, 1700, Spain, personified by that piteous creature, Charles II of the House of Hapsburg, lay prone in a bed over which death was impatiently hovering. Yet it was a bed draped with flags that were banners, and the banners were fluttering already in the new breeze arising in readiness for a new day. Through the close-pressing gloom peopled with gruesome phantoms and terrors conjured up by a superstition indescribable, tumultuous echoes of distant warfare subtly stirred: the cannon at Cartagena, the guns at Caledonia, the staccato musketry and prayers of triumphant thanksgiving at Tayasal—all made mirages of sound in that Spanish darkness prior to the dawn. In Charles's fear-ridden mind the proud thought may have lurked, half formed and never expressed: "We of the Spanish Hapsburgs have fought our enemies staunchly during two hundred years, yet they have taken from us half of Hispaniola—St. Christopher—Martinique—Guadeloupe—a few other islets—and Jamaica. But they will take no more." On the breath of a quavering sigh the King's soul took flight, and a bugle-call rang through the expectant palace. Taps? No! Reveille!

Notes to Chapter X

[1] The foregoing is based upon my book, *History of the Spanish Conquest of Yucatan and of the Itzas,* in Vol. VII of the Papers of the Peabody Museum, Cambridge, Massachusetts, 1917, in which work many authorities ancient and modern are cited and quoted; and also upon Francisco de Elorza y Rada, *Nobiliario de el valle de la Valdorba,* published at Pamplona in 1714, pp. 207 to 279 of that work containing the *Conquista de la Provincia Del Ytza, en la Nueva España, por el Conde de Lizarraga Vengoa.* Of those pages a facsimile edition, with a translation into English by Philip Ainsworth Means, was brought out in two volumes in Paris by Les Éditions Genet, in 1930.

[2] Bourne, 1904, pp. 206–211. Simpson, 1929, especially pp. 30–33. Hanke, 1935, Chs. i and ii.

[3] Author unknown to me, and also to Professors J. D. M. Ford and Guillermo Rivera, of Harvard University.

[4] Angel Rosenblat, in the careful study already cited on p. 25, calculates that in 1570 the indigenous population of Mexico was 3,500,000, that of Ecuador, Peru, and Bolivia together being 2,600,000. In 1825 there were 3,700,000 Indians and about 1,000,000 mestizos (Indian-White mixture) in Mexico and, in the three Andean countries, 2,830,000 Indians with about 800,-000 mestizos. Needless to say, these figures are only approximations; but they serve to show that the Indian population at least held its own in Mexico and the Andean area during the colonial period and that it also mingled with the white upper class to a considerable extent.

[5] As Spanish history is less well known to Americans than is either English or French, it is well to cite here several easily found books in which plentiful source materials are referred to. See, therefore: Peers, 1929, Ch. ii (by the Rev. H. J. Chaytor), and ii (by E. A. Peers); Chapman, 1918, Chs. xviii–xxvi; Sedgwick, 1925, Chs. xiv–xxxvi.

[6] A sagacious French ecclesiastic, the Abbé Coyer, perceiving the utter uselessness of the French nobility, wrote a book in which he suggested that noblemen be encouraged to go into trade and into empire-building. Very little, if anything, came of this sane hint. See: *La Noblesse commerçante,* London and Paris, 1756. See also, Saint-Léger and Sagnac, 1935, especially pp. 167–207.

[7] On all this see: Andrews, 1934, Chs. iii and iv.

BIBLIOGRAPHY

BIBLIOGRAPHY

ABBAD Y LASIERRA, Friar Iñigo:
Historia geográfica, civil y natural de la isla de San Juan Bautista de Puerto Rico, . . . Puerto Rico, 1866. (First edition, 1788.)

ABBOTT, Wilbur Cortez:
The Expansion of Europe. New York, 1924. 2 vols.

ABERCROMBY, John:
A Study of the Ancient Speech of the Canary Islanders. Harvard African Studies, I, 95–129. Cambridge, Mass., 1917.

ADAMS, James Truslow:
The Founding of New England. Boston, 1921.

ALCEDO, Antonio de:
The Geographical and Historical Dictionary of America and the West Indies. Edited, with additions, by G. A. Thompson. London, 1812–1815. 5 vols. and Atlas.

ALCEDO Y HERRERA, Dionisio de:
Aviso histórico, político, geográphico, . . . del Peru, Tierra Firme, Chile, y Nuevo Reyno de Granada, . . . Madrid, 1740.

ALTAMIRA Y CREVEA, Rafael:
Historia de España y de la civilización española. Barcelona, 1913–1914. 4 vols.

ANDERSON, C. L. G.:
Old Panama and Castilla del Oro. Washington, 1911.

ANDREWS, Charles M.:
Our Earliest Colonial Settlements. New York. (N. Y. University Press, 1933.)
The Colonial Period of American History. I. The Settlements. New Haven. (Yale University Press, 1934.)

ANDREWS, William Loring:
New Amsterdam, New Orange, New York. New York, 1897.

ANGELIS, Pedro de:
Collección de obras y documentos relativos a la historia antigua y moderna de las provincias del Río de la Plata.
Buenos Aires, 1835–1837. 6 vols., folio. (Reissued in 1910.)

ARGÜELLO, Friar Tomás de:
Monarchia de España. MS. 9475, Biblioteca Nacional, Madrid, 1681.

ARTÍÑANO Y DE GALDÁCANO, Gervasio de:
Historia del comercio con las Indias durante el dominio de los Austrias. Barcelona, 1917.

ASPINALL, Sir Algernon:
The Pocket Guide to the West Indies. London, 1931.

BARALT, Rafael María; and DIAZ, Ramón:
Resúmen de la historia de Venezuela. Curaçao, 1887. 3 vols. (1st edn., Paris, 1841, 3 vols.)

BARBOUR, James Samuel:
A History of William Patterson and the Darien Company. Edinburgh and London, 1907.

BARLOW, Roger:
A Brief Summe of Geographie. Edited by E. G. R. Taylor. London. (Hakluyt Society, 1932.)

BAUDIN, Louis:
L'empire socialiste des Inka. Paris. (Institute d'Ethnologie, 1928.)

BEAZLEY, C. Raymond:
John and Sebastian Cabot. The Discovery of North America. London, 1898.

BEER, George Louis:
The Origins of the British Colonial System. 1578–1660. New York, 1908.
The Old Colonial System. 1660–1754. New York, 1912. 2 vols.

BELLOC, Hilaire:
Cromwell. Philadelphia and London, 1934.

BELTRÁN Y RÓZPIDE, Ricardo:
Cristóbal Colón y Cristóforo Colombo. Madrid, 1918.
América en tiempo de Felipe II según

el cosmógrafo-cronista Juan López de Velasco. Madrid, 1927.

BENSON, E. F.:
Sir Francis Drake. New York and London, 1927.

BERTONI, Moises Santiago:
La civilizacion guarani. Puerto Bertoni, Paraguay, 1922.

BEUCHAT, Henri:
Manuel d'Archéologie Américaine. Paris, 1912.

BISHOP, Morris:
The Odyssey of Cabeza de Vaca. New York, 1933.

BLANCO FOMBONA, RUFINO:
El conquistador español del siglo XVI. Madrid, 1922.

BLANCO, TOMÁS:
Prontuario histórico de Puerto Rico. Madrid, 1935.

BOGOTTE, Félix E.:
Colón y su descubrimiento. Caracas, 1904–1905. 3 vols.

BOURNE, Edward Gaylord:
Spain in America. New York ana London, 1904.
The Voyages of Columbus and of John Cabot. New York. (Scribners, 1906.)

BRADFORD, William:
History of Plymouth Plantation. Edited by William T. Davis. New York. (Scribners, 1908.)

BRAU, Salvador:
Historia de Puerto Rico. New York, 1904.
La colonización de Puerto Rico. San Juan, Puerto Rico 1930.

BREBNER, John Bartlet:
The Explorers of North America, 1492–1806. New York, 1933. (The Pioneer Histories.)

BREVOORT, James Carson:
Verrazano the Navigator. New York, 1874.

BRIDGES, The Rev. George Wilson:
The Annals of Jamaica. London, 1827–1828. 2 vols.

BUCHAN, John:
Oliver Cromwell. Boston, 1934.

BURNEY, James:
History of the Buccaneers of America. London, 1912. (Reprinted from the 1816 edition.)

CALZADA, Rafael:
La Patria de Colón. Buenos Aires, 1920.

CASANOVA, Abbé Martin:
La vérité sur l'origine et la patrie de Christofe Colom. Bastía, 1880.

CASAS, Bishop Bartolomé de las:
Historia de las Indias. Ed. by the Marqués de la Fuensanta del Valle and José Sancho Rayón. Madrid, 1875–1876. 5 vols.

CASTELLANOS, Juan de:
Primera Parte, de las Elegias de Varones Ilustres de Indias. Madrid. (Viuda de Alonzo Gomez, 1589.)

CASTILLA, Julián de: See Wright, 1923.

CAULIN, Father Antonio de:
Historia Coro-Graphica Natural y Evangelica de la Nueva Andalucia, Provincias de Cumaná, Guayana y Vertientes del Rio Orinoco; . . . Madrid, 1779.

CHAMPLAIN, Samuel de:
A Narrative of a Voyage to the West Indies and Mexico in the Years 1599–1602. Transl. by Alice Wilmere; ed. by Norton Shaw. London. (Hakluyt Society, 1859.)
Œuvres. Ed. by Abbé C.-H. Laverdière. Quebec, 1870. 6 vols.
The Works of . . . Ed. by H. P. Biggar. Toronto. (The Champlain Society, 1922–1933.) 5 vols. and Portfolio.

CHAPMAN, Charles Edward:
A History of Spain. New York, 1918.
Colonial Hispanic America: A History. New York, 1933.

CHARLEVOIX, Father Pierre-François-Xavier de:
Histoire de l'Isle Espagnole ou de S. Domingue. Paris. (Hippolyte-Louis Guerin, 1730–1731.) 2 vols.

CHEYNEY, Edward Potts:
European Background of American History, 1300–1600. New York, 1904.

CHIDSEY, Donald Barr:
Sir Walter Raleigh, That Damned Upstart. New York, 1931.

CHURCH, George Earl:
The Aborigines of South America. London, 1912.

CIEZA DE LEÓN, Pedro de:
The War of Chupas. Transl. and ed. by Sir Clements R. Markham. London. (Hakluyt Society, 1918.)

COLL Y TOSTE, Cayetano:
Colón en Puerto Rico. Puerto Rico, 1893.

CONSTANTIN-WEYER, M.:
Champlain. Paris, 1931.

CORBETT, Julian S.:
Drake and the Tudor Navy. London and New York, 1898. 2 vols.
The Successors of Drake. London and New York, 1900.

CORTÉS, Fernando:
The Letters of Fernando Cortés . . . to the Emperor Charles V. Transl. and ed. by Francis Augustus MacNutt. New York, 1908. 2 vols.

[CROMWELL, OLIVER:]
A Declaration of His Highness, By the Advice of his Council; Setting forth, On the Behalf of this Commonwealth, the Justice of their Cause against Spain. London. (Henry Hills and John Field, 1655.) Dated Friday October 26th, 1655. (Copy in The John Carter Brown Library.)

CRONAU, Rudolf:
The Discovery of America and the Landfall of Columbus. New York, 1923.

CUNDALL, Frank:
Studies in Jamaica History. London, 1900.

CUNDALL, Frank; and PIETERSZ, Joseph L:
Jamaica under the Spaniards. Kingston. (Institute of Jamaica, 1919.)

CÚNEO-VIDAL, Rómulo:
Historia de las guerras de los últimos Incas Peruanos contra el poder español. Barcelona, 1925.
Vida del conquistador del Perú Don Francisco Pizarro y de sus hermanos Hernando, Juan y Gonzalo Pizarro y Francisco Martín de Alcántara. Barcelona, 1925a.

CUNNINGHAM, Charles Henry:
The Audiencia in the Spanish Colonies. Berkeley. (University of California, 1919.)

DAMPIER, William:
A New Voyage Round the World. Ed. by Sir Albert Gray. London. (The Argonaut Press, 1927.)

DAU, Frederick W.:
Florida Old and New. New York and London, 1934.

DELGADO CAPEÁNS, Father Ricardo:
Un problema histórico europeo relativo al descubridor del Nuevo Mundo. Bol. de la Acad. Nac. de Historia, IX, 208–220. Quito, 1924.

DIAZ DE GUZMAN, Rui:
Historia Argentina del descubrimiento, población y conquista de las provincias del Rio de la Plata. In vol. I of Angelis, which see. (Written about 1612.) 1835.

DÍAZ DEL CASTILLO, Bernal:
A True History of the Conquest of New Spain. Transl. and ed. by Alfred Percival Maudslay. London. (Hakluyt Society, 1908–1916.) 5 vols.

DIAZ PIMIENTA, Francisco:
Relacion del Svcesso qve tvvo . . . en la Isla de santa Catalina. . . Madrid. (Iuan Sanchez, 1642.)
Relacion del Svcesso qve tvvo . . . en la Isla de S. Catalina. . . Seville. (Francisco de Lyra, 1642a.)
(Copies of these rare and informative items exist in The John Carter Brown Library.)

DIXON, Roland Burrage:
The Building of Cultures. New York and London. (Scribners, 1928.)

DNB—Symbol used to indicate *Dictionary of National Biography*, London.

DOMÍNGUEZ, Luis L.:
The Conquest of the River Plate (1535–1555). London. (Hakluyt Society, 1891.)

DOMÍNGUEZ, Manuel:
El Chaco. Rev. del Instituto Paraguayo, IV, 14–65. Asunción, 1904.

DROUIN-DE-BERCY, M.:
Histoire civile et commerciale de la Jamaïque; . . . Paris, 1818.

ERRARA, Carlo:
La spedizione di Sebastiano Caboto al Rio della Plata. Florence, 1895.

ESPINOSA, Alonso de:
The Guanches of Tenerife. Transl. and ed. by Sir Clements R. Markham. London. (Hakluyt Society, 1907.)

ESQUEMELING, John:
The History of the Bucaniers: . . . London. (Thos. Malthus, 1684.)
Bucaniers of America. London. (William Crooke, 1684–1685.)
The Buccaneers of America. London and New York, 1893.
The Buccaneers of America. Ed. by William Swan Stallybrass. Introd. by Andrew Lang. London and New York. (Broadway Translations, N.D.)

EXQUEMELIN, Alexandre Olivier:
De Americaensche Zee-Roovers. Amsterdam, 1678. Same writer as Esquemeling, whom see.

FANSHAWE, Ann Lady:
Memoirs. London and New York, 1907.

FECUNDO Y CARVAJAL, Francisco:
Relacion de la Vitoria, qve han tenido las Armas de Sv Magestad, (Dios le guarde) en la Ciudad de S. Domingo, Isla Española, contra la Armada Inglesa de Guillermo Pen. Seville. (Iuan Gomez de Blas, 1655.) Copy of this rare work exists in The John Carter Brown Library.)

FERNÁNDEZ DE ENCISO, Martín:
Suma de geographia . . . Seville. (Jacobo Cronberger, 1519.)
Suma de geographia . . . Seville. (Andres de Burgos, 1546.)
Barlow, whom see, based his work upon this book.

FERNÁNDEZ DE NAVARRETE, Martín:
Biblioteca marítima Española. Madrid, 1851. 2 vols.

FERNÁNDEZ DE OVIEDO Y VALDÉS, Gonzalo:
Historia general y natural de las Indias . . . Ed. by José Amador de los Ríos. Madrid. (Real Academia de la Historia, 1851–1855.) 4 vols.

FERNÁNDEZ DE PIEDRAHITA, Bishop Lucás:
Historia general de las conquistas del Nuevo Reyno de Granada. Antwerp. (Juan Bautista Verdussen, 1688.)

FERNÁNDEZ DURO, Cesáreo:
Armada Española desde la unión de los Reinos de Castilla y León. Madrid, 1895–1903. 9 vols.

FISKE, Amos Kidder:
The West Indies. New York, 1899.

FISKE, John:
Old Virginia and Her Neighbours. Boston, 1897. 2 vols.

FUENTES Y GUZMAN, Francisco Antonio de:
Historia de Guatemala. Ed. by Justo Zaragoza. Madrid, 1882. 2 vols.

FUGGER NEWS-LETTERS.
Ed. by Victor von Klarwill. First series transl. by Pauline de Chary; second series by L. S. R. Byrne. New York and London, 1924–1926. 2 vols.

GAFFAREL, Paul:
Histoire de la découverte de l'Amérique. Paris, 1892. 2 vols.

GAGE, Thomas:
The English-American his Travail by Sea and Land: or, a New Svrvey of the West-India's, . . . London. (R. Cotes, 1648.)
A new Survey of the West-India's: or, The English American his Travail by Sea and Land: . . . London. (E. Cotes, 1655.)
A New Survey of the West Indies, 1648. Ed. by A. P. Newton. New York, 1929.

GALVANO, Antonio:
The Discoveries of the World, from their first Original unto the year of our Lord 1555. Ed. by Vice-Admiral Bethune. London. (Hakluyt Society, 1862.)

GANDÍA, Enrique de:
Historia crítica de los mitos de la conquista americana. Madrid, 1929.
Historia del Gran Chaco. Madrid, 1929a.
Historia de la conquista del Río de la Plata y del Paraguay. Buenos Aires, 1932.

GARCÍA DE LA RIEGA, Celso:
Colón, Español. Madrid, 1914.

GARDINER, Samuel Rawson:
History of England from the accession of James I. to the outbreak of the

civil war, 1603–1642. London, 1884–
1886. 10 vols.
*History of the great civil war, 1642–
1649.* London, 1898–1901. 4 vols.
GARDNER, W. J.:
History of Jamaica. London, 1873.
(Second edn., 1919.)
GONZALES CARRANZA, Domingo:
*A Geographical Description of the
Coasts, Harbours, and Sea Ports of
the Spanish West-Indies; . . . To
which is added an Appendix contain-
taining Capt. William Parker's own
account of his taking the Town of Porto
Bello, in the Year 1601.* London.
(Caleb Smith, 1740.)
GOSSE, Philip:
The History of Piracy. London and
New York, 1932.
GOULD Y QUINCY, Alice:
*Nueva lista documentada de los tripu-
lantes de Colón.* Bol. R. Acad. Hist.,
vols. LXXXVI, LXXXVII, XC,
and XCII. Madrid, 1925–1928.

HAKLUYT, Richard:
*The Principal Navigations Voyages
Traffiques & Discoveries of the Eng-
lish Nation.* Glasgow, 1903–1905.
12 vols. (Also, Hakluyt Society,
London.)
HAMILTON, Earl J.:
*American Treasure and the Price
Revolution in Spain, 1501–1650.*
Cambridge, Mass., 1934.
HANKE, Lewis:
*The First Social Experiments in
America.* Cambridge, Mass., 1935.
*Studies in the Theoretical Aspects of
the Spanish Conquest of America,*
1935a. Ms. Thesis, seen by P. A. M.,
through Author's kindness.
HARCOURT, Robert:
A Relation of a Voyage to Guiana.
Ed. by Sir C. A. Harris. London.
(Hakluyt Society, 1928.)
HARING, Clarence Henry:
*The Buccaneers of the West Indies in
the XVII Century.* New York, 1910.
*Trade and Navigation between Spain
and the West Indies in the time of the
Hapsburgs.* Cambridge, Mass., 1918.
HARLOW, Vincent T.:
*The Voyages of Captain William

Jackson, (1642–1645.)* London, 1923.
(The Camden Miscellany, vol. XIII.)
*Colonising Expeditions to the West
Indies and Guiana, 1623–1667.* Lon-
don. (Hakluyt Society, 1925.)
A History of the Barbados, 1625–1685.
Oxford, 1926.
Ralegh's Last Voyage. London. (The
Argonaut Press, 1932.)
HARLOW-RALEGH: See, Harlow, 1932,
and Ralegh, 1928.
HARRISSE, Henri:
*John Cabot, the Discoverer of North
America, and Sebastian his Son.*
London, 1896.
HART, Francis Russell:
Admirals of the Caribbean. Boston
and New York, 1922.
The Disaster of Darien. Boston and
New York, 1929.
*Spanish Documents Relating to the
Scots Settlements in Darien.* Boston,
1931.
HAZARD, Samuel:
*Santo Domingo, Past and Present;
with a Glance at Hayti.* New York,
1873.
HELPS, Sir Arthur:
The Spanish Conquest in America.
London, 1855–1861. 4 vols.
HERRERA Y TORDESILLAS, Antonio de:
*Historia General de los Hechos de los
Castellanos en las Islas i Tierra Firme
del Mar Oceano . . .* Madrid, 1601–
1615. 4 vols., folio.
HISTORICAL PORTRAITS.
*Lives by C. R. L. Fletcher, and por-
traits chosen by Emery Walker.* Ox-
ford, 1909–1919. 4 vols., folio.
HUME, Martin A. S.:
The Spanish People. London, 1901.
The Court of Philip IV. London,
1907.
Two English Queens and Philip. New
York and London, 1908.

INSH, George Pratt:
*The Company of Scotland Trading to
Africa and the Indies.* London and
New York. (Scribners, 1932.)

JANE, Cecil:
*Select Documents illustrating the four
voyages of Columbus.* Transl. and ed.

by Cecil Jane, vol. II containing a supplementary Introduction by E. G. R. Taylor. London. (Hakluyt Society, 1930–1933.) 2 vols.

JOHNSON, Captain Edward:
Wonder-Working Providence (1628–1651). Ed. by J. Franklin Jameson. New York. (Scribners, 1910.)

JOS, Emiliano:
La expedición de Ursúa al Dorado y la rebelión de Lope de Aguirre. Huesca, Spain, 1927.

JURAS REALES, el Barón de:
Entretenimientos de un prisionero en las provincias del Río de la Plata. Barcelona, 1828. 2 vols.

KERVYN DE LETTENHOVE, Baron:
Relations politiques des Pays-Bas et de l'Angleterre, sous le règne de Philippe II. Brussels, 1882–1891. 10 vols., folio.

KIRKPATRICK, F. A.:
The Spanish Conquistadores. London and New York, 1934. (The Pioneer Histories.)

KONETZKE, R.:
Sir Walter Raleigh und der Englisch-Spanische Kampf um Amerika. Ibero-Amerikanisches Archiv, VIII, 133–152. Berlin, 1934.

LABAT, Father Jean-Baptiste:
Voyages aux Isles de l'Amerique (Antilles) 1693–1705. Ed. with Introd. by A. t'Serstevens. Paris, 1931. 2 vols.

LANNOY, Charles de; and, VANDER LINDEN, Herman:
Histoire de l'expansion coloniale des peuples européens. Brussels and Paris, 1907–1911. 2 vols.

LAUDONNIÈRE, René de:
L'Histoire notable de la Floride sitvée es Indes Occidentales, . . . Paris. (Guillaume Auuray, 1586.) (In The John Carter Brown Library.)

LECLERC, Charles:
Bibliotheca Americana. Paris, 1878.

LEE, Bertram T.:
Algunos documentos sobre los primeros conquistadores. Revista Histórica, VIII, 366–375. Lima, 1928.
Una relación desconocida sobre Sir Francis Drake. Rev. Hist., IX, 88–93. Lima, 1928a.

LEE-MEDINA: See: Medina, 1934.

LIGON, Richard:
A True & exact History Of the Island of Barbadoes. . . . London. (Peter Parker, 1673.)

LINNÉ, Sigvald:
Darien in the Past. Gothenburg, 1929.

LONG, Edward:
The History of Jamaica. London, 1774. 3 vols.

LÓPEZ DE GÓMARA, Francisco:
Primera y segunda parte dela historia general de las Indias. . . . Saragossa. (Miguel Capila, 1553.) (Numerous later editions.)

LÓPEZ DE VELASCO, Juan:
Geografía y descripción universal de las Indias. Ed. by Justo Zaragoza. Madrid, 1894. (Author flourished 1571.)

LOTH, David:
Philip II of Spain. New York, 1932.

MacNUTT, Francis Augustus:
Bartholomew De Las Casas. New York, 1909.

MAGGS BROTHERS:
Bibliotheca Americana. London, 1922–1930. 9 vols.

MARCEL, Gabriel:
Les Corsaires Français au XVIe Siècle dans les Antilles. Paris, 1902.

MARIÉJOL, Jean H.:
Philip II, The First Modern King. Transl. by Warre B. Wells. New York, 1933.

MARKHAM, Sir Clements R.:
The Conquest of New Granada. London, 1912.

MARTYR D'ANGHERA, Peter:
De Orbe Novo. Transl. and ed. by Francis Augustus MacNutt. New York, 1912. 2 vols.

MEANS, Philip Ainsworth:
History of the Spanish Conquest of Yucatan and of the Itzas. Cambridge, Mass., 1917. (Peabody Museum.)
A Note on the Guarani Invasions of the Inca Empire. Geog. Rev., IV, 482–484. New York, 1917a.
Ancient Civilizations of the Andes.

New York and London. (Scribners, 1931.)

Fall of the Inca Empire and the Spanish Rule in Peru: 1530–1780. New York and London. (Scribners, 1932.)

Gonzalo Pizarro and Francisco de Orellana. Hispanic Amer. Hist. Rev., XIV, 275–295. Durham, N. C., 1934.

MEDINA, José Toribio:
Descubrimiento del Río de las Amazonas . . . Seville, 1894.
El Veneciano Sebastián Caboto al servicio de España. Santiago de Chile, 1908. 2 vols., folio.
El Portugués Estéban Gómez al servicio de España. Santiago de Chile, 1908b.
Los viages de Diego García de Moguer al Río de la Plata. Santiago de Chile, 1908c.
El descubrimento del Océano Pacífico. Santiago de Chile, 1913–1920. 4 vols.
The Discovery of the Amazon. Transl. by Bertram T. Lee and ed. by H. C. Heaton. New York. (American Geographical Society, 1934.) (Referred to as Lee-Medina in the Notes.)

MÉTRAUX, Alfred:
La civilisation matérielle des tribus Tupi-Guarani. Paris, 1928.
Études sur la civilisation des indiens Chiriguano. Tucumán, Argentina, 1930.

MIMS, Stewart L.:
Colbert's West India Policy. New Haven. (Yale University Press, 1912.)

MONTEIRO, Mario:
Aleixo Garcia, descobridor Portuguez em 1524–1525; . . . Lisbon, 1923.

MONTEMAIOR DE CUENCA, Juan Francisco de:
Discvrso Politico: Historico Juridico Del derecho, y Repartimiento de presas y despojos apprehendidos en justa guerra. . . . Mexico. (Ivan Rrviz, 1658.) (The John Carter Brown Library has this very rare work.)

MONTESINOS, Father Fernando:
Anales del Perú. Ed. by Víctor M. Maúrtua. Barcelona, 1906. 2 vols.
Memorias antiguas historiales del Peru. Transl. and ed. by P. A.

Means, with Introd. by Sir C. R. Markham. London. (Hakluyt Society, 1920.)

MORISON, Samuel Eliot:
Builders of the Bay Colony. Boston and New York, 1930.
The Founding of Harvard College. Cambridge, Mass., 1935.

N. N.:
America: or An exact Description of the West-Indies: More especially of those Provinces which are under the Dominion of the King of Spain. . . . London. (Ric. Hodgkinsonne for Edw. Dod., 1655.) (See Ch. VIII, Note 42, for further data.)

NABER, S. P. L'Honoré; and WRIGHT, Irene A.:
Piet Heyn en de zilvervloot, .¦. . Utrecht. 2 vols. in 1.

NEWTON, Arthur Percival:
The Colonising Activities of the English Puritans. New Haven and London, 1914.
The European Nations in the West Indies, 1493–1688. London and New York, 1933. (The Pioneer Histories.)

NILES, Blair:
Colombia, Land of Miracles. New York, 1924.

NORDENSKIÖLD, Baron Erland:
The Guarani Invasion of the Inca Empire in the Sixteenth Century. Geog. Rev., IV, 103–121. New York, 1917.
An Ethno-Geographical Analysis of the Material Culture of Two Indian Tribes in the Gran Chaco. Gothenburg, Sweden, 1919.
De Geografiska Upptäckternas Historia Sydamerika. Kampen om Guld och Silver, 1498–1600. Uppsala, Sweden, 1919a.

NUIX Y PERPIÑÁ, Abbé Juan:
Riflessioni imparziali sopra l'umanitá degli Spagnuoli nell' Indie. Venice, 1780.
Reflexiones imparciales sobre la humanidad de los españoles en las Indias, . . . Madrid. (Joachin Ibarra, 1782.)

NUTTALL, Zelia:
New Light on Drake. London. (Hakluyt Society, 1914.)

NYS, Ernest:
Les publicistes espagnoles du XVIe siècle et les droits des indiens. Revue de Droit International et de Législation Comparée, XXI. Paris, 1889.

ORDENANÇAS para remedio de los daños, e inconuenientes, que se siguen de los descaminos, y arribadas maliciosas de los nauios que nauegan a las Indias Ocidentales. Madrid. (Viuda de Alonso Martín, 1619.)

PALAU Y DULCET, Antonio:
Manual del Librero Hispano-Americano. Barcelona, 1923–1927. 7 vols.

PEDREIRA, Antonio S.:
Bibliografía Puertorriqueña. Madrid, 1932.

PEERS, E. Allison: Editor.
Spain; a companion to Spanish studies. New York, 1929.

PELLEPRAT, Father Pierre:
Relation des missions des PP. de la Compagnie de Jesvs Dans les Isles, & dans la terre ferme de l'Amerique Meridionale. . . . Paris. (Sebastien Cramoisy & Gabriel Cramoisy, 1655.)

PRESTAGE, Edgar:
The Portuguese Pioneers. London and New York, 1933. (The Pioneer Histories.)

RALEGH, Sir Walter:
The Discoverie of the large and bewtiful Empire of Guiana. Ed. by V. T. Harlow. London. (The Argonaut Press, 1928.) (Cited as Harlow-Ralegh, 1928, in the Notes.)

RAMIREZ, Juan:
Las Pragmaticas. Alcalá de Henares. (Lançalao Polono, 1503.) (Unique copy in the British Museum. For notes on this work and on other editions of it see: Maggs Brothers, VI, pp. 224–231.)

RAYNAL, Abbé Guillaume-Thomas:
Histoire philosophique et politique des Établissens et du Commerce des Européens dans les deux Indes. Geneva. (Jean-Leonard Pellet, 1782.) 10 vols. and Atlas.

RESTREPO, Vicente:
Los Chibchas antes de la conquista española. Bogotá, 1895.

RICHMAN, IRVING BERDINE:
The Spanish Conquerors. New Haven, 1919.

RIONEGRO, Friar Froilán de:
El fundador de Carácas Don Diego de Losada, Teniente de Gobernador y Capitán General en estas Provincias. Caracas, 1914.

ROBERTS, W. Adolphe:
Sir Henry Morgan, Buccaneer and Governor. New York, 1933.

ROCHEFORT, Charles de:
Histoire natvrelle et morale Des Iles Antilles de L'Amerique. Rotterdam. (Arnout Leers, 1665.)
The History of the Caribby-Islands, . . . Translated by John Davies of Kidwelly. London, 1666. (Printed by J. M. for Thomas Dring and John Starkey.)

RODRÍGUEZ, Father Manuel:
El Marañón, y Amazonas. Madrid. (Antonio Gonçalez de Reyes, 1684.)

RODRÍGUEZ FRESLE, Juan: (Writing in 1636.)
Conquista y descubrimiento del Nuevo Reino de Granada, . . . Bogotá, 1890.

ROGERS, Cameron:
Drake's Quest. Garden City, New York, 1927.

ROWLAND, Donald:
Spanish Occupation of the Island of Old Providence or Santa Catalina, 1641–1670. Hispanic Amer. Hist. Rev., XV, pp. 298–313. Durham, N. C., 1935.

S., I.:
A brief and perfect Journal of The late Proceedings and Successe of the English Army in the West-Indies, Continued until June the 24th 1755. . . . London, 1655. (This work is in The John Carter Brown Library.)

SAINT-LÉGER, A. de; and, SAGNAC, Philippe:
La prépondérance française. Louis XIV. (1661–1715.) Paris, 1935.

SANTELLI, Ramón L.:
Cristoforo Colombo o Cristóbal Colón. Carupano, Venezuela, 1919.

SARMIENTO DE GAMBOA, Pedro:
History of the Incas. Transl. and ed. by Sir Clements R. Markham. London. (Hakluyt Society, 1907.)

SCELLE, Georges:
La traite négrière aux Indes de Castille. Paris, 1906. 2 vols.

SCOTT, James Brown:
The Spanish Origin of International Law. Francisco de Vitoria and his Law of Nations. Oxford and London, 1934. (Cited in the Notes as Scott-Victoria.)

SCOTT-VICTORIA, see: Scott, James Brown.

SEDGWICK, Henry Dwight:
Spain. A short history of its politics, literature, and art from the earliest times to the present. Boston, 1925.

SIMÓN, Friar Pedro:
Primera Parte De las Noticias historiales de las Conquistas de tierra firme en las Indias Occidentales. Cuenca, Spain. (Domingo de la Iglesia, 1627.)
The Expedition of Pedro de Ursua and Lope de Aguirre in search of El Dorado and Omagua in 1560-1561. Transl. from Simón's Sixth Historical Notice by William Bollaert, with Introd. by Clements R. Markham. London. (Hakluyt Society, 1861.)
Segunda y Tercera Partes de las Noticias Historiales .'. . Bogotá, 1892. 4 vols. (Printed from the original Ms. in the National Library of Colombia.)

SIMPSON, Lesley Byrd:
The Encomienda in New Spain. . . . Berkeley, Calif., 1929.

SLOANE, Sir Hans:
A Voyage to the Islands of Madera, Barbados, Nieves, S. Christophers and Jamaica, with the Natural History . . . of the last of those Islands. London, 1707.

SOSA, Juan B.:
Panamá la Vieja. Panama, 1919.

SOUTHEY, Robert:
The expedition of Orsua; and the Crimes of Aguirre. London, 1821.

STERNBECK, Alfred:
Histoire des Flibustiers et des Boucaniers. Paris, 1931.

STRONG, Frank:
The Causes of Cromwell's West Indian Expedition. Amer. Hist. Review, IV, 228-245. 1899.
A forgotten Danger to the New England Colonies. Ann. Report, Amer. Hist. Assoc. for 1898, 77-94. 1899a.

TARDUCCI, Francesco:
John and Sebastian Cabot. Transl. by Henry F. Brownson. Detroit, Mich., 1893.

TAVERA-ACOSTA, B.:
Un dogma histórico que va deschaciéndose. Bol. Acad. Nac. de Hist., V, 79-84. Quito. 1922.

TAYLOR, Eva G. R.:
Roger Barlow: A New Chapter in Early Tudor Geography. Geog. Jour., LXXIV, 157-169. London, 1929.

TAYLOR, Eva G. R.: See Barlow, 1932; also under Jane, Cecil.

TERTRE, Father Jean-Baptiste du:
Histoire generale, des Isles de S. Christophe, de la Gvadelovpe, de la Martiniqve, et avtres dans l'Ameriqve. Paris. (Iacqves Langlois, 1654.)
Histoire generale des Antilles habitées par les François. Paris. (Thomas Jolly, 1667-1671.) 4 vols.

TESSMANN, Günter:
Die Indianer Nordost-Perus. Hamburg, 1930.

THURLOE, John:
A Collection of the State Papers of John Thurloe. . . . London, 1742. 7 vols.

TORRES CAMPOS, Rafael:
Carácter de la conquista y colonzación de las islas Canaries. Madrid, 1901. (R. Academia de la Historia.)

TOYNBEE, Arnold J.:
A Study of History. Oxford, 1935. 3 vols. (1st edn., 1934.)

TRAPHAM, Thomas:
A Discourse of the State of Health in the Island of Jamaica. London. (R. Boulton, 1679.) (See Ch. VIII, Note 45.)

URTEAGA, Horacio H.:
El fin de un Imperio. Lima, 1933.

URTEAGA, Horacio H.; and ROMERO, Carlos A.:
Fundación española del Cusco y Ordenanzas para su Gobierno. Lima, 1926.

VALCÁRCEL, Luis E.:
Final de Tawantisuyu. Rev. del Museo Nac., Lima, II, 79–97. Lima, 1933.

VELASCO, Father Juan de:
Historia del Reino de Quito. Quito, 1841–1844. 3 vols.

VENABLES, Robert:
The Narrative of General Venables, with an Appendix of papers relating to the expedition to the West Indies and the conquest of Jamaica, 1654–1655. Ed. by C. H. Firth. London. (Royal Hist. Society, 1900.)

VICTORIA, Friar Francisco de: See Scott, James Brown.

VIGNAUD, Henri:
Histoire critique de la grande entreprise de Christophe Colomb. Paris, 1911.

VILLESTREUX, Général de la:
Les Flibustiers aux Antilles. Paris, 1930.

WAFER, Lionel: (Flourished 1680–98.)
A New Voyage & Description of the Isthmus of America. Ed. by L. E. Elliott Joyce. Oxford. (Hakluyt Society, 1934.)

WALDMAN, Milton:
England's Elizabeth. Boston and New York, 1933.

WATTS, Arthur P.:
Une histoire des colonies anglaises aux Antilles (1649–1660.) Paris, 1924.

WEST INDIES:
A Book of the Continuation of Forreign Passages. . . . London. (Printed by M.S. for Thomas Jenner, 1657.) (A rare book, to be found in The John Carter Brown Library.)

WILGUS, A. Curtis:
A History of Hispanic America. Washington, D. C., 1931.
The Histories of Hispanic America. Washington, 1932. (Pan American Union Bibl. Ser. No. 9.)
An Atlas of Hispanic American History. Washington, D. C., 1932a.
Maps relating to Latin America in books and periodicals. Washington, 1933. (Pan American Union Bibl. Ser. No. 10.)

WILKINSON, Henry:
The Adventurers of Bermuda. London, 1933.

WILLIAMSON, James A.:
English Colonies in Guiana and on the Amazon, 1604–1668. Oxford, 1923.
The Caribbee Islands under the Proprietary Patents. London, 1926.
Sir John Hawkins. The Time and the Man. Oxford, 1927.
The Voyages of the Cabots and the English Discovery of North America under Henry VII and Henry VIII. London. (The Argonaut Press, 1929.)

WINSHIP, George Parker:
Some Facts about John and Sebastian Cabot. Worcester, Mass. (American Antiquarian Society, 1900.)
Cabot Bibliography with an Introductory Essay on the Careers of the Cabots. London, 1900a.
Sailors Narratives and Voyages along the New England Coast, 1524–1624. Boston, 1905.

WINSOR, Justin: Editor.
Narrative and Critical History of America. Boston and New York, 1889. 8 vols.

WINTHROP, John:
History of New England. (Journal.) Ed. by James Kendall Hosmer. New York. (Scribners, 1908.) 2 vols.

WISSLER, Clark:
The American Indian. New York, 1922. (2nd edn.)
The Relation of Nature to Man in Aboriginal America. New York, 1926.

WRIGHT, Irene A.:
Early History of Cuba, 1492–1586. New York, 1916.
The English conquest of Jamaica; an account of what happened in the island of Jamaica, from May 20 of the year 1655, up to July 3 of the year 1656. By Julián de Castilla. Transl. and ed. by Irene A. Wright, from the original Ms. in the Archives of the Indies. London, 1923. (Camden Miscellany, XIII.)
The Coymans asiento (1685–89.) Ed.

by I. A. Wright. The Hague, 1924.
Spanish Narratives of the English Attack on Santo Domingo, 1655. Ed. by
I. A. Wright. London. (Royal Historical Society, 1926.)
Spanish Documents concerning English Voyages to the Caribbean, 1527–1568. Transl. and ed. by I. A.
Wright. London. (Hakluyt Society, 1928.)
Documents concerning English Voyages to the Spanish Main 1569–1580. Transl. and ed. by I. A. Wright.
London. (Hakluyt Society, 1932.)
WRIGHT, Irene A.: See also: Naber and Wright, 1928.

INDEX

INDEX

Absolutism: comparison of Spanish and French, 245–247.
Adanero, Count of: 233–234.
Africa: see Slaves and Slavery, Negro.
Aguarico River: 109.
Aguirre, Lope de: 99; journey of from Peru to the Spanish Main by way of the Amazon, 115–118; death of, 118.
Albemarle, Duke of: 190–191.
Alexander VI, Pope: 16–17; his Demarcation Line, 53–54. See Demarcation Line, Papal.
Alfinger (Ehinger), Ambrose: 102.
Almagro, Diego de: 100–101.
Alva, Duke of: 81.
Alvarado, Pedro de: 33, 232.
Amazon, the: 6; 16; 39–40; Barlow's plan to invade Peru by way of, 48; 100; 106; Orellana on, 111–114; El Dorado somewhere on, 119; English adventurers on, 151–152.
Anglo-Dutch wars: 204.
Ango, of Dieppe: 59.
Antigua: 189.
Antilles, the: 10–11. See also Caribbean; Lesser Antilles; Greater Antilles.
Aparia the Greater: 112.
Aparia the Lesser: 111.
Arawak Indians, the: 11; 12; 15; 21; 120; 128; 130; 137–138. See Caribs; Indians.
"Archaic" Culture: See Intermediate Culture.
Arias de Ávila, Pedro: 35; 37.
Armada, the Spanish: 93.
Aruba Island: 165; 189.
Asientos (slave-trading contracts): 60; 205; 220. See also Slaves and Slavery, Negro.
Association Island: see Tortuga.
Asunción, Paraguay: Sebastián Cabot at, 42.
Atienza, Inés de: 116–117.
Avendaño y Lóyola, Father Andrés de: 233–237.
Ayscue, Sir George: 187; 203.
Aztecs: conquered by Cortés, 30–32; 232.

Barbados: 155; English colonization on, 157–159; Jackson at, 186; Royalists defeated on, 187; 189; 191; Penn and Venables at, 193; 203.
Barlow, Roger: with Sebastian Cabot, 41–45; plans invasion of Peru by way of the Amazon, 48; 105; 138; 190.
Baskerville, Sir Thomas: 93–94.
Bastidas, Rodrigo de: 46.
Bell, Governor (of Bermuda and of Providence) Philip: 176; and *passim* in Ch. VIII, Section 2.
Benalcazar, Sebastián de: 101; 104.
Benavides y Bazán, Juan de: defeated by Piet Hein, 165–166.
Bermejo River: 39.
Bermuda: 20; English colony on, 176–177; 189.
Bernaldez, Alonso: 63; 65.
Berrio, Antonio de: his quest for El Dorado and his career, *passim* in Ch. VI, and especially pp. 125–138.
Blake, Admiral Robert: 196.
Blondel, Paul: 78; 82.
Bogotá: 6; 46; 103–104.
Bontemps, Jean: 65.
Booties and Ransoms: 71; 86; 89; 91; 92–93; 103; 165–166; 211; won by Morgan at Panama, 213; taken at Cartagena, 219. See Piracy.
Boriquén: Carib name for Puerto Rico, which see.
Bourbon, Philip of, becomes Philip V of Spain: 206.
Brazil: 16; 39–40; 61; 66; 120.
Breda, Treaty of: 216.
"Brethren of the Coast": 207–208; 211.
Buccaneers: See Contraband; Interlopers; Piracy.
Buckingham, Duke of: 152.
Buen Aire Island: 165; 189.

Cabot, John: 19.
Cabot, Sebastian: expedition of to the River Plate, 41–45; 52; 56; 105.
Cabral, Pedro Alvares: 40.
Calderón, Hernando: 42; 44.
Caledonia: *passim* in Ch. IX, Section 5.
Calvin, John: 171–173.
Canary Islands: 9; 10–11; 28; Hawkins at, 61; Drake near, 84; Drake and Hawkins repulsed from, 93–94; Blake at, 196.
Canek, King of the Itzas: 232–240.

271